PLURAL FEMINISMS

PLURAL FEMINISMS

Navigating Resistance as Everyday Praxis

Edited by
Sohini Chatterjee and Po-Han Lee

BLOOMSBURY ACADEMIC
LONDON • NEW YORK • OXFORD • NEW DELHI • SYDNEY

BLOOMSBURY ACADEMIC
Bloomsbury Publishing Plc
50 Bedford Square, London, WC1B 3DP, UK
1385 Broadway, New York, NY 10018, USA
29 Earlsfort Terrace, Dublin 2, Ireland

BLOOMSBURY, BLOOMSBURY ACADEMIC and the Diana logo are
trademarks of Bloomsbury Publishing Plc

First published in Great Britain 2023
Paperback edition published 2025

For legal purposes the Acknowledgements on pp. xv–xvi constitute
an extension of this copyright page.

Cover design by Adriana Brioso
Cover image © Separisa/Adobe Stock

A catalogue record for this book is available from the British Library.

Library of Congress Cataloging-in-Publication Data
Names: Chatterjee, Sohini, editor. | Lee, Po-Han, editor.
Title: Plural feminisms : navigating resistance as everyday praxis /
edited by Sohini Chatterjee and Po-Han Lee.
Description: New York : Bloomsbury Academic, 2023. |
Includes bibliographical references and index.
Identifiers: LCCN 2023009476 (print) | LCCN 2023009477 (ebook) |
ISBN 9781350332737 (hardback) | ISBN 9781350332720 (epub) |
ISBN 9781350332713 (pdf) | ISBN 9781350332706
Subjects: LCSH: Feminism.
Classification: LCC HQ1111 .P58 2023 (print) | LCC HQ1111 (ebook) |
DDC 305.42–dc23/eng/20230321
LC record available at https://lccn.loc.gov/2023009476
LC ebook record available at https://lccn.loc.gov/2023009477

ISBN: HB: 978-1-3503-3273-7
         PB: 978-1-3503-3269-0
         ePDF: 978-1-3503-3271-3
         eBook: 978-1-3503-3272-0

Typeset by Integra Software Services Pvt. Ltd.

To find out more about our authors and books visit www.bloomsbury.com
and sign up for our newsletters.

This book is dedicated to those who have not had their experiential knowledge validated, who have not felt, seen, heard and understood many times over, and whose stories of resistance are in the process of transformative unfolding

CONTENTS

Part II
ANTI-NORMATIVE POSSIBILITIES AND EVERYDAY RESISTANCE

Part III
CRITICAL PEDAGOGY AS FEMINIST INTERVENTION

ABOUT THE EDITORS AND CONTRIBUTORS

Editors

Sohini Chatterjee is a PhD Candidate and Vanier Scholar in the Department of Gender, Sexuality and Women's Studies at the University of Western Ontario, Canada. Her work has recently been published in *QED: A Journal in GLBTQ Worldmaking, Lateral: Journal of the Cultural Studies Association, Women's Studies: An Inter-disciplinary Journal, South Asian Popular Culture*, and *Fat Studies*. Her research interests revolve around trans and queer activism, queer cultural studies, trans and queer disability studies and resistance movements in India. Sohini was previously a Non-Fiction Project Editor at HYSTERIA: Feminisms Radicalism Periodical and Activist Platform.

Po-Han Lee is Assistant Professor in the Global Health Program and the Institute of Health Policy and Management at National Taiwan University. Previously trained in International Law and Political Sociology, he has been studying the construction, circulation and consumption of the right to health discourse in health social activism and global health governance. Po-Han has been a member of *Feminist Review Collective* and a senior editor for *Plain Law Movement*, the first multimedia platform for legal and human rights education in Taiwan. He recently published the book *Towards Gender Equality in Law* (2020), which he co-edited with Gizem Guney and David Davies.

Contributors

Maria Silvia D'Avolio is Postdoctoral Researcher in Architecture at the ZHAW Zurich University of Applied Sciences, Switzerland. She has cultivated an interdisciplinary background obtained from educational and professional experience in architecture, sociology and the social sciences. Between 2016 and 2022 she had taught sociology, criminology and gender studies in the UK at the University of Sussex and the University of Brighton. Her research approach is aimed at analysing intersecting inequalities in various contexts and exploring forms of social, urban and environmental harm from a feminist perspective. She is currently working on a three-year project that explores the role of socialist and communist women architects in the political and architectural context of 1960–1980s Milan, Italy.

Madeline Bass has an undergraduate degree in Sociology and Anthropology from Wells College in Aurora, New York, and an MS in Sociology from Portland

State University in Portland, Oregon. Her MS was received as part of Peace Corps' Masters International programme, and she lived and worked in Oromiya, Ethiopia, from 2014 to 2017. Each of these moves has guided me to the work I hope to do with the MOVES research programme, funded by the European Union's Horizon 2020 research and innovation.

Renée E. Mazinegiizhigo-kwe Bédard is of Anishinaabeg, Kanien'kehá:ka, and French-Canadian ancestry. She is a member of Okikendawdt (Dokis First Nation). She holds a PhD from Trent University in Indigenous Studies. Currently, she is Assistant Professor at Western University in the Faculty of Education. Her areas of publication include practices of Anishinaabeg motherhood, maternal philosophy and spirituality, along with environmental issues, women's rights, Indigenous Elders, Anishinaabeg artistic expressions and Indigenous education.

Maddie Brockbank is a PhD candidate and Vanier Scholar in the School of Social Work at McMaster University. Maddie has her Bachelor of Social Work (2019) and Master of Social Work (2020) from McMaster. Her research, practice experience and community organizing initiatives have been in the area of anti-violence work with men, specifically in exploring the links between sexual violence prevention, masculinities, anti-carceral feminisms and engaging men in primary prevention efforts. Additionally, she has research experience in the areas of houselessness, disability, social systems, curriculum development and creating safety for marginalized students in university pedagogy. Maddie has been recognized for her academic excellence and community leadership as a recipient of the Young Woman of Distinction Award (YWCA Hamilton), the President's Award for Excellence in Student Leadership (McMaster University), a Hamilton Hero award (Hamilton Ticats), a Women Who Rock award (EMPOWER Strategy Group) and a Mary Keyes Award for Outstanding Service and Leadership (McMaster University).

Roxana Pessoa Cavalcanti is a British-Brazilian critical social scientist at the University of Brighton, UK. Since completing her PhD (2017) and taking her second career break for maternity leave (2018), she has been an active member of international networks, including the Urban Violence Research Network, the Feminist Urban Violence Research Collective, which she co-founded, and European Group for the Study of Deviance and Social Control. Her book, published by Routledge in 2020, examines the governance of violent relations in Brazil. She has written about urban violence, insecurity, feminism, cities, criminology, police violence and the criminalization of dissent in Latin America. She is currently working on a project that examines the current context and struggles faced by feminist movements in Brazil. https://orcid.org/0000-0003-3885-8603

Simten Coşar was Visiting Professor of Political Science at the University of Pittsburgh before returning to Turkey in July 2021. She is currently affiliated with the Carleton University as an adjunct associate researcher. Her MS progressed; she started a new medication programme until June 2023.

Deanna Dadusc is Senior Lecturer in Criminology at the University of Brighton.

Cienna Davis is a Black feminist community organizer and scholar. She received her bachelor's degree in Ethnic Studies and Communication from the University of California San Diego where she was a McNair Scholar. She then completed her master's in North American Studies at the John F. Kennedy Institute of the Freie Universität Berlin, and is doing her doctoral study at the Annenberg School for Communication at the University of Pennsylvania. Her writing and speaking on Afrofuturism, Black feminism, colourism, digital blackface, popular culture and community organizing has been published in academic journals, books and newspapers in the United States, Germany and Switzerland. Davis is one of the original founders of Soul Sisters Berlin, a diasporic, Black feminist network where she organized workshops, social events, performances, roundtable discussions and retreats with the goal of educating, empowering and connecting Black womxn and femmes in Berlin.

Yi-Hui Lin is an independent researcher. Her current research interests include the everyday in international politics, traumatic memory, nationalism and sovereignty, and feminist methodologies. She holds a research master's degree in Public Administration and Organizational Science from the University of Utrecht.

Elizabeth Chelsea Mohler is a PhD candidate in Occupational Science at the University of Western Ontario, Canada. Elizabeth has worked for National Educational Association of Disabled Students (NEADS), Balance for Blind Adults and Ryerson Magnet. Elizabeth's Doctoral research will explore the impact that access to direct funding has on the occupational performance and engagement of people with disabilities (PWDs), who receive funding from the Ontario Direct Funding (ODF) programme to 'self-manage' their attendant services. Elizabeth is the co-author of *Creating a Culture of Accessibility in the Sciences* (2016).

Kody Muncaster is PhD candidate in Gender, Sexuality, and Women's Studies at Western University. Their research and consulting interests include queer and trans health, HIV/AIDS, queer suicide, trauma, psychotherapy and queer Buddhist studies. They recently released the chapter 'PrEP Will Not Save Us: The Ghosts of AIDS and Suicide' in Mattilda Bernstein Sycamore's edited collection *Between Certain Death and a Possible Future: Queer Writing on Growing Up with the AIDS Crisis*.

Nasheeka Nedsreal is a Berlin-based dancer, choreographer and artist working with movement, music and visual art. Often exploring subjects related to identity, ritual, futurism and improvisation, her work incorporates uses of voice, collage, found objects, textiles and masking. As a choreographer her work has been showcased at Ballhaus Naunynstrasse, HAU Hebbel Berlin, Savvy

Contemporary, Ada Studios and nGbK. As a video artist, her work has been showcased at Sadler's Wells London, Kampnagel Hamburg, Floating University Berlin and Gallery Am Tacheles Berlin. Having dropped out of university during her second year, Nedsreal considers herself to be an autodidact artist. She is currently a member of the Schauspielhaus Dance Ensemble Zürich. In late 2022, she travelled to Dakar as a participant in the Black Rock residency programme.

Gülden Özcan was Assistant Professor in the Department of Sociology at the University of Lethbridge, Alberta, Canada. She completed her MA (2007) and PhD (2017) at Carleton University in Ottawa, ON, Canada. The title of her PhD dissertation in Sociology was entitled 'Orchestrating the Public: A Contribution to the Critique of Modern Police Power'. Her work included involvement in radical theatre, with Scholars at Risk and in critical police studies. Özcan also worked at challenging and disrupting systemic and social injustice issues on campus. She was the first ever recipient of the SNAC+ (Support Network for Academics of Colour Plus) Excellence in Equity Award in January 2022. Özcan was also an active member of the Equity subcommittee of the Canadian Sociological Association. Özcan published in English and Turkish on critical security studies, feminist knowledge production, and social justice issues. She was a founding member of the *Feminist Asylum: A Journal of Critical Interventions*.

Corin Parsons is a PhD candidate in geography at the University of British Columbia and teaches at Langara College. He is writing his doctoral dissertation on cats, gender and domesticities. He is also an advocate for queer, crip and trans issues.

Rowan J. Quirk recently received a master's in Global Health from National Taiwan University, where they conducted a scoping review investigating non-monogamous health concerns across a global context. At the moment, their research interests include queer intimacies, (trans)gender theorizing and expansive/non-nuclear family issues. Additionally, they are a passionate educator – most notably presenting a guest speaker series, entitled *Non-monogamy Affirming Therapeutic Practices*, at the Denver Family Institute.

E. Scherzinger is a postdoctoral fellow at McMaster University in the Department of Pediatrics. Her research interests focus on poststructuralist feminist theory, Mad/disability studies, child and youth studies, and more. She has published on gender studies, *Alice in Wonderland*, and superheroes.

Kascindra (Kascie) Shewan is a Postdoctoral Fellow in Art History & Communication Studies at McGill University, Canada. She has published on sexualized violence prevention and filmic representations of gender-based violence in *Atlantis: Critical Studies in Gender, Culture & Social Justice* and *The Canadian Journal of Film Studies*. Currently, Kascie is exploring new research fields, including how feminist agency is defined and navigated through Neo-Pagan and occult practices, and the identity/figure of the witch.

Laetitia Walendom is a tricontinental writer, urbanist and producer currently based between Dakar and Berlin. She has worked as Communications Director of Cinelogue, a Berlin-based streaming platform engaging films from the Global South, and is currently a Fulbright Fellow researching art restitution and circulation in Senegal. When in the United States she is the Projects Director of Lalibela Baltimore, a film production, tech and creative innovation collective building novel forms of creative equity in historically disenfranchised Black Baltimore.

ACKNOWLEDGEMENTS

This project gained momentum through an unusual queer friendship. In 2016, Po-Han submitted an essay that contextualized queer politics in East Asia to *HYSTERIA: Feminisms Radicalism Periodical and Activist Platform* – which was founded by the members of the School of Oriental and African Studies (SOAS) Feminist Society, even though the magazine ran independent of both the university and the society as long as it was in publication – and Sohini served as *HYSTERIA*'s Non-Fiction Project Editor at the time. A while later, around mid-2018, when Sohini thought of collecting and documenting lived realities and resistance practices of feminists, Po-Han was invited to contribute a chapter. Later, Po-Han decided to join Sohini as the project's co-editor – a very exciting moment for both of us. This project has been in the making since 2018, and we experienced many transitions in life while developing it. In 2020, Sohini started her PhD at the University of Western Ontario, Canada, during the challenging pandemic time, and Po-Han returned to Taiwan for his first academic position after concluding his PhD at the University of Sussex in 2020 – that very same year. Diasporic experiences, however, have strengthened our queer friendship and expanded our understanding of community, feminisms and resistance. We developed this project in phases in India, Canada, the UK and Taiwan, and it has been nearly five years in the making.

Along such a long journey, we have accumulated immense debts of gratitude. We cannot thank the contributors of this volume enough for trusting us with their stories. They have shared deeply complex and vulnerable knowledge about themselves in the pages of this book and provided us, in the process, with affective and intellectual resources to carry on with the project and with life, in more ways than one. We put this volume together, marvelling at the power of their narratives, and we will remain forever grateful for their generosity in sharing with us their life-affirming knowledges of resistance.

We would like to thank editors, artists, contributors and writers who were involved with *HYSTERIA* as long as it existed and made it a robust platform of creation and activism for many years. *HYSTERIA* enabled the coming together of feminists from around the globe, including Sohini and Po-Han, and if this book has an origin story, *HYSTERIA* figures prominently in it.

Sohini would like to thank professors and mentors at the Department of Gender, Sexuality, and Women's Studies at the University of Western Ontario, particularly Bipasha Baruah, Chris Roulston and Pamela Block, who offered her the flexibility required to work on this book during the first, second and third years of her doctoral study while she simultaneously worked on and took her candidacy examination, and wrote her doctoral thesis proposal. Their encouragement and mentorship makes Sohini want to do better. She would also like to thank Dr Erica Lawson for her support, warmth, generosity and transformative pedagogy, and Dr Laurel Shire for teaching an invaluable course on the History of Sexuality that opened new intellectual horizons for her. She remains grateful for her generosity with time and guidance.

Sohini also remains deeply grateful to professors at South Asian University, New Delhi, Jayashree Vivekanandan, Soumita Basu and Nabarun Roy, whose support has made it possible for her to undertake her doctoral journey and make the important transition from one disciplinary home to an interdisciplinary academic environment. Without such transition, this book would not exist. Ama Josephine Budge, Bjørk Grue Lidin and Emma Saperstein cannot be thanked enough for their support, encouragement and feminist solidarity over the years. They make feminist world-making possible and an absolute joy to witness. Ratna, Sohini's mother – who has been a working single parent since Sohini was 13 – needs to be acknowledged for giving her the space, time and understanding required to work on this book, for teaching her by example that it is possible to lead a life outside of heteronormative institutions, cultivate affirming relationalities, find joy in old and new friendships, and that it is important to value un/learning as we move through life. Her mother's life gives her the resource to carry on and is an ode to feminist resistance. Sohini would also like to thank her friends – and friendships past and present – in Kolkata, New Delhi and London, Ontario, for their world-expanding love, care and kindness, which breathes life into her every day. Sohini receives funding from the Social Science and Humanities Research Council of Canada (SSHRC) as a Vanier Scholar and would like to thank the donors for their support.

Po-Han expresses gratitude for the feminist comrades at *Feminist Review*, who have been a great and constant source of inspiration regarding feminism and feminist practices. He would also like to thank his family and partners, Alvaro and Eric, and his colleagues and friends at the National Taiwan University and the University of Sussex, who encouraged him to pursue projects like this one out of passion rather than the demands of 'quantitative metrics'.

Last but certainly not least, we would like to thank Olivia Dellow, Assistant Editor at Bloomsbury, who believed in our project, and let us tell the stories we wanted to tell and needed to share with the world. She made our long-cherished and hopefully nurtured dream – of giving this book a world – come true. We could not thank her enough for it.

EDITORIAL INTRODUCTION

Sohini Chatterjee and Po-Han Lee

Introduction

Feminism is the inheritance of resistance. Variously marginalized people and their communities of belonging offer each other joy amidst devastation, affirmation amidst derogation, point each other towards possibilities of subversion, trust each other with the gift of critique, wilfully deliver and receive care (and negotiate the terms of giving/receiving care), bequeath intergenerationally creative and political means of survival and sustenance, impart disruptive knowledge, hand down and recreate/resignify strategies of dissent, develop everyday ways of bringing communities together, advance methods of fostering trust between Traumatized, vulnerable, agential people, demand equity, hold space for desire in its complexity, provoke each other's rebellious imagination and labour towards knowing differently – even before they come to feminisms.

We learn about their rich and complex lives, just mutual aid and collective care practices, dissident aspirations and subversive dreams, in community spaces and with counterpublics of various forms, in conversations with our friends and lovers, and in intergenerational dialogues with kin who are often unaware of the life-saving resource they are providing us with in the form of uncovered (resistant) knowledge when they talk about those who came before and passed on more than they knew they were leaving behind. We learn how to honour their unarchived legacies, craft our lives in ways that do justice to their resistances and carry on another day knowing we have ancestors who dreamt the dissidence we live today, and we live our lives learning from feminists whose dreams and desires remain unhinged today and every day.

We revel in the disobedience posed by the bodyminds of those who were not honoured by history, who have been ignored by dominant social movements and undone by 'radical' exclusionary politics, and whose stories are considered not worth recounting. Today, despite limitations inevitably associated with our locational specificities, we strive to know differently, and have collected stories that are not understood very often, even if they are told many times over in bits and pieces, time and time again. This book archives the dissident desires, resistance practices and critical relational wisdom embodied by those who wanted their stories to be told.

We begin with the acknowledgement that many of us who have come together to develop this volume simultaneously occupy positions of privilege and penalty, and our lives are an ode to complexities posed by such simultaneity. This collection does not claim to represent all marginalized communities – or all experiences of marginalization within a community of resistance – but has collected stories to validate our lived, embodied and embodiminded experiences of resistance, engagement with feminisms and beyond. Our contributors are trans and/or queer and/or disabled and/or neurodivergent people and feminists, anti-carceral feminists, Black femme feminists, feminists whose work goes beyond the Anglo-American academy, indigenous feminists and feminists who are questioning the limits of feminisms – we are all united by the recognition of resistance as an invaluable resource in our lives. We issued a public call for chapters with the audacious hope of putting this volume together in February 2021. We knew very little about publishing when we started out. We began slowly, and somewhat, hesitantly. As our networks expand, and we have the courage to invite more people to contribute chapters (and are able to compensate them for their labour), we remain hopeful that we will, collectively, be able to tell many different stories not covered in the pages of this volume. We began by recognizing that we are not entitled to stories of people's experiences of marginalization, oppression and resistance. An open call ensured that we reached many who were interested in sharing their knowledges with us, and it is their openness and trust that make this book what it is. Because of our locational specificities in the academy, many contributors to this volume are primarily early career researchers, writers, scholar-activists and graduate students who navigate conditions of precarity in the neoliberal academy and inhabit multiply marginalized and stigmatized as well as sociopolitically dominant identities. This book holds in its pages stories of certain aspects of their lives, first-person narratives of their engagement with and investment in feminisms, and that which goes beyond what we identify as 'feminisms'. It bears witness to their resistance practices, and is brought into existence because of their will to write and share their stories. We are frequently asked to discount theoretical insights gained from our quotidian lived realities. When we want to write about our lives and relationalities, and the effects structural violence has on them, by putting our bodyminds on the line, it is neglected as 'me-search', and even though some of us are experts by virtue of experience, we are rarely identified as such. This book dissents against calls to write ourselves out of resistances we pose on the daily, which keep our communities and us afloat – resistances that make survival, kinship, activism and academic, intellectual and affective labour possible for us. It holds space for feminist reflections inspired by transformative resistance practices, uncovering in the process what is expected to remain hidden in plain sight.

Accordingly, this collection explores how we embrace feminist resistance praxis and how our constantly evolving feminist praxis transforms us. It evidences how we offer dissident strategies of resistance through autoethnography of our lived and embodiminded realities. Drawing on multiple understandings of feminisms, this volume archives how we engage with feminisms and imagine the mundane as a feminist site of resistance against multiple and intersectional forms of marginalization, privilege and oppression. This book spurs a discussion about how structural violence is identified and resisted, and the invisible, uncompensated and affective labour that goes behind this resistance, and documents the resistance strategies feminists deploy on a daily basis to survive and live, and form and sustain dissident kinships that remain unread, unheard, overlooked and excluded from dominant discourses of being and becoming. Detachments and brackets have made us disobedient and, at times, 'inconvenient' subjects who desire to experiment, breaking and forming relations from within the world: a world that needs disturbing (Berlant 2022). Through autoethnography, feminist, queer, trans and/or genderqueer, indigenous, Black and racialized, disabled and neurodivergent scholars in the academy reflect on their engagement with feminisms as well as their unique resistance methods exceeding its limits – embracing and exploring complexities and challenges that both entail. This book foregrounds the critical importance of first-person narratives in developing a capacious understanding of what it means to inhabit the world as feminists, as disabled people, neurodivergent people, trans and queer people, as Black femmes, as indigenous people and as people whose identities are always getting shaped and reshaped by their lives multiply journeys. It reflects on how dissidence looks in the lives of people whose bodyminds and ways of living, being and knowing do not conform to the normative in various ways – whose assertions challenge normativity and the desire for the status quo. Since spaces are seldom held for such articulations of resistance, and because the knowledges of people bearing complex identities, who are not yet established writers, are rarely privileged, this book brings together their critical 'situated knowledges' (Haraway 1988) as they reflect on themselves, and their life-worlds and worldmaking, as an act of resistance in and of itself.

Epistemological accounts: A pluralistic approach to feminism

Resonant with Catriona Macleod's work on *Radical Plural Feminisms and Post-Apartheid South Africa*, this edited collection aims to explore feminism in its plural form where multiple resistance strategies are emphasized with the help of a conceptual framework that enacts the 'both/and' function rather than 'either/or'. Our work is guided by the awareness that 'feminist political practice becomes a matter of alliances rather than one of unity around a universally shared interest' (Macleod 2006: 378). This anti-oppression, anti-normative, affect-centric, subversive, coalitional framework allows us to explore the following questions: How do feminists imagine the regular and the mundane as feminist sites of resistance? How do we put our feminisms into quotidian practice as resistance? How do we undertake various embodiminded journeys, and what unlearning and relearning take place through them? How do we define the 'political' and understand the affective, and what does 'resistance' mean to us? What structural disadvantages hinder our being and becoming, and how do we confront its oppression and exclusion? How are we shaped by contradiction, self-reflexivity, ambivalence, intentionality, dissidence and critique? How do we build communities and kinship networks against violence and precarity in various garbs as we give meaning to not only the specificities of our contexts but also the world at large?

The volume privileges autoethnographic modes of knowing that are devalued, by positioning the self as an active knower as well as a witness to various forms of knowing, questioning and resisting. Quotidian lived realities of the knower, and their 'minor feelings' (Hong 2020), are given critical importance in the pages of this volume, since, for those of us shifting between margins, what constitutes life, living, surviving and resisting is often shrouded in obscurity to the greatest degree. We are also often disallowed the space to arrive at expansive ideas of resistance, feminist, as well as trans, queer, neurodivergent, disabled, Black, indigenous subversive imaginings. This project affirms dissident iterations by those who are starting out, exploring their interests, discovering the significance of their multiple positionalities, learning to understand their own journeys and are witnessing their stories as they unfold. This volume is an effort to resist alienation from the self, stories of our lives and the resistance practices that make us who we are and are not.

We believe in 'narrative power', to borrow Ken Plummer's (2019) words. Through narrativizing lived experiences and feminist reflections, we aim to think through dynamic processes of enacting resistance – those dissident practices that accompany us when we confront oppressive structures – that inform various forms of knowing and strengthen our resistances. Our edited collection intends to understand how the mundane and the extraordinary imbue our feminist ideas, imagination, feelings, identities and the ways in which they have brought us to feminisms – propelling us to explore, expand, challenge and revolutionize feminism itself. It offers minoritized, anti-normative, queer, crip, neurodivergent, trans, non-binary, Black, indigenous, Traumatized and racialized voices to demonstrate the power over their narratives through reconstruction. It also explores how feminists negotiate with and subvert power in myriad ways, and how we contribute to care, resistance, politics and those that exceed its terms, while navigating our histories, cultural realities and socio-economic contexts.

We believe in the power of storytelling. Sara Ahmed writes about early feminist work that 'emphasized the importance of women telling their own stories that dislodged the happiness myth, stories that are not simply about unhappiness but about the complex, ambivalent, and messy feelings that women have' (Ahmed 2017: 57). We hold space for the messy, complex and ambivalent, and offer this book as a space to co-think what feminisms offer our lives, what resistance means as well as what it means to resist. To borrow from Ahmed (2017), this book is 'an unhappy archive' just as 'feminism is an unhappy archive' (Ahmed 2017: 60). We recognize that 'feminist history is affective' (Ahmed 2017: 65). This collection of essays is hence rooted in understanding the world through affect, embracing feminist unhappiness, and the complexities of quotidian resistance. We also explore in this volume how authors' identities are evolving through contextualized feminist resistance praxis in the everyday. How do we become a feminist from incurring penalties in our everyday even if we embody certain privileges, and how do our feminisms re/signify our identities? How do our experiences of both privilege and marginalization inform our politics? How does our politics inform our agency? How do we problematize and interrogate our daily lives through the lens of identity as process rather than a stable category? What does our resistance praxis look like? How have our understandings of resistance evolved and transformed, and how do we engage with feminisms, queerness, transness or disability justice, because of it? We stay with these questions.

Methodological concerns: Novel ways of doing autoethnography

To open up the possibilities for transnational and intersectional feminist narratives to emerge, this volume uses autoethnography as a resistance methodology to interrogate the formation, transformation and evolution of identities and resistances as processes in fervent motion. We also deploy different feminist strategies to achieve our goal, including Mary Macleod Bethune's *intellectual activism*, María Lugones's *world-travelling*, Rosi Braidotti's emphasis on *feminist multiplicity* and Cynthia Enloe's *feminist curiosity*. They have all required us to not only unlearn and re-world our feminist selves and epistemologies but also taught us to be 'constantly vigilant and reflective in terms of self, other, context, process, assumptions and theory' (Macleod 2006: 382).

Autoethnography allows us to reflect on our lives and critique the worlds where we are located, as we think about resistance, how we enact it and our quotidian commitment to feminisms. What renders our autoethnographic method novelty in this volume is that we think about resistance together from our differing, and sometimes, converging identity locations and attempt to co-create (and re-create) an 'unhappy archive' that also holds possibilities of joy. We resist essentialism by denouncing the universal figure of the 'feminist academic' by taking into account our varied and differential negotiations with the world as well as the academy – also by being cognizant of our critical embodiminded differences – which influence how we resist as well as invest in feminisms. Autoethnography and theorizing of the self form a methodology that values reflexivity and 'situated knowledges' (Haraway 1988), resists silencing and has been a core resistance method for disability justice knowledge building as well as feminists of colour theorizing (Moraga & Anzaldúa 1981). Autoethnography conducted by variously marginalized people allows us to re-centre identities, knowledges, experiences and resistance enactments, which are always decentred in dominant discourses. This volume challenges dominant attempts to alienate us from ourselves as we welcome embodiminded insights and practices of worldmaking in its pages.

In *Autoethnography as Feminist Method: Sensitising the Feminist 'I'*, Elizabeth Ettorre posits that autoethnography requires writers to be rigorously self-aware of the complex relationships between one's socially coded categories – the enforced differences embedded in different power relations (Ettorre 2017: 6). And, according to Carolyn Ellis and Tony Adams, 'the power of these accounts rests on an author's ability to use personal hopes, fears, and investments to provide complex and engaging descriptions of cultural life' (Ellis & Adams 2016: 261). We are thus mindful of marginalized identities and knowledges that cannot be simplified and subsumed under unitary modes of analyses and challenge essentialism through attention to difference. We have encouraged contributors to engage with intersections of differences and reflect on differences as critical practice in writing as resistance. We have welcomed analytic, interpretive, evocative, critical and collaborative autoethnographic chapters in this collection.

The editors of this volume are queer feminist academics. A book project that holds space for stories of different lives in various contexts, we believe, is an important attempt to archive many histories, narratives, praxes and moments of grief, anger, joy, love, life, failure and triumph. It is also a documentation practice of our protests and silences as resistance which are helping us explore our journeys and our lived realities as everyday feminist praxis. To narrativize the ordinary is a form of feminist resistance. By doing so, we own and author our stories, acknowledge our histories of dissidence and share it with those who offer various resistances on the daily.

Chapter outline

Part I (Witnessing and Inhabiting Intersectional Lives) opens with the chapter by Corin Parsons, who reflects on his transition as a form of dissent against cisnormative conceptions of masculinity and refuses to establish his proximity to cisness, or cishet masculinity, in order to affirm his trans masculinity. Parsons's powerful autoethnographic reflection allows insights into his shifting feminist praxis as he begins the process of transition. In this chapter, Parsons co-thinks with Chela Sandoval about the nuances and complexities of feminism and resistance, reflects on various incarnations of trans time and represents transness as a veritable modality of feminist resistance.

Maddie Brockbank's feminist autoethnography serves as a critical tool for analysing service provisions within social work settings. Autoethnography and feminist social work's conceptualization of reflexivity invites Brockbank to unpack her experiences conducting workshops on and researching men's violence intervention and prevention efforts. In this chapter, she reflects on her feminist positionality and uncovers the challenges of embodying feminist values in social work settings, expanding the understanding of feminist resistance in the process.

Kody Muncaster powerfully queers experiences of post-traumatic stress disorder and complex trauma in the third chapter of this volume through the method of 'traumatic autoethnography'. Deploying crip theory, drawing on Mad Studies and utilizing Ann Cvetkovich's depathologizing conceptual framework on trauma, Muncaster depathologizes their own experiences of trauma and reflects on negotiating crip and Mad identity politics and world-making by traumatized Mad and crip queers, and presents resistance as the honouring of collective pain.

Madeline Bass, Cienna Davis, Nasheeka Nedsreal and Laetitia Walendom have conducted collective autoethnography and sensory ethnography in Germany's underground public transit U-Bahn for this chapter ode to Black resistance. Honouring their Afro-diasporic lives in Germany, the authors reflect on Black feminist spatiality of resistance, space-making as resistance, and reflect on the possibilities of finding and making a life that can be called beautiful in the face of oppression, hostility and marginalization – a life which offers strength and becomes the site of meaning-making.

By voicing women architects' concerns, Maria Silvia D'Avolio's chapter has demonstrated that architecture is still primarily a white-male-dominated profession lacking diversity in Europe. Maria has integrated rich narrative data with the critical work done by feminist writers to interrogate this reality. She has comprehensively mapped out the terrain of women's marginalization in the field of architecture, focusing particular attention on the depiction of women architects' strategies of negotiating gender norms and toxic work culture.

Part II (Anti-Normative Possibilities and Everyday Resistance) begins with Po-Han Lee's chapter, which reflects on inhabiting multiple selves and closets at different points in time and points towards those who are rarely seen as being closeted. He begins by recounting how closets can be inhabited variously and then reflects on his 'closeting' experiences variously. His autoethnography explores fatphobia, racism, classism, politics of desire and desirability and their association with structural violence, lateral violence and discrimination. He identifies resistance as a method of building alliances and creating possibilities for critical thinking.

Drawing on the notion of autoethnography as 'neuroqueer methodology', Sohini Chatterjee's reflexive and reflective account forms a powerful critique of the invisiblization of neurodiversity as embodied by queer people. She traces her journey through cities to gain a sense of neuroqueer becoming, reveals possibilities, opportunities and limitations of care work, and explores what it means to resist a neurotypical system that is intertwined with cisheterosexism and upholds compulsory ableism and sanism and privileges certain manifestations of 'ability'. By deconstructing the hierarchy between ways of relating as structural violence, her chapter provokes a rethinking of normativity in everyday life.

Renée E. Mazinegiizhigo-kwe Bédard's chapter explores the concept of 'aazhawigamig' – the space between – to conceptualize a sense of movement and fluidity, drawing on the life and philosophy of the Anishinaabeg people. Based on this, she develops an Indigenous matricentric feminist praxis, which enables her, as an Anishinaabeg mother, to articulate maternal resistance and resilience as part of the decolonization process in everyday life. Bédard's theorization of 'aazhawigamig' has retained the elasticity of how Anishinaabeg people use the term. The dynamics of such liminality illustrated by her are helpful in visualizing and problematizing gender inequities and colonial institutions altogether. The integration and reconciliation of indigenous and feminist philosophies/activisms – constituted by reflections on the proposed Indigenous-matricentric feminist praxis – is illustrated powerfully through her nuanced autoethnographic account.

Rowan J. Quirk dissents against compulsory relating and reflects on possibilities of resistance inherent in polyqueer kinship and kinship-building practices, which also poses a veritable challenge to neoliberal rationales. Quirk's chapter offers an expansive understanding of how polyqueer intimacies can dissent against settler colonialism, settler citizenship and settler modes of nation-building, opening up provocative, subversive and alternative universes of relating queerly and dissidently.

E. Scherzinger offers autotheory as a form of resistance in this volume where they explore their affective worlds produced by, as well as against, reproductive futurity, whiteness, heteronormativity, erasure of queerness, normativities associated with the figuration of the ideal female citizen, expectations of perfect girlhood and the threat of the 'apocalyptic child'. Their narrative addresses structural violence produced by neoliberal capitalism, disablement induced structurally, writing against the hegemony of meaning imposed on their bodymind and offering autotheory as a survival strategy.

In her chapter, Yi-Hui Lin offers an autoethnographic account of gender socialization and upbringing, her experiences of being a racialized, first-generation Taiwanese immigrant being raised in a working-class household in the United States, and the vulnerabilities produced therein. Her chapter explores issues of sexual abuse and the silences around it, vulnerability produced by immigration status and the complexities of feminist resistance, which, she argues, cannot always be expected to be coherent when variously marginalized subjects reflect and resist.

Part III (Critical Pedagogy as Feminist Intervention) of the book starts with Gülden Özcan and Simten Coşar's collaboration. They reveal their distinct and yet interrelated experiences as feminist academics in the higher education sites that are gendered, racialized and 'neoliberalized'. Their stories spanning two decades – in different societies in Turkey, Canada and the United States – contain extensive and insightful reflections. Simten and Gülden have told stories centring their presences and the affects generated by them 'being there' confronting, negotiating with and navigating the intersections of gender, racial norms and neoliberal logic. With the emphasis on ethnographic writing and feminist autoethnography, the erasure of individual stories is addressed and repaired by collective efforts geared towards 'horizontal knowledge production', as identified in their chapter.

Kascindra Shewan's honest and moving story illustrates hardships at both material and affective levels experienced by her during uncertain Covid times. Her story is presented through conceiving, preparing for and delivering a course on 'Witchin' in online spaces. She presents a comprehensive introduction to and application of spiritual activism, its relationship with feminist autoethnography and links 'witchy' practices to feminisms in transformative ways. This chapter puts feminist writers in dialogue with each other, and conversations of this nature have allowed Kascindra to find inner peace and peace with those she cares about.

Elizabeth Chelsea Mohler offers a robust critique of neoliberal universities and academia where disabled students continue to be marginalized and invisibilized and where they have to manage their own access needs and are made responsible for it. Her account explores the ableism and sanism of academia and the politics of disablement induced by it.

Maria Silvia D'Avolio, Roxana Pessoa Cavalcanti and Deanna Dadusc offer a strong critique of carceral feminism through a powerful conversation and complex exchange of ideas with each other and address how carceral logics have individualized the responsibility of gender-based violence by stigmatizing and incarcerating individual perpetrators instead of collectively coming together and organizing to mitigate such violence and its effects. They reflect on how carceral feminism has advocated for increasing punishment, imprisonment and isolation of individuals. Their conversation also leads to a powerful critique of state-centric imaginaries within the field of criminology. Primarily aligning and slightly differing from Simten and Gülden's chapter in its methodology – which uses the third-person tone to compare two people's experiences – the employment of the method of 'conversation as praxis' in this chapter presents the whole conversation as a dialogue taking place in real time. Doing so enables them to uncover diverse possibilities of 'autoethnography' as a method. They have also clarified the relationship between carceral feminism and the paternalistic approach that is dominantly taken to represent gender equality in the name of 'protecting women and girls'. Their chapter points out the limitations and dangers of relying on such an approach to gender equality.

References

Ahmed, S. (2017). *Living a Feminist Life*. Durham: Duke University Press.

Berlant, L. (2022). *On the Inconvenience of Other People*. Durham: Duke University Press.

Ellis, C. & Adams, T. E. (2016). 'The Purposes, Practices, and Principles of Autoethnographic Research'. In Patricia Leavy (ed.). *The Oxford Handbook of Qualitative Research*. New York: Oxford University Press, pp. 254–76.

Ettorre, E. (2017). *Autoethnography as Feminist Method: Sensitising the Feminist 'I'*. Oxon: Routledge.

Haraway, D. (1988). 'Situated Knowledges: The Science Question in Feminism and the Privilege of Partial Perspective'. *Feminist Studies* 14 (3): 575–99.

Hong, C. P. (2020). *Minor Feelings: An Asian American Reckoning*. New York: One World.

Kafai, S. (2021). *Crip Kinship*. Vancouver: Arsenal Pulp Press.

Macleod, C. (2006). 'Radical Plural Feminisms and Emancipatory Practice in Post-Apartheid South Africa'. *Theory and Psychology* 16 (3): 367–89.

Moraga, C. & Anzaldúa, G. (1981). *This Bridge Called My Back: Writings by Radical Women of Color*. Watertown: Persephone Press.

Plummer, K. (2019). *Narrative Power: The Struggle for Human Value*. London: Polity Press.

Part I

WITNESSING AND INHABITING
INTERSECTIONAL LIVES

Chapter 1

MULTITEMPORALITY AND FEMINIST RESISTANCE IN TRANSITION

Corin Parsons

practitioners enact any position only insofar as they are ultimately

hoping to transform both the position they hold and the reality it acts upon.

– *Chela Sandoval, p. 101 of* Methodology of the Oppressed.

'trans AF'– my notes in the margin on p. 101

of Methodology of the Oppressed

Introduction

This is a chapter about having no idea what I am doing – and the process of trying to figure it out. Different subjectivities do different things and make different things doable in different spaces, so as a disabled and queer trans man early in my medical transition, I want to know how enacting feminist resistance might change along with my understanding of self and others' perceptions of me. I owe my interpretation of feminist resistance to Chela Sandoval's 'Methodology of the Oppressed'; for Sandoval (2000), resistance is fundamentally about addressing power differentials. What I am struggling with is not defining but *enacting* resistance at a point in my transition that is characterized by uncertainty: uncertainty about how I am read, uncertainty about what is expected of me and uncertainty about how to deliver on or disrupt those expectations.

In this chapter, I steer into that uncertainty, which primarily hinges on the question, *what sort of feminist subject am I?* My hope is that understanding how I now find myself positioned vis-à-vis the feminist project will clarify how to enact feminist resistance. To guide my investigation, I revisit Sandoval; as Ahmed (2017, 5) observes, '[w]here we find feminism matters; from whom we find feminism matters.' Sandoval's work fundamentally shaped my understanding of feminist praxis – and, specifically, feminist resistance – when I first read it a decade ago, before coming into my transness. In my present moment of uncertainty, it therefore seems like the right place to begin looking for answers.

In 'Methodology of the Oppressed', Sandoval aims to understand how actors can intervene in the social world with the objective of redistributing power. She focuses specifically on feminist approaches for decolonizing the imagination. Although it would be inaccurate and inappropriate for me to claim that I am decolonizing anything in this chapter (Liboiron 2021, Tuck & Yang 2012), I am nevertheless working with and from Sandoval's text for several reasons: first, the redistribution of power is central to Sandoval's aims and my own questions. Second, our respective emphases, while distinct, are interrelated; the dominant construction of gender in the (so-called) North American context in which I live and write is inextricably intertwined with colonization and racialization, so any feminism worth enacting must be intersectional, anti-racist and anti-colonial (Lugones 2016, Spillers 1987). Third, the spirit of Sandoval's text is, in her words, to 'advance the possibility of connection, of a "coalitional consciousness" … across racialized, sexualized, gendered theoretical domains' (79). In order to do this, she draws together eclectic texts not because she conflates their distinct lineages, concepts and goals but because she is more focused on the overall 'shape', dynamics and functioning of the theories with which she works. I am attempting to approach her insights in a similar fashion, so although we may not be writing *to* precisely the same experiences, my hope is that we might be writing towards each other in a coalitional sense.

The feminist subject that emerges out of this chapter is a multitemporal one, consistent with crip, queer and trans scholarship that takes a critical view of *chrononormativity*. This literature disrupts and interrogates dominant assumptions around futurity, synchronicity, orderly life stages, pace and indeed the very notion of progress (Halberstam 2005, Kafer 2013, Muñoz 2009, Price 2014). In what follows, I examine first the shortcomings of resistance rooted in a chrononormative relationship to my sex assigned at birth and lived gender. I then bring together Sandoval's insights with my own experiences to argue that multitemporality makes transness particularly well suited to the sort of resistance that Sandoval describes. This is all a bit speculative; I am a trans scholar and not a scholar of transness, so my representational loyalties lie with the sausage-making process rather than the charcuterie platter.

The once and future feminist versus 'The Man'

I am a trans man and locate myself under the broader 'trans masc' umbrella.[1] Transness does not caveat my masculinity; it both defines and affirms it. The

---

1. Trans masculinity is also the space from which I write, and I would therefore discourage speculation about trans women's experiences on the basis of this chapter. The experiences of trans men and trans women are neither identical nor the inverse of one another, particularly when approached intersectionally. Trans women are the best sources for engaging with trans women's experiences, and trans men's perspectives are valuable in their own right.

reductive refrain 'trans men are men' serves a purpose for educating cis people but can also collapse trans masculinities into a cis-centric definition of 'man'. Because cis men are not more 'authentically' men, I prefer 'some men are trans men' (or, if I am feeling cheeky, 'some men are cis men'). The 'self-evident', 'fundamental' character awarded to cisness is a reflection of cisnormative society and its racist, classist and ableist foundations – not the bodyminds assigned to its categories. My goal is not to approximate cisness; I value having arrived at my gender by way of transness.

However, together with the joy and relief of coming into my transness, I have also experienced an undercurrent of dread owing to the potential minefield that comes with inhabiting the unfamiliar social position of a white man. Cis and nonbinary friends have told me that I do not need to change anything about how I relate to others – 'just be yourself' – but the fact is: how others relate to *you* changes depending on how they read you; even one's same actions can register differently. Therefore, as my perceived gender and thus social position have shifted, so too must the contours of my feminist praxis. For example, the assertiveness that was a survival skill as a small, disabled, queer 'woman' has become a liability when being perceived as a white man. A recent professional interaction underscored this point: an instructor who is older than me, has several decades more experience and holds institutional power over me gave me some pedagogical advice while repeating the entire time that she hoped I would not be angry with her for doing so. Meeting her suggestions with curiosity and gratitude was not enough; she just switched to thanking me for not being angry. It was a new experience. For most of my life, anger has been treated as both unexpected and unwarranted.

When I started being read as a man, one of the first things I noticed was that the frequency and type of interactions with other men changed. Strangers began treating me like an acquaintance. They would nod in passing and I would be expected to 'shoot the shit' should we end up sharing an elevator or waiting in the same line. At first, I would rack my brain for any memory of having previously encountered this person because of the tone of conspiratorial conviviality – and it did feel 'conspiratorial', although not in an ominous sense but rather like being in on a shared experience or inside joke. I had expected my disability to create distance, but I quickly learned that the boys' club has its own 'accessible entrance'. When I use my crutches, men eagerly approach me to swap sports-related war stories (assuming that I am temporarily injured rather than permanently disabled). When I use my wheelchair, they treat me to disorienting spectacles of jocular bravado (presumably believing that I was injured doing something 'badass' while also reassuring me that I 'still count' as one of them). Meanwhile, it took me much longer to realize when women began reading me as a man because the change was marked instead by *non*engagement; with their gaze, body position and navigation of space, women within about ten years of my own age began to pre-emptively dodge any potential interaction.

In short order, I had become 'just some guy' – which is fine! But as I blunder through unfamiliar social situations, I want to avoid being 'that guy' who makes others feel devalued, afraid, invisible, inadequate, powerless, etc. (whether deliberately or precisely because of a *failure to be deliberate* about how one wields the 800-pound gorilla subjectivity of a white man). I am not motivated by the conceit of 'innocence' or the need to be a 'protagonist'; rather, it is the desire to engage in feminist praxis and enact feminist resistance. Ahmed (2017, 2) tells us that the key to doing feminism is 'to make everything into something that is questionable', but frankly my main question continues to be what if I have no idea what I am doing in general?

Cis friends have insisted I should not worry because I have 'been there' – on the receiving end of misogyny – and thus will not be 'that kind of man'. This assertion has a clear temporal directionality: having 'been a woman' in the past will make me a 'better kind of man' in the future. The argument is seductive, but it relies on an essentialized, static understanding of privilege and gives far too much weight to intentions, as if either of those things might compensate for potential harm (even though we know that whiteness and maleness operate beyond the bodies categorized as white and male and often irrespective of how those same bodies may be marginalized along other axes of social difference like class, disability or sexual orientation). It also assumes that, in terms of perception and legibility, my transness will and should always supersede or at least soften my masculinity – which is becoming less and less true by the day. (At times I have even caught a glimpse of my changing features in the mirror and, by force of habit, subconsciously prepared to duck an unsolicited opinion or advance before sheepishly realizing I was seeing my own reflection!)

Assuming that trans men will instinctively 'get it' also seems to suggest that feminist consciousness arises from having personally experienced misogyny and gendered violence – a sort of inoculation against perpetuating gendered oppression. This ignores the existence of internalized and lateral misogyny (both of which are, by definition, perpetuated by the same people who experience misogyny) as well as its systemic manifestations. Moreover, it is a politically limiting assumption. If the path to desiring justice has to be routed through facing that same injustice oneself, there is no hope for intersectional analyses or coalitional consciousness and the beneficiaries of oppression are completely let off of the hook.

Perhaps the most troubling thing about attributing innate feminist consciousness to having grown up 'girled' is that it positions anyone presumed female – if not assigned such at birth – as the de facto feminist subject. This is problematic on several fronts. First, women of colour have never had the same access to the category of 'woman', with its racist and colonial underpinnings, or enjoyed any reassurance of shared purpose with white feminists. Next, if simply being declared female at birth or raised presumedly female grants a person favoured access to feminist consciousness, some women and femmes will automatically be excluded. At what point would someone become 'woman enough' to be considered a feminist subject? Where would nonbinary and intersex people 'rate'? Would anyone other than (implicitly white) cis women 'count' as a feminist subject, and would everyone else be left to imitate a truer 'natal' feminism that footnotes their experiences or even their existence? This circumscribed and reductive feminist subject is inadequate for addressing the realities of gender and gendered oppression, perpetuating the injustices feminism purportedly seeks to address (Butler 2006). In other words, this is a feminist subject that fails even its own immunity titre.

In contrast to the once-and-future-feminist argument, some people in my life have instead (jokingly?) 'congratulated' me on becoming the newest member of 'the patriarchy' or gravely 'reminded' me to be cognizant of my 'male privilege'. Once again, there is an underlying temporal assumption with transition marking a rupture from a past self. This too would be easier to navigate than the situation in which I find myself (after all, I have very clear ideas about how I wish many white cis men might have acted when previously encountering me as a 'woman'); however, presuming trans men no longer 'get' – or, through transition, magically forget – misogyny hinges on an understanding of privilege that does not accurately reflect trans men's relationship to male privilege. Some trans men may benefit from it some of the time, but male privilege is not meant for us, so it is a contingent and costly relationship at best. Moreover, trans men continue to live with misogyny as men. In the United States and elsewhere, anti-trans (and quietly white supremacist) laws are being passed in order to 'protect' (read: control) the bodies and reproductive capabilities of (implicitly white) 'little girls' (Petrovnia 2022). Trans men who can get pregnant are subject to the same anti-abortion laws as women and face similar (and often greater) barriers to reproductive care. Trans men may also experience systemic misogyny (inextricably intermixed with cissexism), such as medical misogyny and a persistent wage gap (Rummler 2022). On an interpersonal level, trans men frequently encounter interwoven misogyny and cissexism with respect to interests, behaviours, presentation, embodiment, etc. Privilege – male or otherwise – is relational and operates at multiple scales and temporalities simultaneously. For trans men, even just within the category of gender, there are many tensions and outright contradictions in how we may be read and misread or treated and mistreated. That does not mean, however, that as a trans man I retain the *same* relationship to misogyny that I once had – nor can I do feminist resistance in the ways that I once did.

Ultimately, neither a presumption of male privilege nor a supposed immunity from perpetuating misogyny is all that helpful to me. These framings force trans masculine ways of being into a cisnormative frame that misrepresents trans men's experiences, flattens feminist subjects, undermines feminist objectives and offers little guidance with respect to feminist resistance. Furthermore, they subtly impose an unhelpful chrononormativity on the experience of transition. In need of a framework that lets me explore my uncertainties while still attending to power, plurality and resistance, I therefore turn my attention to what Chela Sandoval calls her 'model for the self-conscious production of resistance' and bring this together with a multitemporal trans masc feminist subject (43).

Feminist resistance in transition

In 'Methodology of the Oppressed', Sandoval deliberately and generously works across the insights and practices of thinkers and activists from a range of backgrounds and contexts, including racialized feminists; queer and trans folk; and white (mostly male) theorists of postmodernity. She seeks out and amplifies points of resonance to identify patterns in how oppression is theorized, resisted and subverted. She enrols the scholarship of several white men (including Roland Barthes, Fredric Jameson and Michel Foucault) into the project and even asks whether such scholars may be considered decolonial thinkers insofar as they cannily perceive the social landscape shifting beneath the feet of 'the formerly centred and legitimated bourgeois citizen-subject of the first world (once anchored in a secure haven of self)' (27); however, she also identifies where they reach a dead end when attempting to operationalize resistance – succumbing instead to alienation and despair.

This hopelessness, Sandoval observes, is rooted in 'a lost time and place where it was once possible to know exactly who you were and where you stood' and, as a result, how to enact resistance (23). For me, from this body in transition, Sandoval's words hold an unanticipated resonance. I too find myself nostalgic for positioning that allowed me to comprehend 'the place' – my place – 'in the social order from which one is expected to speak' (23). Whether my previous positioning as a white 'woman' was ever so self-evident is obviously debateable, but the fact remains: I am currently more uncertain than ever about where I stand in the social order.

Sandoval proposes a way through the alienation and despair of the white male theorists: she suggests that the transformative potential of their insights is actually realized and mobilized in the work of activists and thinkers engaged in what she calls U.S. Third World Feminism of the 1970s and 1980s (referring to the internationally minded, US-based feminist of colour- and queer-led scholarship and organizing of that time). Sandoval's resulting framework, which she titles 'the methodology of the oppressed', is made up of three interrelated components: oppositional social movements, technologies and consciousness. Taken together, these are 'techniques for moving energy' or 'oppositional technologies of power' – in short, resistance (82). I relate each of these components to three of the four attributes of the multitemporal subject I describe: synchronicity, intertemporality, and suspension. (Meanwhile, the fourth – anticipation – lets me stumble towards a conclusion.)

Sandoval begins with oppositional social movements, examining movements' approaches to transforming power relationships. The first four categories Sandoval identifies are (1) an equal rights approach that seeks duplication, integration and assimilation vis-à-vis the dominant social order; (2) a revolutionary stance that seeks to fundamentally restructure the categories underpinning the dominant social order; (3) a supremacist posture that seeks to provide 'a higher ethical and moral vision' than that of the dominant social order; and (4) a separatist attitude that seeks 'complete separation from the dominant social order' (57). The danger for social movements, as Sandoval sees it, lies in viewing these as mutually exclusive, stand-alone categories (which she suggests has been the downfall of white feminist organizing).

Looking to U.S. Third World Feminism, Sandoval thus introduces a fifth category of oppositional social movements: the differential. The differential category is related to the other four categories much like 'the clutch of an automobile, the mechanism that permits the driver to select, engage, and disengage gears in a system for the transmission of power' (58). This opens up the possibility for social movements composed of 'manifold positions for truth' by allowing for tactical positioning among differences such that they do not 'become opposed to each other' and wind up (re)producing relations of domination.

When I first encountered Sandoval's work, these were the insights that stood out, bringing into relief the history and pluralism of feminist social movements and instructing me on how to do feminism as a white 'woman' wanting to act in solidarity with BIPOC feminists by reading 'the current situation of power and self-consciously choosing and adopting the ideological stand best suited to push against its configurations' (60). Returning to the text now, I see an expanded coalitional potential in what Sandoval suggests. Because Sandoval's framing primarily attends to *power*, there is no de facto feminist subject; rather, as Sandoval writes, 'practitioners of the differential mode of social movement develop and mobilize identity as political tactic in order to renegotiate power' (162). One characteristic of trans temporalities – simultaneity – seems particularly well suited to this approach.

That I am a trans man is both a realization I came to in my thirties *and* something I have known forever. I have always been a trans man, even before I knew that was 'an option' and before I had the language to express what I knew about myself; however, that is not all I have ever been. As an elementary schooler, I announced to my mother I was 'bisexual', as in 'a boy and a girl'. She chuckled at my etymological overconfidence and told me, 'that's not what that word means'. As an adolescent, I tried to tuck my 'boy' self into my sexuality instead, alternately identifying as a bisexual woman or a lesbian. Although queerness was ultimately an accurate frame for my sexuality, it was an inadequate solution with respect to gender. Still, there were hints! For instance, in a high school art class I painted a self-portrait as Thomas Gainsborough's 'Blue Boy'. My parents made the questionable decorating decision to hang the 5'8" canvas in the dining room and, even though this gender-swapped self loomed over dinnertimes, none of us read into it any further. Meanwhile, I was navigating the world consciously as a young woman. It was not the totality of my experience, but it felt like an accurate descriptor of many parts of my life. I even attended a women's college for undergrad (and there I was introduced to the possibility of deliberately anti-patriarchal masculinities). As new words like gender queer and gender fluid entered my vocabulary over the next decade, I tried them on. I wondered whether I should take the average of my gender feelings; was I reaching for androgyny? The exploration was instructive, but nothing felt quite right. By the time pronouns became a standard line in email signatures, I had all but thrown up my hands: 'I don't know! Any pronouns, I guess?' People began assuming I identified as nonbinary and defaulting to 'they', which felt close but was somehow even more frustrating – like having the right word on the tip on my tongue. It was finally as a trans man that I found the greatest level of comfort with not just my own gender but also the many ways that I have been oriented towards gender over the course of my life.

These experiences are part of my transness as well as my man-ness – they *are* what makes me a man – but they are also experiences in their own right; they are the various ways that I have made sense of myself and that I have been perceived, positioned and treated. I do not see this simultaneity as contradictory or a sort of 'in-between' gender. Likewise, I am neither 'still a woman' nor have I been at any point 'not a man'. Trans temporalities in defiance of chronormativity are what make this possible, and such simultaneity offers a way to think about how these gendered and gendering experiences *persist into the present* with varying levels of salience in different concentrations and situations, thus potentially facilitating the necessary mobility and responsiveness to align oneself with what Sandoval calls 'manifold positions of truth' in order to deliver on the differential form of social movement.

Sandoval turns from social movements to practices of meaning making, identifying five technologies for consciously shifting patterns of meaning. Revisiting this text in transition, this second type of differential movement – a power-sensitive mobility in the service of meaning-making – also felt freshly relevant. The first three technologies that Sandoval proposes are semiotics ('reading signs for power'), deconstruction (deconstructing those 'sign-systems') and meta-ideologizing ('creating new, "higher" levels of signification') (110). The fourth, democratics, orients these technologies towards the redistribution of power, and the fifth echoes Sandoval's differential category of social movements; she terms this tactic 'differential' as well, and it similarly moves across and within the other four technologies, connecting them and ensuring agility when 'shifting gears' depending on the ideological terrain.

I see these practices at work in my experiences of transness as well, specifically when it comes to the second example of trans multitemporality: the intertemporality (and, in this case, intergenerationality) of gendered meaning-making. This is a dynamic that Butler has spoken to, stating that one of their goals in theorizing gender performativity was to 'open up the field of possibility' for previously unnamed ways of being (Butler 2006, p. viii). They have since observed that, when they wrote Gender Trouble, 'there was no category for "nonbinary"', but they now use the term to describe their relationship to gender (Gleeson 2021). I also have 'trans elders' younger than myself to thank for giving me ways to think about my gender that propelled me into my transness.

For years I had been embracing a masculine presentation, using 'any pronouns', binding my chest, and – when pressed – identifying myself as 'gender "meh", I guess?' or 'I dunno ... Is "hobbit" a gender?' But *a man*?! I would periodically research testosterone and contemplate top surgery without understanding these as the actions of a trans man. After all, the dominant depiction of trans men in media is generally a lesbian so butch that 'she' becomes 'a he'. This trajectory is characterized by dysphoria and the goal is to approximate cisness. Despite knowing trans men who did not fit this stereotype, I had subconsciously internalized these assumptions and therefore thought I could not possibly be a man; I was not femme, but I was feminine (although not in the ways that male femininity is predominantly portrayed, which is to say as either flamboyant or a joke – and sometimes both).

I am one of the many people for whom hours of 'doom scrolling' to break the monotony and anxiety during the early days of the Covid-19 pandemic resulted in a radically changed understanding of self. The eerily perceptive TikTok algorithm filled my For You Page with feminine masculinities that I had rarely seen represented: men (cis and trans) being publicly, deliberately and earnestly pretty, gentle or nurturing; men (cis and trans) sincerely and enthusiastically demonstrating their feminized interests and hobbies; trans men expressing attraction to other men; superficial bro culture set-ups being instructively rescripted to showcase deeper care practices; etc. Despite largely adhering to an 'unveiling' format, many of these memes were more of a mischievous revelation than an unsettling 'reveal' – skilfully faking towards, but ultimately evading, the harmful trans 'trap' trope. They tended to sparkle with a sense of irreverent 'gender euphoria' (a term that itself calls up but redirects away from defining transness primarily through the medicalized, defect-centric lens of dysphoria). One account described gender euphoria as looking in a mirror and seeing yourself reflected (as in *oh, there you are*). The creators of these TikToks were announcing 'here I am' and, reflected therein, I saw a self that I had always been but had not yet known existed.

What all of this content had in common was Gen Z and younger Millennials' knack for meaning making through meme, serving up repurposed audio and visuals with the intent of creating, in Sandoval's words, new orders of meaning. When severing the signified from signifier, they would invoke the assumptions that usually fill the space between before replacing them with new meaning – and a flourish and a wink. Creators gleefully engaged in the 'meta-ideologizing' of masculinity, manhood and transness. Even the very word 'gender' seems to have acquired new a meaning, standing in for a deeply felt but unspecified (unspecifiable?) affinity, presentation or genre of being when used in phrases such as 'this is so *gender*' and 'I feel very *gender*' or in the concept of 'gender envy' illustrated through the short-lived 'gender envy but it makes less and less sense to cis people' meme. In it, the content creator would post a succession of pictures that caused them 'gender envy', starting with recognizable gender presentations from fashion photographs, film stills and illustrated fictional characters but moving towards what might be called 'a vibe': objects, landscapes, paintings, lighting, patterns, fabrics, colours – even states of overgrowth, dilapidation or decay. (Mere months earlier, I had half-jokingly created a 'gender mood board' with Pippin from Lord of the Rings, Farmer Hoggett from Babe, Michael from The Good Place and Arnold Lobel's Frog and Toad. I now understand this as an exercise motivated by gender envy.) These practices follow the contours laid out by Sandoval: reading for power, disrupting and subverting dominant understandings, and rewriting and repurposing meaning towards liberatory gender possibilities both individually and collectively.

Although I do not yet feel capable of so skilfully exercising the sort of deliberate political strategizing or semiotic disobedience associated with the first two types of differential movement that Sandoval describes, it is the third type – differential consciousness – that gives me hope for being able to enact similar practices. I would even go so far as to argue that transness itself may offer access through a third temporality: suspension. Describing differential consciousness, Sandoval states that it cannot be expressed through words or viewed head-on. She identifies its workings across the writings of activists and thinkers including Frantz Fanon, Gloria Anzaldúa, Trinh Minh-ha, Cherríe Moraga, Patricia Hill Collins, Audre Lorde, Gayatri Spivak, Donna Haraway, Roland Barthes, Jacques Derrida and Hayden White. She characterizes differential consciousness as a sort of 'no place' in which potential meanings are 'available in a constant tumult of possibility' (141).

To make use of differential consciousness requires that we embrace a technology of 'drifting' among these meanings, attentive to what she calls a 'third meaning' beyond binary opposition. Sandoval writes, 'every exchange can be understood as suffused with this meaning as it shimmers around what appears to be concrete. It is an extra, uncategorizable, unnameable meaning haunting all human need to name, classify, order, and control' (144). Although not stated outright, 'third' appears to refer not to the number of possible meanings – which would reasonably be as uncountable as they are unnameable and uncategorizable – but rather to how these potential meanings operate: Sandoval is speaking about possibilities that cannot be distributed into the binaries structuring Western thought without some sort of remainder that is 'unintelligible to the dominant order' (150). Sandoval writes that this is a characteristic shared with marginalized constituencies, and I would suggest that transness offers one such example with suspension operating like the 'drifting' that she describes.

Although I carry an awareness of the simultaneous and cumulative character of my gender into my interactions, people I meet for the first time (particularly cis people) seem to glimpse only facets of this trajectory and treat them as evidence for the purposes of categorization. I never enter a situation confident in how I will be read – how the other party will distribute decades of experiences, behaviours, affinities, presentations and desires into gendered categories. Recently, a new volunteer at wheelchair racing practice defaulted to 'she/her' pronouns for me after I mentioned the topic of my dissertation research (cats, gender and domesticities), yet only weeks before another racer's father had suggested the need for sex-segregated practices while gesturing towards me as a specimen of hulking masculinity relative to his (ironically, more athletic) daughter. Neither of them asked my pronouns or gender, and I do not know if they know I am trans. I therefore wonder how they arrived at their conclusions, which I suspect reveal at least as much about their own conceptualizations of gender as they do about my presentation.

Most interactions with strangers have this suspended, 'Schrödinger's gender' quality until the other person says or does something that reveals their assumptions –

as illustrated by a phone call I received about pie. The woman on the other end of the line worked for a gluten-free bakery. They were out of the pumpkin pie I had ordered; would I take blueberry instead? I eagerly agreed to the substitution, but the woman belaboured the point – a bit too apologetic for a conversation about pie – and gilded the interaction with an oddly flirtatious giggle. I reassured her that I was equally excited about blueberry, thanked her and hung up a bit bewildered. It was the first time I had heard that giggle directed towards me; *why* would she be flirting? It took me a moment to realize that she was *actually* engaged in emotional management; she had expected me to react negatively to being told I could not have the pie I presumably wanted. I remember having behaved similarly towards white men in particular when working in the service industry. It was important to massage any 'no'; upfront emotional labour could save considerably more on the backend. I had been selling cheese rather than pie, but I was aware of the need to make men feel desirable and in control even in such low-stakes transactions. I then understood: the bakery worker had perceived my voice as a man's voice (a correct assumption) and was treating me accordingly in case I took the pie selection as an affront (an assumption that I certainly hoped to be incorrect but that I was helpless to change until it was too late to do so).

This dynamic can present a further problem when it is unclear which classificatory systems are in play. For example, at about four months on testosterone, I was taking a neighbourhood walk with my crutches at dusk. On an otherwise empty street, I saw a man and a woman around my age coming towards me on the sidewalk. I could tell that the man was inebriated and agitated. As he passed me, he slowed, leaned in slightly and let out a quiet wolf whistle. The woman, appearing unbothered, herded him forward. As my uneasiness began to ebb a few blocks away, I wondered what to make of the situation. I knew that I felt unsafe and targeted, but I did not know in which way: misogyny, transphobia, homophobia or ableism (all of which have been grounds for street harassment of one sort or another in the past). Sometimes an interaction reveals the assumptions of the other party, and sometimes it does not. I am relieved that this situation did not escalate enough to find out.

More recently, I wondered aloud to my boyfriend (himself a trans man) whether this state of suspended subjectivity is a feature or a bug of the trans masc experience. He vigorously interjected, 'oh yeah that feeling never goes away.' To a certain extent, one may learn the rules of engagement (i.e. how to operate relative to the binary); however, transness also eludes and exceeds such conventions, holding the same 'grammatical position' in the social order as Sandoval's 'third meaning'. According to Sandoval, to operationalize the third meaning in the service of differential consciousness requires a 'punctum' – a rupture – that 'breaks through social narratives to permit a bleeding, meanings unanchored and moving away from their traditional moorings' (140). As it happens, breaking through social narratives is something I do a lot – albeit by accident, as illustrated by an exchange outside of my doctor's office:

I had parked in the accessible space out front and was transferring into my wheelchair when a beefy, bald man standing behind my car barked in an aggressively jovial tone, 'Hey! Did you see that asshole parked here?!'

Unsure where this was going, I responded to his question with a straightforward answer: 'Oh, I missed him, but yeah it happens all the fucking time.'

There had been a break in the traffic and the man was about to jog across the road, but he halted abruptly mid-action and did a doubletake before mumbling an explanation, sounding confused and almost hurt: '... plumbing van.'

I did not know quite what I had done – only that I was read as a 'fellow man' and somehow breached 'protocol'. I asked trans friends and social media mutuals, and they explained: the man was soliciting casual comradery. He was acknowledging me, and I was supposed to reciprocate. I had been expected to match his tone with something like 'yeah what an asshole' or 'fuck that guy'. Instead, I injected information into what was intended to be a fleeting and superficial bonding exercise – and, worse, I turned *down* the aggressiveness of the interaction to the point of dismissal, batting away the figurative fist bump he was extending to me.

Over and over again, I have found that my transness has granted me the ability to disrupt the 'normal' course of events. Unfortunately, at this point, it is usually completely unintentional on my part. As 'punctums' go, my transness is currently making Swiss cheese of social interactions – not at all the deliberate challenging and channelling of power that Sandoval encourages us to practice, so now I come to this chapter's fourth incarnation of trans time: anticipation. In short, hoping that my future self with greater experience is a little bit wiser for it. This is not unique to transness, of course. In follow-up reflections on their seminal works, feminist scholars such as Judith Butler, Gayatri Spivak and Donna Haraway have written about how their ideas have continued to change with further feedback and reflection (Butler 2006, Spivak 2010). Every publication is only ever a snapshot of how the author makes sense of the topic at the time of writing. Perhaps one difference, however, is the omnipresence of 'known unknowns'. I am gently haunted by the 'ghost of transness future', who I fully expect to look back at my present efforts and shake his head – hopefully because he feels much better equipped to enact feminist resistance.

A provisional conclusion

This chapter began with a clumsy admission of uncertainty, and now it concludes in a similarly inelegant manner: what can I say but, um, this is as far as I have gotten with things? It is all admittedly quite shaky, but it would be disingenuous for me to 'fake it 'til I make it' when my transition is presently characterized primarily by ongoing questions and (re)adjustments.

The question motivating this chapter was, quite simply, how do I do feminism when I feel as though I have no idea what I am doing more broadly? The first step to answering this question was figuring out how my relationship to feminism has changed through transition; what kind of feminist subject am I? It would be inaccurate to say either that my relationship to feminist praxis remains unchanged or that being a man automatically makes me 'The Man'. I therefore returned to a text that oriented my feminist journey pre-transition: Chela Sandoval's 'Methodology of the Oppressed'.

Although I am still trying to grasp in concrete terms the ways that my relationship to feminist resistance has changed, Sandoval's work has given me some possibilities for framing my experiences and some potential directions to explore. I have brought her insights together with four incarnations of trans time (simultaneity, intertemporality, suspension and anticipation) to suggest that transness may itself function as an avenue for feminist resistance through responsive and agile negotiations of power – even if the execution may take a bit more practice.

References

Ahmed, Sara. (2017). *Living a Feminist Life*. Durham, NC: Duke University Press.

Butler, Judith. (2006). *Gender Trouble: Feminism and the Subversion of Identity*. New York, NY: Routledge.

Gleeson, Jules. 'Judith Butler: "We Need to Rethink the Category of Woman"'. *The Guardian*. Guardian News and Media, 7 September 2021. https://www.theguardian.com/lifeandstyle/2021/sep/07/judith-butler-interview-gender.

Halberstam, J. Jack. (2005). *In a Queer Time and Place: Transgender Bodies, Subcultural Lives*. New York, NY: New York University Press.

Kafer, Alison. (2013). *Feminist, Queer, Crip*. Bloomington, IN: Indiana University Press.

Liboiron, Max. (2021). *Pollution Is Colonialism*. Durham, NC: Duke University Press.

Lugones, Maria. (2016). 'The Coloniality of Gender'. In The Palgrave Handbook of Gender and Development. London: Palgrave Macmillan, pp. 13–33.

Muñoz, José Esteban. (2009). *Cruising Utopia: The Then and There of Queer Futurity*. New York, NY: New York University Press.

Petrovnia, Alex. Twitter Post. 29 March 2022, 08:56. https://twitter.com/AlexPetrovnia/status/1508835392480501763.

Price, Margaret. (2014). *Mad at School: Rhetorics of Mental Disability and Academic Life*. Ann Arbor, MI: University of Michigan Press.

Rummler, Orion. '"Those Dollars and Cents Add up": Full-Time Trans Workers Face a Wage Gap, Poll Finds.' The 19th, 27 January 2022. https://19thnews.org/2022/01/transgender-workers-wage-gap-lowest-paid-lgbtq/.

Sandoval, Chela. (2000). Methodology of the Oppressed. Minneapolis: University of Minnesota Press.

Spillers, Hortense J. 'Mama's Baby, Papa's Maybe: An American Grammar Book'. *Diacritics*, 17 (2): 65–81. https://doi.org/10.2307/464747.

Spivak, Gayatri Chakravorty. 'In Response: Looking Back, Looking Forward'. In Rosalind C. Morris (ed.), *Can the Subaltern Spaek?: Reflections on the History of an Idea*. New York: Columbia University Press, pp. 227–36.

Tuck, Eve & K. Wayne Yang. (2012). 'Decolonization Is Not a Metaphor'. *Decolonization: Indigeneity, Education & Society*, 1 (1): 1–40.

Chapter 2

WALKING THE 'FEMINIST TIGHTROPE': NAVIGATING FEMINIST IDENTITIES WITHIN ANTI-VIOLENCE WORK WITH MEN

Maddie Brockbank

Introduction

When thinking of autoethnographic methodologies, we might initially conceptualize it solely as a qualitative research practice that can assist us in connecting our personal stories, identities and experiences to broader structural forces and influences through critical self-reflection (Allen & Piercy 2005; Ettorre 2016). As Allen & Piercy (2005) suggest, '[a]utoethnography is the practice of going back and forth between inner vulnerable experience and outward social, historical, and cultural aspects of life, searching for deeper connections and understanding' (p. 155–6). In this process, the autoethnographic method aligns well with feminist approaches to research, which actively seek to challenge androcentric, objectivist frameworks claiming the existence of a singular empirical truth by exploring personal subjectivities, partial truths and contested histories (Allen & Piercy 2005; Ettorre 2016; Kirby & McKenna 2004). Ettorre (2016) suggests that autoethnography 'is an active demonstration of the "personal is political"' (p. 6).

While feminist autoethnography indeed serves as a qualitative methodology that can uncover subversive histories and centre marginalized stories through research, it can also serve as a practical tool guiding the critical analysis of service provision (e.g. counselling, group therapy, intake, assessment and other therapeutic practices involved in social service work) and the foundational discourses that they are built upon, such as integrating considerations of a service provider's identity and positionality in relation to the service users that they are working with for the purposes of imagining socially just practice (Ettorre 2016; Kirby & McKenna 2004; Pillow 2015). Specifically, within social work praxis, the concept of reflexivity closely aligns with feminist autoethnography, whereby we are required to think critically about the work we are doing, why we are doing it and what assumptions underpin the conceptualization and operationalization of the social problem our practice is seeking to address (D'Cruz, Gillingham, & Melendez 2007). However, social work continues to undergo systemic attempts to professionalize, institutionalize and bureaucratize the work in order to 'legitimize' it and reject its perceived origins as a 'semi-profession' characterized by 'seemingly natural feminine qualities of listening and caring' (Weigmann 2017: 101). Professionalization involves a decided shift away from exploring the subjective realms of service providers and service users to instead prioritize more objective forms of practice, including overreliance on standardized assessments, strict adherence to practice theories, documentation, treatment plans and ethical policies seeking to identify reporting procedures regarding perceived risk (Beres, Crow & Gotell 2009; Hancock, Mooney & Neal 2012; Leotti 2021; Smith 2008).

In this chapter, I seek to bridge feminist autoethnography with feminist social work's conceptualizations of reflexivity to unpack my experiences of facilitating and researching men's violence intervention and prevention. Specifically, I seek to draw on these methodologies to reveal the ways in which feminist subjectivities and resistances play out in a practice setting, where my feminism was constantly in flux, under attack and challenged by the confines of social work practice settings. To do so, I will narrativize and metaphorize three significant vignettes of my experiences in anti-violence work to explore the interplay between personal feminist subjectivities and socio-structural discourses. In this process, I aim to demonstrate how reflexivity tends to be gendered labour that exposes the limitations and deficits of current men's anti-violence programming and theorizing. In naming reflexivity as a gendered demand that can lend to important insights to the power dynamics governing the systems we work in, I also seek to name how this feminist praxis can act as everyday form of resistance to pressures of professionalization and individualization of social work practice with men who use violence. Put simply, centring feminist subjectivities can both implicitly and explicitly challenge the ways in which anti-violence work has become increasingly alienating, bureaucratic and removed from the social contexts that it is operating within.

A note on feminist social work

Dominelli (2002) describes feminist social work praxis as 'a form of social work practice that takes women's experience of the world as the starting point of its analysis and by focusing on the links between a woman's position in society and her individual predicament' (p. 7). Feminist social work is deeply connected to the popular motif of the 'personal as political', where shared experiences among women have been recognized as matters requiring public attention (Dominelli 2002; Ettorre 2016). While consensus would suggest that feminist social work practice seeks to better women's social conditions and communities by politicizing previously labelled 'private troubles', feminisms in practice cannot be oversimplified or essentialized as women do not agree about the sources of their oppression and marginalization (Dominelli 2002). Further, when feminist theory – and feminist social work – maintains its roots in whiteness by historically centring, uplifting and pursuing white women's concerns and interests, reducing the source of women's oppression to 'patriarchy' is often deemed a counterproductive attempt to 'whitestream' the feminist movement (Bates 2020; Grey 2004; Sheehy & Nayak 2020).

While it is outside the scope of this chapter to address these tensions, it is important to note that my understanding of feminist social work as it pertains to facilitating violence intervention with men does not encompass the myriad of approaches, conceptualizations and ideas put forth by feminist researchers and practitioners. In this way, some of my reflections are quite myopic; however, I feel that articulating my personal experiences can link to some of these tensions of whitestreaming in the feminist movement against gender-based violence, where the structure of anti-violence work relies on specific assumptions about perpetrators of violence and the programmes that they should be mandated to attend.

A note on reflexivity in social work

While reflexivity is a frequently used concept in feminist autoethnography, it is also a tool readily integrated into critical social work pedagogy and variously defined in social work literature. D'Cruz, Gillingham and Melendez (2007), in particular, provide a relatively comprehensive overview of the different conceptualizations of reflexivity in social work literature. In their discussion, they make distinctions between types of reflexivity, ranging from deeply micro-level practices of self-actualization to considerations of the ways in which power shapes knowledge curation, and differentiate processes of 'reflection' from these dynamics. For the purposes of this discussion, I turn towards their third version of reflexivity, which aims to both (1) acknowledge one's own cognitions, emotions and positionality in knowledge production and (2) mobilize a critical awareness of self to influence their practice and action (D'Cruz, Gillingham and Melendez 2007). This third variation rejects an objectivist framework for social work practice to instead embrace the subjective, dynamic interplay between a practitioner's emotions, thoughts and subsequent knowledge production. Here, emotion plays a key role in how a service provider undertakes service provision and demonstrates self-awareness of how their own perspectives may shape their work.

I also seek to pull from Pillow's (2015) notes on feminist reflexivity, which acknowledges the origins of this work as lying within women of colour's resistance to former conceptualizations of reflexivity as a 'knee-jerk reaction'. Instead, reflexivity is framed as an intentional process with the potential for transformative interactions, where one can exercise 'the ability to reflect inward toward oneself as an inquirer; outward to the cultural, historical, linguistic, political, and other forces that shape everything about inquiry; and, in between researcher and participant to the social interaction they share' (p. 421). This approach prompts researchers and practitioners to consider the ways in which they are always 'caught in representation' (Pillow 2015: 421) and may be demonstrative of power dynamics determining who can represent who.

Women in anti-violence work: Locating the author

As a white, cisgender woman interested in anti-violence work with men, it is important for me to identify myself and the origins of my reflections in this autoethnographic chapter. I occupy a unique position, where I am caught up in various representations: the power of being a white woman in men's violence prevention is underpinned by the ways in which white women's stories have been – and continue to be – centred in mainstream coverage of gender-based violence (Bates 2020; Grey 2004; Phipps 2016; Phipps 2021; Sheehy & Nayak 2020). Simultaneously, my vignettes focus on being isolated as a woman in anti-violence work, where I am frequently framed as representing all women in a room of men. Despite the potential for me to centre my gender in these reflections as my most salient characteristic that subverts me in these contexts, I hope to also resist picking apart and dichotomizing identity markers. In other words, my whiteness is inseparable from my gender; neither is more visible or more important. Rather, they interact to produce my experiences and my myopic accounts of being a woman in anti-violence work. They cannot be individually unpacked for they have material and historical origins, where white women's roles in upholding white, colonial, imperialist cisheteropatriarchy continue to be of significant concern (Gregory 2021; hooks 2004; Joseph 2015).

In the broader context of existing literature on women's roles in anti-violence work, gender has been framed as the most salient characteristic shaping women facilitators' experiences. Research has indicated that, while men facilitators are preferred in anti-violence programming, women facilitators and a co-gender model have proven merit (Flood 2019; McCallum 1997; Piccigallo, Lilley, & Miller 2012; Tyagi 2006). For instance, McCallum (1997) suggests that the inclusion of women in a facilitation role prompts men to consider the impacts of their diction and language in group sessions, appreciate the integration of a woman's point of view, and respond positively to women facilitators' empathy by exercising honesty and accountability (McCallum 1997). Similarly, Flood (2019) indicates that women facilitators can effectively engage and sensitize men and boys in violence prevention through creating space for them 'to hear of women's experiences and concerns and to further mobilize their care for the women and girls in their own lives' (p. 212). A co-gender model, where groups are moderated by one man and one woman, can model an egalitarian relationship and challenge traditional gender stereotypes (Flood 2019; McCallum 1997; Tyagi 2006).

Despite the potential positive aspects of women's facilitation in men-focused anti-violence work, Allen (2005) and Tyagi (2006) identify potential limitations. For example, Allen (2005) reflects on her experiences of facilitating all-men focus groups and the risks of women facilitators inadvertently perpetuating and imposing expectations of cisheteropatriarchal masculinity by implicitly suggesting what is/ is not acceptable behaviour for men. These impositions of traditional masculinity might include making assumptions about their personal (hobbies, interests, etc.) and social (race, class, sexual orientation, etc.) identities. Additionally,

Tyagi (2006) notes that women facilitators might endure an uncomfortable and/ or hostile environment as participants direct misogynistic comments or 'gender-specific anger' (p. 5) towards the only woman in the room, particularly in the context of mandated group settings, based on the assumption that she is there to challenge or police them. Flood (2019) and Tyagi (2006) both indicate that men often do not take a woman's role seriously in anti-violence work as she is perceived as a gendered token that is required to meet a programme expectation, a staple to maintain a cisheterosexual group dynamic, or a fulfilment of feminine stereotypes (e.g. taking on the 'nurturing' or 'empathic' role). These factors become exacerbated by a co-gender model that recreates gendered power dynamics, where the man facilitator takes up significant space, implicitly (or explicitly) undermines the woman facilitator's authority, 'rescues' the woman facilitator or consistently qualifies her statements (Tyagi 2006). Simultaneously, women facilitators may be forced to undertake the burden of sensitizing men to this topic by disclosing personal experiences or pushing participants to consider how violence could affect them personally (e.g. popular motifs around 'what if this happened to your sister/partner/friend/mom?'). The amalgamation of these factors might result in significant barriers to women's participation in anti-violence work

Vignettes from a woman in men's anti-violence

I identify with the reflections posed in previous literature on this subject as they are ones that I have intimately experienced as a woman in violence intervention and prevention. I utilize some of these discussions to ground my exploration of three autoethnographic accounts of my experiences in men's anti-violence work. The details of these stories are drawn from reflective papers submitted for my courses, journals I wrote in and my distinct memories of significant events that have shaped my feminist praxis. These vignettes are broader metaphors that will be linked to the dynamic (re)negotiations and (re)imaginations of feminist subjectivities and identities in decidedly anti-feminist spaces, where I will reflect on my various resistances and complicities that often troubled me.

Vignette #1: Feminist failures

As an eager undergraduate student, I pursued a project on exploring men university students' perspectives of sexual violence on Ontarian university campuses. The project had emerged out of conversations I had with my second-year instructor for a feminist social work class. She believed that I was onto something when I declared that I wanted to talk to men about sexual violence. With her support, I drafted questions, conducted interviews and mini-focus groups, and performed data analysis for the first time. It was unlike anything I had ever done before, and I firmly believed that it was filling a necessary gap in feminist research on anti-violence with men.

Emboldened by my passions and curiosities, I entered dialogues with seven young men over the course of one summer. What began as something exciting quickly evolved into something unsettling. One interaction, a focus group with two young men, continues to haunt me. While discussing the gaps in existing policies and educational programmes about sexual violence on campus, the conversation veered into a territory that I was not prepared for. The conversation was documented in the transcription as follows:

> **Greg:** Like, I just think people need a more holistic understanding of what consent is. People just think consent is something that's, like, 'do you wanna have sex, yes or no?' And they think if someone's absolutely obliterated and they say 'yes,' then that's okay.
> **Interviewer:** And you think that should be taught more?
> **Kyle:** Yeah. Well, unless it's your girlfriend, like, that's a perfect example. If you go to a bar and some girl or guy is, like, really drunk and gives consent, it's a grey area because you don't know if it's real. If it's your girlfriend, it's different. You've built a relationship with trust and all that. But, with a random person, I don't know. Like, that's the problem, right? Like, most of these sexual encounters would be at a bar or possibly there could be some drinking going on.
> **I:** Hmm.

Within this dialogue about developing educational programmes and resources about sexual violence, Kyle articulated an understanding of consent that deeply troubled me. I remember sitting across from him, discomfort churning my stomach, as I wrestled with my feelings. *Should I intervene? Should I correct him? Should I ask him to elaborate?* I questioned my own perspectives and understandings: *Am I misinterpreting him? Is my definition of consent too restrictive? Do I understand the social context that he is referring to?* I was so caught up in my own reaction to what he said and how it landed with me – *he is saying that alcohol makes consent a grey area and that consent is assumed when you're in a relationship* – that the conversation naturally progressed while I sat in this excerpted moment for hours afterward.

Ultimately, I felt like a failure. While I could rationalize the decision not to say anything as a purely research-related exercise in letting the dialogue flow, I felt troubled by the reality that Kyle may have walked out of that room feeling as though conversations about consent and sexual violence did not apply to him based on his belief that he knew enough about it or that he did not see himself as a perpetrator of sexualized harm.

Olive and Thorpe's (2011) discussion of negotiating identity in feminist ethnographic fieldwork provides a sound summary of what I was wrestling with. Their discussion dedicates space to exploring the concept of 'feminist failures', where confounding moments, disruptions or inactions can facilitate a perceived disconnect between our research practices and our own values. While they acknowledge that it is an uncomfortable and distressing process, they also indicate that it is a contextual tactic allowing researchers to work within and against anti-feminist spaces by drawing on multiple positionalities. Here, Olive and Thorpe (2013) draw on the Bourdieusian concept of 'regulated identities' to point to the ways in which individuals occupy and negotiate multiple identities and locations to maintain access, navigate relationships and confront troubling moments in their interactions within the field. In this dynamic, we come to recognize how women may simultaneously adhere to and resist sociocultural norms governing femininity to navigate a space where a feminist identity might be unwelcome or might become a barrier to further engagement. This process is particularly significant in ethnographic praxis, whereby researchers are expected to navigate, balance and conform to the dichotomy between adherence and resistance in an effort to create space for understanding and avoid unduly influencing subjects' participation (Olive & Thorpe, 2013).

Drawing on Olive and Thorpe's (2013) theorizing, my monosyllabic response ('*hmm*') could be perceived as both a feminist failure and a tactic of resistance that was appropriate for the ethnographic context, particularly as it links to facilitating space for participants' values, perspectives and languages to emerge without interference. If I had corrected Kyle, I might have shut down communication completely and caused harm. However, I also feel that I abandoned some aspects of my feminist identity, a concession that did not sit well with me. By simply responding with an 'hmm', I did not voice my support of his comments, but I also did not intervene in a way that could have potentially ended the discussion. Interestingly, in his own way, Greg also expressed his resistance by redirecting the conversation after Kyle had finished speaking. Neither of us acknowledged Kyle's comments, which might have been a form of resistance in itself. Here, feminist failures can bring us to new understandings and insights about the dynamics and processes of research and where feminist identities come into play. In this way, they can also be necessary; these failures can evoke opportunities for both researcher and participant reflexivity that happens throughout the interaction and enhances our critical understandings of ethnographic praxis.

Vignette #2: Identity work

Early in my fourth-year social work field placement, I was tasked with co-facilitating the Partner Abuse Response (PAR) programme. The PAR programme is a mandated anti-violence group for people who have been criminalized for domestic violence-related offences. Pioneered by Todd Augusta-Scott (2017), the programme seeks to undertake an invitational and accountability-driven approach to violence intervention and prevention by integrating narrative therapeutic techniques with educational elements about a range of topics, including abuse, communication, conflict resolution, substance use, anger and gender norms, among others. While the group structure ranges depending on the context, the PAR programme at the agency I was placed at tended to have around thirty men per group.

Initially, I expected to be a third facilitator that eased into a leadership role in the group. Instead, I became the woman facilitator, paired with a man facilitator who had been doing this work for over twenty years, about four weeks into my placement. I considered myself lucky to have a great co-facilitator who knew the ropes and was willing to mentor me, but I was also inundated with nerves. My co-facilitator's encouragement was well intentioned and kind, but it also failed to account for the complexity of what was being asked of me. Here I was, a 21-year-old BSW student, an unpaid intern, a young, white woman, and relatively inexperienced, stepping into a room where I was the only woman. The men had only gotten used to seeing me observe sessions, make an occasional comment and assist with activities on the whiteboard. They had never seen me step up and take the lead.

Over the course of the next ten weeks, several interesting dynamics and tensions emerged. First, marring some of the positive experiences I had – where I felt like the men really heard and absorbed what I was saying in the group – were instances where I felt undermined. For example, after every session for about ten weeks, one man participant would hug me before leaving for the day. One man handed me an incredibly crass and overtly sexual joke, typed up on a piece of paper, at the break during one Saturday morning group. A few joked around with me in a way that bordered on flirtatious; one man made me deeply uncomfortable during a one-on-one intake with comments about my appearance and bodily movement that eventually invaded my personal space. And, on the feedback form they fill out after completing the programme, one man wrote, 'I really liked Chris and the girl facilitator.' I was frequently called 'Natalie' or 'Maggie' for all ten of the weeks I co-facilitated. They never forgot my co-facilitator's name.

Simultaneously, I also had experiences where I bore the brunt of participants' frustration with being forced to complete the programme. It was difficult not to notice the ways in which participants would nod, make eye contact, laugh and jump off Chris's points, while most of what I said was followed by a stretch of awkward silence, men's gazes fixed on the floor, their postures slumped as if I wasn't even speaking. I distinctly remember one participant nearly falling asleep when I led a section of the group. Contrastingly, some participants, especially early in the programme, would make eye contact with me when they would make a misogynistic comment. 'All women are crazy.' 'Why don't you guys do a women's group?' 'All women do is lie.' 'Why isn't she here, doing this group, when she's the one that started it?' Their gazes would linger on me, as if they were gauging my reaction or waiting for me to blow up, waiting for me to prove their point.

I would often leave the group exhausted. I began to dread the days where I had to facilitate. I began to doubt my own abilities. *Why don't they take me seriously? What am I doing wrong? Why am I so bad at this?* The knot in my stomach eventually felt like a permanent fixture. At times, I felt crushed. Other times, I felt completely apathetic.

In her research on utilizing focus groups as a methodology for working with men, Allen (2005) utilizes the term 'identity work' to refer to how men in her study constructed masculinity linguistically, behaviourally and relationally through gendered socialization and 'performing' gender. In a similar vein, I feel that my experiences in the PAR programme were largely reflective of my own identity work, where my feminist identity was deeply contextual, dynamic and challenging to present in my language, behaviour and interactions with service users. When participants would engage in flirtation with me, it was a case-by-case decision that I often attempted to rationalize. For example, while I wanted to reject one participant's departing hugs, I found myself instead justifying my passivity: *if I hug him, that'll be easier than trying to exert a boundary and explain to him why it's inappropriate. I don't need another guy in this group hating me.* It was a contextual subversion of my feminist subjectivity that I engaged in based on my concerns that my overt resistance would result in hostile reactions.

However, it is also important to note that the men who were most forward with me were all white, cisgender, heterosexual men over the age of forty. While there were many racialized men in the group, several of whom did not use English as their first language, they were, contrastingly, quite wary and did not engage much with me, nor openly with the group. White men tended to verbally dominate the space. On average, in a group of thirty men, three to four men were usually the most active while the rest were sat quietly; of those who were most active, they were usually white, cis-hetero, English-speaking men. Most of the men participating in the group were also working class and talked openly about financial concerns that persisted throughout their lives. In understanding men's positions entering the group, some of my decisions to subvert feminist subjectivities were in relation to positionality; as a young, white, educated, middle-class woman, I was forced to think critically about standards of professionalism that I may have been imposing upon them and that reflected largely white, Western and colonial understandings of appropriate conduct. In this, my decisions not to 'call them out' on certain behaviours could have been considered a form of resistance to classist and racist logics that demand men perform identity in a way that is deemed acceptable by white, capitalist, colonial systems.

I also identify with what Vera-Gray and Kelly (2020) call 'safety work' (p. 269), which refers to the invisible labour that women often undertake to prevent violence from happening. As Vera-Gray and Kelly (2020) aptly note, '[l]ike other forms of invisible work, safety work is hidden because it is related to the very core of what being a woman is – not seen as something women do but as something that they are' (p. 269). I felt that I frequently engaged in discretionary safety work, where I contextually decided 'what hill to die on'. In this way, I stretched and subverted my feminist values to accommodate my perceptions of men participants' attitudes toward me. To avoid experiencing further violence in the group, such as being the subject of misogynistic comments, I turned back towards Olive and Thorpe's (2013) concept of working within and against anti-feminist spaces by adapting to the climate, engaging in subtle resistance and exercising a regulated identity. In this, my efforts to compartmentalize and contextualize my identity and feminist values were a resistance to falling into the binary categories often assigned to women facilitators in anti-violence work: passive token or harsh disciplinarian. Instead, I chose to integrate contextual considerations – such as participants' identities, the space, the topic, the time and my own capacities – before I expressed myself. I can only describe it as waiting to jump into double Dutch: you carefully assess your surroundings, wait for the perfect moment and then jump in to express your feminist beliefs when you know it is safer to do so. I managed to do that by the end of my placement, but it certainly took a significant amount of feminist complicity.

Vignette #3: Disrupting carceral logics

As many social workers know, responding honestly to the question, 'so what do you do for a living?' is often met with raised eyebrows, sympathetic grimaces and slightly disapproving *tsks* about how difficult and underpaid the work is. In my case, my standard description – *I work in anti-violence with men* – tends to evoke some interesting reactions: ears perk up in a cartoonish fashion and they ask me a relatively standard set of questions about what exactly I do, what the men in mandated violence intervention programmes are like, what they did to get into the PAR programme and what made me want to go into this work. I think many expect a deeply personal narrative to emerge as many assume social workers go into the profession to heal from some of their own traumas. I think they also expect some horror stories about my experience co-facilitating PAR, including the gritty details of police reports and accounts of violent outbursts happening during group programming.

I experience this dynamic most often when guest-speaking about feminist social work and violence intervention in a variety of social work courses. After discussing the complexities and promises of the work, the question I am asked the most by burgeoning social work students, many of whom haven't yet worked in the field, is, '*so are the guys in the group scary?*' Usually, I give a half-hearted answer about 'scary moments, not scary people'. However, during the most recent talk I gave to a feminist social work class, I tried to expand on this further, albeit in what felt like an unsuccessful response.

'Well,' I remember saying.

> There are certainly moments that can be uncomfortable and challenging. But it feels reductive to say that they scare me. The men in the group are not monsters; they are people in your community. And, yes, they perpetrated harm in their relationships, but it'd be unfair to say that they do that to everyone and that I'm scared that they'd do it to me. It might negate the experience of the survivor, and it might paint the men in the group as some sort of deviant criminal that behaves as such. It perpetuates myths about intimate partner violence. In reality, they are people who have caused harm, and we have had some incredible conversations about that and all the things that shaped that. So, I guess the long-winded answer is that I actively resist the impulse to be scared of them because I think it might be … counterproductive.

My answer ended in an uncertain mumble, which was prompted by the blank stares I received on the screen of the Zoom call. I'm not sure that what I said landed well. I wrestled with how I phrased things; I worried that I might've said something that could be perceived as being dismissive about the harm of intimate partner violence. It was a tension that expanded beyond the confines of that presentation and one that I have named 'the feminist tightrope': How do you balance the need for accountability in men's violence intervention, while also resisting common tropes that stigmatize, pathologize and criminalize those who use violence in unhelpful ways?

To explore and settle these tensions, I turn to anti-carceral feminist theorizing. Returning to my comments about the ways in which whiteness has been centred in mainstream accounts of gender-based violence, I feel that it is important to understand the whitestreamed narrative of the feminist movement against violence and how it has intentionally individualized the issue and constructed perpetrators of violence as the 'bad', 'violent', Other (Ahmed 2013; Gottzen 2013; Taylor 2019). Here, popular motifs about criminalized perpetrators of violence are underpinned by carceral logics that facilitate the individualization of social problems and the shift away from recognizing white, colonial, imperialist cisheteropatriarchy as a social structure facilitating this violence (Bumiller 2008; hooks 2004; Taylor 2019). In the process of upholding pathologized images of perpetrators, we reify myths about intimate partner violence that distance 'normal', 'good' people from the deviant, violent monster perpetrating violence against the community (Ahmed 2013; Levine & Meiners 2020; Taylor 2019). However, anti-carceral and Black feminist theorizing, which I have used to ground my doctoral work, presents feminist resistance to such practices of dehumanization via challenging these binaries and naming the systems that facilitate and uphold these images (Levine & Meiners 2020; Taylor 2019).

My thinking around this subject has been the result of relatively intense self-reflection and reflexivity, where I have pushed myself to consider where my fears of PAR participants originated, what assumptions those fears are predicated on and what kinds of harms might be inflicted if I treat service users as the violent Other. Namely, I had to push myself to confront the deeply classist and racist origins of these fears, where white women, in particular, have perpetuated carceral constructions of the violent Other via 'the Brute Caricature' and other images that often depict perpetrators as racialized, poor strangers (Pilgrim 2012). It is considerably tough work: my experiences of practising safety work and feeling embodied tensions as the only woman in the room during PAR sessions are certainly built on very real experiences that women have; however, confronting your own biases, assumptions and fears that are built on white, colonial, capitalist and carceral foundations can be unsettling and shameful. Nonetheless, in some incredible moments facilitating the group, I was able to have in-depth conversations with men about their lives, values, feelings, goals and relationships and got to witness them arrive at a place of accountability seemingly on their own, which presented some fascinating opportunities to resist and rewrite carceral logics in real time.

These experiences defied the racist, classist and carceral logics that suggest 'bad' men are mandated and criminalized while 'good' men roam free. Additionally, carceral assumptions that gender-based violence is sufficiently addressed through arrest, incarceration and/or mandated rehabilitation negate the realities that most instances of intimate partner and sexual violence go unreported and less than 1 per cent of perpetrators of sexual violence face conviction and sentencing (Johnson 2012; Kim 2018; Taylor 2018). In other words, constructing carceral interventions as effective and perpetrators as deserving of punitive treatment programming deliberately ignores the failures of the carceral state to actually protect survivors, which has been widely recognized and named by prison abolitionists and Black feminists (see Davis et al. 2022; Kim 2018; Levine & Meiners 2020; Taylor 2018). As they identify, the carceral state commits mass violence against both survivors and perpetrators of violence to obscure the realities that social structures are at fault for the continued prevalence of gender-based violence (Kim 2018; Taylor 2018; Taylor 2019).

Despite the personal strides that I have made in my own theorizing, it continues to be a difficult conversation to have with most people, where many still believe in the efficacy of the carceral state and feel comfortable individualizing violence in reductive ways. Further, many emerging social work students may feel bonded to the criminal justice system based on social work's alliance with the carceral state. In this way, it can be incredibly challenging to practice anti-carceral reflection or action in a social work organizational setting due to the reality that the agency you are working in likely receives funding from carceral bodies. The PAR programme, in particular, is an extension of police, the court and probation offices, and we must adhere to policies that extend the surveillance, power and control of the carceral state. Here, we begin to uncover the confining structures of social work as a profession, where feminist subjectivities must also be flexed to accommodate the mandate of the agency you are working within. Nonetheless, integrating anti-carceral feminist reflexive and autoethnographic praxis into your everyday work – via challenging images of the violent Other and resisting pathologizing practices – can offer an avenue for enacting feminist resistance to the deeply carceral systems that we operate and live in.

Discussion and conclusion

This discussion has sought to autoethnographically explore the tensions of navigating feminist identities in anti-violence settings. My accounts have discussed the dynamics of 'feminist failures', where feminist practitioners and researchers are often burdened with feeling that they have abandoned their values to accommodate anti-feminist spaces, rhetoric and ideas in the name of organic research (Olive & Thorpe, 2013). Further, I discussed the discomfort tied to being 'caught up in representation' as the only woman in the room during men's PAR programmes and the kind of 'safety work' that women often undertake to prevent and avoid further violence, which often involves feminist complicity and discretional feminist expression (Vera-Gray & Kelly 2020; Allen 2005). Lastly, I attempted to challenge the carceral logics frequently underpinning the conceptualization of mandated anti-violence programme participants as being inherently reflective of whitestream feminist motifs about gender-based violence (Grey 2004; Kim 2018; Sheehy & Nayak 2020; Taylor 2018).

From my stories and reflections about my five years in this work, I have taken away that this kind of feminist reflexivity, where we are constantly flexing our identities, strategically negotiating and communicating our values, and questioning the production of assumed knowledge, is gendered labour that women practitioners and researchers frequently bear the brunt of (Olive & Thorpe 2013; Pillow 2015; Vera-Gray & Kelly 2020; Tyagi 2006). When subjectivity, emotion and vulnerability are implicitly framed in social work as 'feminine' practices (Weigmann, 2017), they become the subject of scrutiny, dismissal and erasure in projects of professionalization, thus undermining the significance of reflexive praxis (Smith 2008; Beres, Crow, & Gotell 2009; Hancock, Mooney, & Neal 2012; D'Cruz Gillingham, & Melendez 2007). Moreover, these dynamics often result in women being forced to accommodate professionalized, bureaucratized, individualized and androcentric spaces by subverting their feminist values and identities, questioning their own abilities and practices, and feeling unfit to work within the confines of an organization that does not support them (Smith 2008; Beres, Crow, & Gotell 2009; Hancock, Mooney, & Neal 2012). However, feminist practitioners also resist these violent structures in their everyday praxis via centring humanization, socio-structural analyses, awareness of positionality and a willingness to challenge the deeply white, colonial, capitalist and carceral constructions governing the systems we work in.

In this work, reflexivity can often feel like a fruitless task: How can I engage in any kind of transformation and social change when working within restrictive boundaries and anti-feminist spaces? However, I have come to appreciate that resistance does not always need to be explicit, loud, and jarring; rather, it can be a slow process that is exercised strategically. Maybe it is not groundbreaking; perhaps you feel a bit like a failure when it is done. Nonetheless, these resistances are important pieces to a larger puzzle about feminist subjectivity and resistance. We must often 'collaborate with the very structures [we seek] to transform' (Beres, Crow, & Gotell 2009: 139); however, we can also centre liberatory praxis via feminist reflexivity and resistance. Here, feminisms are pluralities that are dynamic, contextual and ever-evolving, expressed and exercised as resistance when researchers and practitioners are given space to do so. My experiences in anti-violence work point to the complex and contextual nature of this work; however, I see resistance as lived, significant and transformative to, as Davis et al. (2022) suggest, imagine a world that we have not seen yet.

References

Ahmed, S. (2013). *Strange Encounters: Embodied Others in Post-Coloniality*. London: Routledge.

Allen, K. R. & Piercy, F. P. (2005). 'Feminist Autoethnography'. *Research Methods in Family Therapy*, 2: 155–69.

Allen, L. (2005). 'Managing Masculinity: Young Men's Identity Work in Focus Groups'. *Qualitative Research*, 5 (1): 35–57.

Augusta-Scott, T., Scott, K., & Tutty, M. (eds.). (2017). *Innovations in Interventions to Address Intimate Partner Violence: Research and Practice*. New York, NY: Routledge.

Bates, K. G. (2020, May 6). *What Does 'Hood Feminism' Mean for a Pandemic?* NPR. https://www.npr.org/2020/05/05/850963562/what-does-hood-feminism-mean-for-a-pandemic.

Beres, M. A., Crow, B., & Gotell, L. (2009). 'The Perils of Institutionalization in Neoliberal Times: Results of a National Survey of Canadian Sexual Assault and Rape Crisis Centres'. *Canadian Journal of Sociology*, 34 (1): 135.

Bumiller, K. (2008). *In an Abusive State: How Neoliberalism Appropriated the Feminist Movement Against Sexual Violence*. Durham, NC: Duke University Press.

Davis, A. Y., Dent, G., Meiners, E. R., & Richie, B. E. (2022). *Abolition. Feminism. Now* (Vol. 2). Chicago, IL: Haymarket Books.

D'Cruz, H., Gillingham, P., & Melendez, S. (2007). 'Reflexivity, Its Meanings and Relevance for Social Work: A Critical Review of the Literature'. *The British Journal of Social Work*, 37 (1): 73–90.

Dominelli, L. (2002). *Feminist Social Work Theory and Practice*. London, UK: Macmillan International Higher Education.

Ettorre, E. (2016). *Autoethnography as Feminist Method: Sensitising the Feminist 'I'*. New York, NY: Taylor & Francis.

Flood, M. (2019). *Engaging Men and Boys in Violence Prevention*. New York, NY: Palgrave Macmillan.

Gottzén, L. (2013). 'Encountering Violent Men: Strange and Familiar'. In *Men, Masculinities and Methodologies*. London: Palgrave Macmillan, pp. 197–208.

Gregory, J. R. (2021). 'Social Work as a Product and Project of Whiteness, 1607–1900'. *Journal of Progressive Human Services*, 32 (1): 17–36.

Grey, S. (2004). 'Decolonising Feminism: Aboriginal Women and 'Global' Sisterhood'. *Enweyin*, 3: 9–22.

Hancock, L., Mooney, G., & Neal, S. (2012). 'Crisis Social Policy and the Resilience of the Concept of Community'. *Critical Social Policy*, 32 (3): 343–64.

hooks, b. (2004). *The Will to Change: Men, Masculinity, and Love*. New York, NY: Atria Books.

Johnson, H. (2012). 'Limits of a Criminal Justice Response: Trends in Police and Court Processing of Sexual Assault'. *Sexual Assault in Canada: Law, Legal Practice and Women's Activism*, 640: 305–41.

Joseph, A. J. (2015). 'Beyond Intersectionalities of Identity or Interlocking Analyses of Difference: Confluence and the Problematic of 'Anti'-oppression'. *Intersectionalities: A Global Journal of Social Work Analysis, Research, Polity, and Practice*, 4 (1): 15–39.

Kim, M. E. (2018). 'From Carceral Feminism to Transformative Justice: Women-of-color Feminism and Alternatives to Incarceration'. *Journal of Ethnic & Cultural Diversity in Social Work*, 27 (3): 219–33.

Kirby, S. & McKenna, K. (2004). 'Methods from the Margins'. In W. K. Carroll (ed.), *Critical Strategies for Social Research*. Toronto: Canadian Scholars' Press, pp. 67–74.

Leotti, S. M. (2021). 'Social Work with Criminalized Women: Governance or Resistance in the Carceral State?' *Affilia*, 36 (3): 302–318.

Levine, J. & Meiners, E. R. (2020). *The feminist and the Sex Offender: Confronting Sexual Harm, Ending State Violence*. London: Verso Books.

McCallum, S. (1997). 'Women as Co-facilitators of Groups for Male Sex Offenders'. *Social Work with Groups*, 20 (2): 17–30.

Olive, R. & Thorpe, H. (2011). 'Negotiating the 'F-word' in the Field: Doing Feminist Ethnography in Action Sport Cultures'. *Sociology of Sport Journal*, 28: 421–40.

Phipps, A. (2016). 'Whose Personal Is More Political? Experience in Contemporary Feminist Politics'. *Feminist Theory*, 17 (3): 303–21.

Phipps, A. (2021). 'White Tears, White Rage: Victimhood and (as) Violence in Mainstream Feminism'. *European Journal of Cultural Studies*, 24 (1): 81–93.

Piccigallo, J. R., Lilley, T. G., & Miller, S. L. (2012). '"It's Cool to Care about Sexual Violence" Men's Experiences with Sexual Assault Prevention'. *Men and Masculinities*, 15 (5): 507–25.

Pilgrim, D. (2012). 'The Brute Caricature'. *Jim Crow Museum of Racist Memorabilia: Ferris State University*. https://www.ferris.edu/jimcrow/brute/.

Pillow, W. S. (2015). 'Reflexivity as Interpretation and Genealogy in Research'. *Cultural Studies? Critical Methodologies*, 15 (6): 419–34.

Sheehy, C. & Nayak, S. (2020). 'Black Feminist Methods of Activism Are the Tool for Global Social Justice and Peace'. *Critical Social Policy*, 40 (2): 234–57.

Smith, A. M. (2008). 'Neoliberalism, Welfare Policy, and Feminist Theories of Social Justice: Feminist Theory Special Issue: "Feminist Theory and Welfare"'. *Feminist Theory*, 9 (2): 131–44.

Taylor, C. (2018). 'Anti-Carceral Feminism and Sexual Assault – A Defense: A Critique of the Critique of the Critique of Carceral Feminism'. *Social Philosophy Today*, 34: 29–49.

Taylor, C. (2019). *Foucault, Feminism and Sex Crimes: An Anti-Carceral Analysis*. New York, NY: Routledge.

Tyagi, S. V. (2006). 'Female Counselors and Male Perpetrators of Violence Against Women'. *Women & Therapy*, 29 (1–2): 1–22.

Vera-Gray, F. & Kelly, L. (2020). 'Contested Gendered Space: Public Sexual Harassment and Women's Safety Work'. In *Crime and Fear in Public Places*. London: Routledge, pp. 217–31.

Weigmann, Wendy L. (2017). 'Habitus, Symbolic Violence, and Reflexivity: Applying Bourdieu's Theories to Social Work'. *The Journal of Sociology and Social Welfare*, 44 (4): 95–116.

Chapter 3

QUEERLY MAD: CRIPPING GRIEF AND POST-TRAUMATIC FIBROMYALGIA SYNDROME

Kody Muncaster

Introduction

Queer people experience a high prevalence of post-traumatic stress disorder (PTSD) and high rates of exposure to traumatic events (Reisner 2016; Roberts 2010; Shipherd 2011). Yet little work has explored queer experiences of post-traumatic stress disorder and trauma as a disability. This is not surprising since, according to James Berger (2004), trauma studies and disability studies rarely meet. I use crip theory (Kafer 2013) and Mad studies (Menzies, LeFrançois & Reaume 2013) to discuss queer trauma from Ann Cvetkovich's (2003) depathologizing framework. This chapter facilitates a queer dialogue between trauma studies, crip theory and Mad studies. It also represents my own internal dialogue, as I attempt to depathologize my queer experience of trauma, while also negotiating crip and Mad identity politics. Such identity politics involve a complicated dance between demedicalizing narratives and reclaiming psychiatric labels in order to be visibilized in disability justice circles. It is through the work of queercrip and Mad autoethnography, a traumatic autoethnography built from the biblio-therapy of queer theory and the flashbacks of complex PTSD, that I find resistance to dominant narratives around queer trauma. I discuss grief from the AIDS crisis as well as queer and trans suicide in an exploration of queer trauma as Mad, crip and queer world-making. I use my experience of living with fibromyalgia and C-PTSD to explore trauma's impact on the body while resisting dominant medicalized narratives of trauma and chronic pain. I examine the utility of crip and Mad identity for the queerly traumatized to resist, depathologize and politicize queer feelings about cisgender, heterosexual hegemony. To begin, a foregrounding of the relationship between disability studies and trauma studies is germane.

Queer trauma and/as disability

Berger (2004) explains that the disciplines of disability studies and trauma studies rarely meet. He also highlights some differences between approaches in the two fields (Berger 2004). He explains that disability studies scholars often include discussions on their personal experiences of disability, while trauma studies scholars rarely discuss their own experiences of trauma (Berger 2004). However, Berger's article appears antiquated given the burgeoning work of Mad studies and crip theory, two subfields of disability studies that include some work on trauma. Autoethnographic accounts of queer trauma (e.g. see Morrigan 2017a; 2017b; Piepzna-Samarasinha 2018) challenge this notion by integrating the queer person's lived experiences of trauma into their writing. Since Berger's publication in 2004, trauma studies and disability studies have developed a closer relationship, particularly in the intersections of queerness, Mad and crip identity formation. That is not to say that this relationship started following Berger's publication, rather, that these communities have long worked together and their presence in theory has recently become more pronounced.

I resist what Berger argues is a trauma studies tradition of divorcing one's work from one's personal experience. Indeed, Berger's claim may suggest that there is a trauma studies canon, which belies the burgeoning work of queer scholars discussed throughout this chapter. I use autoethnography to theorize about personal experiences that I have had as a traumatized queer person using Mad studies and crip theory. Admittedly, I share Mel Chen's (2012) feelings about the use of personal narrative in academia as 'genuinely risky and threatening terrain, the terrain of the biographical' (p. 273). Indeed, personal narrative is met with suspicion in academia, causing me to share Chen's hesitation to explore it. However, I am resisting the anxious urge to avoid this terrain in hopes that it will provide an analysis of sanism and queerphobia that contributes a queer connection between disability studies and trauma studies.

Medical approaches to queer trauma

In December 2019, I went to a new doctor in London, Ontario, Canada, whom I had never met, to renew my mirtazapine, an antidepressant that can also be used for PTSD. When I told this stranger that I was diagnosed with PTSD at age sixteen, he asked me, in our short interaction, what I had PTSD from. I chose not to explain why that is an inappropriate and obviously triggering question to ask a stranger you are prescribing a common antidepressant for. I also chose not to outline how for queer people, trauma is often ubiquitous, insidious, and sometimes daily experience, rather than a single event. In reality, it was C-PTSD that I was living with, complex trauma from a childhood filled with violence and a life faced with homophobia at every turn, but this was not worth mentioning. Instead, I gave the right answer: an answer of trauma porn to satisfy his voyeuristic curiosity, choosing select experiences from years of child abuse and an account of sexual violence for my testimony. When I finished, he responded with the question: 'so are you gay, heterosexual or non-binary?' I made no mention of queerness, so I wondered if it was the part about sexual violence or the gay sound of my voice telling it that made him ask that question. While I did not pass as straight to this doctor, I passed as a person living with PTSD through my testimony of abuse and violence.

What is queer about queer trauma is not only the fact that it is experienced by queer people. Queer trauma does not fit within dominant approaches to mental health management. The doctor referred me to a trauma support group at a local hospital. When the hospital called me, I was informed that the trauma groups are separated by cis conceptions of binary gender. They told me they did not know what they would do for a genderqueer person such as myself. They told me that they would get back to me and then I never heard from them again. I was unable to access services that were meant for cis straight people. Rosemary Garland-Thomson's (2011) concept of the misfit is interesting here. While Garland-Thomson (2011) suggests that the person with a disability does not fit within social mores of compulsory able-bodiedness/able-mindedness, my queer experience of trauma did not fit within the bounds of the cishetero trauma group. I soon learned that queercrip writing on trauma and Madness would benefit me much more than that group could have. Several years later, I moved to Toronto and was finally able to access services that were targeted towards queer people. I attended a group for gay men and non-binary people that used cognitive processing therapy for PTSD at a new trans and gay men's health organization that offered both STI testing and mental health programmes. The depth of the suffering that these queer men went through was painful to witness, and at the same time the healing community that was formed was more validating than any hetero-dominated group could have ever provided.

Mad studies and crip theory

My formal introduction to Mad communities began in graduate school, when I read about Mad studies. Here, I use the term 'formal introduction' because, little did I know, I had been part of Mad communities my entire life, through the informal Mad networks of people surviving complex mental health challenges. In the introduction to their edited collection, *Mad Matters*, Robert Menzies, Brenda LeFrancois and Geoffrey Reaume (2013) define Mad studies as 'a project of inquiry, knowledge production, and political action devoted to the critique and transcendence of psych-centred ways of thinking, behaving, relating, and being' (p. 13). Mad studies emerged out of the consumer/survivor/ex-patient (c/s/x) movement, critiquing sanism and psychiatry's power, though not all Mad studies scholars are categorically antipsychiatry (Menzies, LeFrançois & Reaume 2013).

It is worth noting that the positionalities of consumer, survivor and ex-patient occupy different relations to psychiatry's power, and one can simultaneously inhabit more than one of these three identities.

Similarly, crip theory is critical of biomedical approaches to disability. While there is some work on crip approaches to mental health (Kafer 2013), crip theory tends to focus more on physical disabilities. Alison Kafer (2013) discusses crip theory's vexed relationship with disability studies. She argues that crip theory examines both the exclusionary practices of identity politics while also examining their utility in disability rights advocacy (Kafer 2013). Crip theory has also been put in conversation with queer theory. Robert McRuer (2006) explains, 'crip theory … should be understood as having a similar contestatory relationship to disability studies and identity that queer theory has to LGBT studies and identity' (p. 35). McRuer employs Judith Butler's explanation in *Critically Queer* (1993) that a failure to adhere to compulsory heterosexuality does not necessarily lead to its subversion. Similarly, McRuer argues for a 'critically disabled' (p. 30) perspective that subverts compulsory able-bodiedness (and, I would add, compulsory ablemindedness) rather than a depoliticized disabled identity. Both Mad studies and crip theory have used a politicization of disability in their discussions of queer trauma (Morrigan 2017a; 2017b; Piepzna-Samarasinha 2018).

Reclaiming queer trauma

Ann Cvetkovich (2003) finds a queer approach to trauma in lesbian public culture that 'seizes control over it from medical experts, and that forge[s] creative responses to it that far outstrip even the most utopian of therapeutic and political solutions' (p. 3). Cvetkovich explicitly resists the diagnosis of PTSD. Instead, Cvetkovich discusses queer trauma as an everyday experience and reconfigures trauma from pathology to explore how queer trauma impacts and is impacted by trauma cultures. She argues that trauma cultures, the public cultures that form around trauma, can have therapeutic effects that extend beyond the limits of the private therapeutic encounter. Moreover, she draws connections between archives of trauma and queer archives; both are ephemeral and challenge that which constitutes an archive. She joins Laura Brown (1991), whose formulation of insidious trauma accounts for the everyday experiences of sexism, oppression and systemic violence. Cvetkovich states, 'the challenge of insidious trauma or chronic PTSD … is that it resists the melodramatic structure of an easily identifiable origin of trauma' (p. 33) such as the origin that my doctor demanded I explain to him in our short interaction. Indeed, those of us living with the insidious trauma of oppression and who have survived repeated exposure to horrific situations that have left us with complex trauma are left asking: Where do I start? How much time do you have?

Cvetkovich (2003) notes that part of her wariness about the pathologization of trauma also stems from the psychiatric pathologization of homosexuality. The American Psychiatric Association declassified homosexuality as a disease in 1973 (Cvetkovich 2003). Though it is important to note that trans experience continues to be pathologized as gender dysphoria in the *DSM-5*, leaving transpeople at the mercy of medical gatekeepers for access to many transition-related services. Cvetkovich (2003) notes that just as doctors and scientists may have 'invented' (p. 45) homosexuality, they similarly created PTSD in the *DSM-III* in 1980 to diagnose the trauma of Vietnam War veterans. She states, 'the parallels with the history of homosexuality serve as a reminder that even if the PTSD diagnosis has certain strategic merits, it is wise to remain vigilant about the hazards of converting a social problem into a medical one' (p. 45). It is worth noting that categories such as PTSD and C-PTSD can enable access to mental health and disability services that, due to the red tape of the medical and social services industrial complexes, may not be available without a diagnosis. These categories can be clarifying and validating for some people. At the same time, they can be limiting, creating an identity in which we cannot escape, in which our reactions to what happened rather than the traumatic events are the problem. The problem is located in our brain chemistry rather than in the brains and fists of our abusers. Some may find it useful to access diagnoses where appropriate and to consider the language of 'trauma' and 'complex trauma' over PTSD and C-PTSD during times in which a depathologizing narrative is more helpful. As someone living with complex trauma, I alternate between both ways of storying my experience. Narrative therapy helps us understand how we live multi-storied lives and sometimes the ways we narrate our experience is informed by oppression or is a replaying of old tapes with the voices of our abusers. We may consider re-authoring the stories we tell ourselves about who we are and what has happened in a way that is more helpful. Sometimes we need to narrate our experience using a certain language that our audience can digest.

Cvetkovich (2003) understands trauma's ability to produce trauma cultures and the relationship between those cultures and queer culture through their ephemerality and their challenge to what which is typically understood as an archive. Cvetkovich's concept of trauma cultures denotes a queer potentiality and capacity for the formation of public cultures. One explicit example of a queer trauma culture can be seen in identity formation among traumatized queer people. Tumblr user ptsdsafe's Traumatized/PTSD LGBT+ pride flags are a notable example of queer trauma's capacity to create public cultures. Ptsdsafe's (2019) mix of various sexual and gender minority flags with a PTSD flag previously created by the user, your-fave-has-ptsd, might suggest an investment in the use of the term PTSD. However, it is important to note that ptsdsafe describes the flags as 'Traumatized/PTSD LGBT+ pride flags', putting the non-pathologizing term first and opening the possibility for traumatized people to use the flag without identifying with the term PTSD. They also state, 'non-traumatized people can interact, but don't use', asserting a political utility for the flags that relies on self-identification as traumatized rather than a medical diagnosis.

These affinities among queer and traumatized community members can be understood as a form of queer worldmaking. Ptsdsafe's (2019) use of the pride flag represents a form of queer world making in which trauma's affects are (counter) public feelings (Cvetkovich 2012). Their flags represent a queer intimacy and comradery around experiences of trauma without reference to the homonormative domesticity and neoliberalism that now proliferates queer politics. The user of the flag admits an inseparability between their trauma and their queerness, a unity between queer cultures and trauma cultures (Cvetkovich 2012). I too, feel an inseparability between my queerness and my trauma, as my queer trauma informs the way I view the world. My life has been spent talking with queerly traumatizied folks about the ways in which we have survived. Cvetkovich's work is grounded in a feminist approach with her discussion of queer trauma culminating in oral history interviews with lesbian AIDS activists. Queer trauma cultures as a concept has strong resonance with feminist notions of collective activism.

The Traumatized/PTSD LGBT+ pride flag politicizes queer trauma as a public feeling, similar to Cvetkovich's (2012) discussion of political depression as a public feeling and a 'sense that customary forms of political response, including direct action and critical analysis, are no longer working either to change the world or to make us feel better' (Cvetkovich 2012: 1). Political depression is a model of understanding that our affect sometimes reflects the outside world and that how we feel can reflect social problems. Perhaps those of us who are queer people living with depression are often the queer people who are paying attention to the cishetero world we are stuck in – and the queer people experiencing multiple forms of marginalization that the more privileged may not be as attuned to. The use of flags suggests a collective affinity among queer people experiencing trauma. Though Alison Kafer's (2013) use of collective affinity suggests an affinity among people of a variety of disabilities who recognize their similarities and differences, it could also apply here to a variety of queer people experiencing various forms of trauma.

Cripping trauma

When I moved to another province to work in queer health, my parents, once again, stopped talking to me and this has continued (perhaps for the better) five years later. After dealing with a few more traumatic events and grief while not being able to keep up with my bills in a city where I knew no one, I began getting pain throughout my body. My finger joints hurt when I typed. Then it spread to my lower back and cervical spine. I was working in the HIV/AIDS sector, and I felt tired all day. I had so many X-rays done that the X-ray technologist asked me if I was sure that I wanted to expose my body to that many carcinogenic atoms and molecules. I had several blood tests for arthritis, an electromyography on my hands to rule out carpal tunnel, and was sent to a back pain specialist whom I later learned, much to my dismay, was not a medical doctor but someone with a PhD in physiotherapy working out of the hospital. Before I realized he was not a medical doctor, he said it may take 5–10 years for me to get a diagnosis of what is likely either fibromyalgia or seronegative rheumatoid arthritis and said, 'I can't help you.' I feared that it was ankylosing spondylitis, one of the diseases my mother has. I am still waiting to get an MRI done to rule that out as it may be comorbid with my current diagnosis. The pain served as a connection to my mother, a constant traumatic reminder that was steeped in the despair of grief. My family doctor told me she had no idea what was wrong with me, so I saw doctors at several walk-in clinics, many of whom said it was likely fibromyalgia but they would not officially diagnose. Eventually, I requested my medical records, printed the over 100 pages out, and brought them to a university doctor with a completed fibromyalgia scoring sheet. She said, 'Kody, I think you need someone to look you in the eyes and tell you: you have fibromyalgia. Many primary care doctors are hesitant to diagnose it even though it does not require a rheumatologist to confirm.' I felt so validated. It took three years.

My current therapist told me that he has had many clients with fibromyalgia and he believes that fibromyalgia is often a physical manifestation of trauma. It is a disease in which you have pain all over your body, brain fog, fatigue and stomach issues with no apparent physical cause, perhaps due to an over-engaged stress response impacting your nervous system. I soon realized that many other queers experienced it too. Mattilda Bernstein Sycamore (2010), writing the introduction to her anthology with voice activation software, explains, 'fibromyalgia is a word for this relentless cycle of pain and exhaustion that is the physical manifestation of my struggles to survive what happened in the house where I grew up, and that still resides in my body, in my brain, *in these poor hands that never could have protected me*' (Sycamore, 2010, p. 14). I broke down crying when I read the last line of this. Indeed, my poor hands could never have protected me from my father's violence, my mother's disgust with me, from the violence of homophobes at school, from the childhood sexual abuse I experienced as a teenager in the hands of older men. My hands ache with a wish that they could have defended me. Leah Lakshmi Piepzna-Samarasinha tries to locate her pain's origin in trauma, interestingly similar to the compulsion to locate the origin of trauma itself. She discusses fibromyalgia as possibly stemming from:

> a childhood filled with abuse, terror, and a need to sleep as much as possible [that] bleeds into chronically tired yet overachieving college years, bleeds into the early twenties when I walked back into my incest memories, got sick, and spent a lot of time on my futon, struggling with fatigue, pain, and shakiness.
> (Piepzna-Samarasinha 2018: 180–1)

Similarly, queer musician Lady Gaga lives with fibromyalgia and PTSD, which she talks about as stemming from sexual violence (Hawa 2018). I soon learned that so many queerly traumatized people in my friend circle also had fibromyalgia. Cohen et al. (2002) found that 57 per cent of their sample of patients with fibromyalgia had clinically significant symptoms of PTSD. It is so common that they hint towards the possibility of a 'post-traumatic fibromyalgia syndrome' (PTFS), with which I would certainly identify. Häuser et al. (2013) found that 45.3 per cent of fibromyalgia patients compared to 3 per cent of the population met the diagnostic criteria for PTSD. While PTFS is not a diagnosis yet, perhaps there needs to be greater recognition of PTFS that honours the relationship between trauma and pain. This is not to say that everyone who has fibromyalgia has trauma. Rather, I want to highlight how significantly trauma impacts the body. How fibromyalgia makes the Mad become corporeally crip. It was validating to see this connection. I often underestimate the impact of my trauma and fibromyalgia forced me to realize that the things that happened to me really were *that bad*. Indeed, they were bad enough to cause physical pain not only during the recurring temporal periods in which I was being beaten but pain that may last a lifetime.

Mad trauma pride

Clementine Morrigan's (2017b) work is an expression of Mad trauma pride that questions the notion of curative time, that people with disabilities are always living in relation to a potential future cure. While some may want a cure, Morrigan (2017b) opts to see PTSD as a different way of living in the world. They *queer* psychiatric constructions of PTSD, instead, opting to understand trauma as a queer temporality of time travel which they call, queer trauma time (Morrigan 2017b). They discuss queer trauma time travel through many of the symptoms I experience daily such as flashbacks, nightmares and hypervigilance (Morrigan 2017b). In their other work exploring self-harm, Morrigan (2017a) explores trauma's so-called 'symptoms', or forms of, 'acting out' (p. 62) as testimony to surviving violence. Morrigan (2017a) asserts that their self-harm was a resistant form of embodied testimony that refused to participate in their family's silence about the sexual abuse that they were experiencing from their grandfather. I spent my teenage years making hundreds of cuts in my own body when I would feel overwhelmed by emotion. Before reading Morrigan's (2017a) work, I thought this was because I did not know how to self-soothe before I started practising meditation regularly when I entered foster care. I now realize that while that is also true, these cuts were also a testimony to the violence that I experienced at home, a refusal to comply with the demands that my body look and act heteronormative. It was a refusal to stay silent, as my scars spoke the abuse for me. Morrigan was psychiatrically incarcerated and forcibly medicated. They explain that 'the location of the problem was shifted from the adults who abused and neglected me to my own body as a chemically imbalanced site of disorder' (Morrigan 2017a: 71). They argue that psychiatric approaches to Madness are designed to produce compliance, and that by telling our stories, Mad people are refusing to comply (Morrigan 2017a).

Their work is resonant with Leah Lakshmi Piepzna-Samarasinha's (2018) discussion of the survival industrial complex (SIC). Piepzna-Samarasinha (2018) explains that the SIC is a network of institutions that manage Madness, including medicine, psychiatry, policing and victim compensation funds. They argue that one way the SIC operates is through the notion of the 'good' and the 'bad' survivor (Piepzna-Samarasinha 2018). The 'good' survivor is a respectable neoliberal citizen that can move on from their trauma and not have it impact their life or their participation in the wage economy (Piepzna-Samarasinha 2018). The 'bad' survivor continues to experience the effects of trauma, despite interventions from psychotherapy, even years after the traumatic event(s) they experienced (Piepzna-Samarasinha 2018). Morrigan's (2017a) argument that Mad people refuse to comply with psychiatry by telling their stories is an example of the 'bad' survivorship that Piepzna-Samarasinha (2018) discusses.

Piepzna-Samarasinha (2018) argues for an alternative, disability justice understanding of the survivor that values the transferrable skills, knowledges and gifts of survivors. Piepzna-Samarasinha posits that some trauma may not be fixable, suggesting a focus on the value of survivorhood itself rather than attempts to cure survivors. Morrigan's (2017a) conceptualization of queer trauma time can be understood as one of the survivor knowledges that Piepzna-Samarasinha (2018) argues we should value rather than focus on curing. Like Morrigan (2017a; 2017b), Piepzna-Samarasinha (2018) includes testimony of their own experience as a 'bad' survivor of trauma, countering the tendency of trauma studies writers to exclude their lived experiences from their work (Berger 2004). Piepzna-Samarasinha (2018) states that they are a 'bad' survivor who is still affected by their childhood sexual abuse despite undergoing psychotherapy, but who is also a person experiencing many joys in their life. They resist the narrative of supercrip while still discussing their complex relationship to a traumatized life's ups and downs (Piepzna-Samarasinha 2018).

Bad survivors haunted by the queer mad (un)grievability of AIDS and suicide

Eve Kosofsky Sedgwick begins *Tendencies* (1993) by stating, 'I think everyone who does gay and lesbian studies is haunted by the suicides of adolescents' (p. 1). Suicide haunts queer communities as the leading cause of death of gay and bisexual men in Canada (Hottes, Ferlatte & Gesink 2015). Suicide also significantly impacts trans people (Bauer, Pyne, Francino, & Hammond 2013; Rood, Puckett, Pantalone & Bradford 2015). I find the metaphor of haunting valuable because it captures the possession that occurs when these losses overtake our minds and we are stricken with grief that can never be fully exorcised. Indeed, many queer people living through this cishetero death world are haunted by the suicides of fellow queers, as well as the deaths of queer people due to a lack of action during the AIDS crisis. My own experience of attempting to exorcise those ghosts has, as of yet, been unsuccessful.

I know eight queer people who have killed themselves, the most impactful for me being the death of the late Logan Cummings. I have tried to consult several people on how to move through my grief, most of which have been unhelpful. In my first session with one psychotherapist, I was asked what lesson I think life is teaching me by having me encounter all these suicides. I responded that perhaps the lesson I have discovered was an article I read, estimating that suicide has surpassed

AIDS-related illness as the leading cause of death of gay and bisexual men in
Canada (Hottes, Ferlatte, & Gesink 2015). That was the wrong answer. I fired
her and went searching for a new therapist. I asked a psychic at the 2020 London
Psychic Expo about a dream I had about Logan. She responded by asking me, in
front of a large audience, if I was dating the queer person I was sitting with (I was).
Then she told me that is imperative that I go back to school to become a counsellor.
I also tried going to a suicide bereavement group to exorcise these ghosts. Each
person introduced themselves, named the person they knew who died by suicide
and graphically described the way their loved ones killed themselves. When it came
to me, I listed several names and explained that I come from a community that has
high rates of suicide. A man in the group immediately responded by asking me if
that community was the gay community. I regretted wearing a colourful shirt that I
figured must have tipped him off. The doctor whom I mentioned earlier, the psychic
and the man at the suicide bereavement group were not interested in witnessing
my testimony. Instead, these people were more interested in finding out if they had
a good gaydar

(other than the psychotherapist, who wanted me to see a life lesson in queer
suicide). Eventually, I found a support group for queer and trans people who have
lost someone to suicide. I was finally among others who shared my experiences
(some of whom experienced multiple losses) without having to worry about
queerphobia.

While being queer has made addressing my grief with heterosexual doctors, psychotherapists, psychics and support groups difficult, I have had some success discussing my experiences with an HIV-positive gay mentor of mine. I was mentored by a man in his sixties, through a grief programme when I worked in AIDS. He explained that during the AIDS crisis, he and his colleagues lost so many people, in such a short time, that traditional models for grief could not capture their complex feelings. This led to the creation of the AIDS Bereavement and Resiliency Program of Ontario (ABRPO), which has been responding to the personal and organizational impacts of AIDS-related grief and loss since its inception in 1994 (Perreault, Fitton, & McGovern 2010). ABRPO's long-term survivors of AIDS-related losses created the AIDS-related Multiple Loss Journey in 2002 to help give voice to these experiences (Perreault 2011). The resistance of dominant approaches to grief counselling through the development of the Multiple Loss Journey model demonstrates how queer resistance need not be confined to protesting; honouring our collective pain is an act of resistance. Though I have yet to lose someone to AIDS-related illness, my mentor used the AIDS-related Multiple Loss Journey model (Perreault 2011) with me to help guide our discussions on my losses to suicide, the loss of my parents and other traumas. The AIDS-related Multiple Loss Journey (Perreault 2011) is emblematic of Piepzna-Samarasinha's (2018) discussion of survivor skills, knowledges and gifts. My mentor's knowledge and skills for working with grief were a queer gift to me that helped our discussions on suicide-related losses and my other trauma. My mentor was a fellow 'bad' survivor (Piepzna-Samarasinha 2018) of loss and was able to teach me some of the skills he gained from his own survivorship.

Jennifer M. Poole and Jennifer Ward (2013) coin the term Mad grief to describe 'a reclaiming of that which has been traditionally used to other, pathologize, and ostracize those who grieve. It may defy categories, binaries of normal or abnormal, may be unstageable, possibly circular, and frequently extended' (p. 95). They name the piece as being born out of the sanist reactions they experienced to their own grief. They situate Mad grief in juxtaposition to dominant psychiatric approaches by arguing against traditional notions of so-called 'normal' vs. 'complicated', grief (Poole & Ward 2013). Their quote that 'we need to think about how someone's self-identified gender, sexuality, and race, for example, will make it more or less safe to grieve Mad' (Poole & Ward 2013: 102) is notable when considered in the context of my earlier story of grieving.

The psychotherapist's insistence that I see a lesson in queer suicide was a sanist reaction to my Mad grief. As a queerly traumatized person, what is truly 'insane' to me is the sanist notion that there is some grand lesson in being surrounded by suicide. Further, to answer Poole and Ward's (2013) call to examine intersectionality and the ability to grieve Mad, it was difficult for me to make outward expressions of grief when the responses were questions about my sexuality. I feel a physical pain in the centre of my chest as I write about this flashback to how after I talked about the horrors of losing so many people suicide, the first thing that a man in this suicide bereavement group cannot restrain himself from trying to find out is whether or not I am gay.

Judith Butler (2016) explains that discursive frames impact whether certain lives are grievable or ungrievable in the public imaginary. Butler explains that 'an ungrievable life is one that cannot be mourned because it has never lived, that is, it has never been counted as a life at all' (Butler 2016: 38). Butler is not stating that nobody grieves these losses; rather, she is discussing how broader public affective responses to loss are determined by larger social structures. She also explains that to be interpellated as a life, a body must also fit within the heterosexual matrix of sex, gender and desire (Butler 1993). The abject bodies (Butler 1993) of queer people and people living with HIV are not interpellated as living and thus are ungrievable. Grieving the ungrievable in a world where queer people are given the status of living dead is Maddening. As Pryor (2017) explains, 'in a culture of forgetting, keeping the dead alive through acts of remembrance is a profoundly subversive act' (p. 31). To insist on grieving the ungrievable is in a cishetero death world is to express Mad grief. Indeed, Mad grief is an affect that has been quintessential in the formation of queer trauma cultures. These cultures conjure spectres of the AIDS crisis, such as that seen in The Names Project's AIDS Memorial Quilt (The AIDS Memorial Quilt, n.d.) in a refusal to forget that which is so often erased from public memory. The trauma of AIDS haunts queer communities through each panel of the AIDS Memorial Quilt. Indeed, grief may have a similar relationship to queer communities that trauma goes.

Mad survivor skills for queer and trans suicide

There was an outpour of queer Mad grief on the microblogging platform Tumblr when trans teens Leelah Alcorn and Zander Mahaffey killed themselves (Hatfield 2019). When Alcorn and Mahaffey took their lives, they scheduled their suicide letters to be posted to Tumblr posthumously (Hatfield 2019). Alcorn's parents and organizations like the American Foundation for Suicide Prevention urged Tumblr to take down Alcorn's letter for fear of suicide contagion (Hatfield 2019). Joe Hatfield (2019) argues that Tumblr's acquiescence with this request constitutes an attempt at queer mnemonicide – the murder of memory. Alcorn's letter states 'People say "it gets better" but that isn't true in my case … Each day I get worse' (Hatfield 2019), refuting the narrative galvanized by the *It Gets Better* campaign that young queers should hope for a promised utopian adult future. Puar (2017) contrasts the approach of the *It Gets Better* project with that of ACT UP, arguing that the former takes an individual approach whereas the latter places the blame for the deaths of queers on government inaction.

The *It Gets Better* narrative risks insisting that queer and trans people comply with neoliberal models of good survivorship by waiting for their assimilation into heteronormative kinship and the capitalist economy. When I was a foster parent for queer and trans youth, my foster son asked me 'does it really get better?' I had spent the past few years of grad school reading critiques of the *It Gets Better* Project; I wanted to be honest with him, but it is difficult when a child you care so much about is looking in your eyes asking for hope. I do not remember exactly what I said, but it was something to the effect that adulthood is indeed so much better, particularly for the privileged, but you live with the trauma and grief of what happened forever. But every day it gets easier, and you think about it a little less, especially as you begin to process it in counselling. It made me think about how far-removed queer theory has become to the actual experiences of queer people. I still agree with many of the critiques of the *It Gets Better* Project, but, as my PhD supervisor pointed out, much of that writing is valuable but also overgeneralized to a collection of over 50,000 videos. It is also important to consider that the intention of the project and to provide reparative readings that include some form of suggestions to improve its aims to reach actual queer and trans children who want to die.

Kate Bornstein (2006) offers many suicide survivor skills in a book where she lists 101 alternatives to suicide (ranging from finishing one's homework first to illegal activity if that is what is takes) and ranks them according to how dangerous they are. I gave it to one of my foster children to read at the hospital after they attempted suicide in my home. In a love letter to femmes who have taken their lives, are thinking about it and/or are supporting people who are, Piepzna-Samarasinha (2018) offers strategies that have helped them not kill themselves while living with the ghosts of queer and trans suicide that haunt them. They state that one thing that has helped them is 'the idea that suicide was a weapon of the abuser and the colonizer, a bomb they plant in our bodies to try to kill us, and that it was political for me to fight to survive and live' (Piepzna-Samarasinha 2018: 202). They explain a friend's perspective that it is ableist to insist that people not kill themselves without changing the conditions that lead to queer suicidality. They mobilize their grief to imagine a queer futurity, stating, 'my grief about femme suicide is the garden where our future grows' (Piepzna-Samarasinha 2018: 204). These gardens of suicide grief are queer trauma cultures of resistance planted with survivor skills (Cvetkovich 2003).

Conclusion

Queer, Mad, crip autoethnographies allow us to unearth not only the effects of trauma but also the skills that have been used for generations of queers to survive them. Queer trauma can sometimes feel debilitating, but it also creates affective public cultures of survival and resistance. Taking a crip approach to queer trauma can depathologize the impacts of homophobia transphobia and allow for crip affiliations amongst the queerly traumatized. Queer Mad grief gives voice to queer experiences of loss that are ungrievable, such as deaths by suicide or AIDS-related losses. Exploring the survivor skills that grow in gardens of grief created through queer loss and queer trauma cultures enable us to understand queer Madness as queer worldmaking. While post-traumatic growth, the positive transformations that often happen to people after we survive trauma, is discussed about primarily in the individual realm of positive psychology, I hope that this work galvanizes future discussions on community post-traumatic growth that are beyond the limits of this chapter. Queer post-traumatic growth happens when grieving and traumatized Mad and crip communities come together and form trauma cultures in which we share our survival skills with one another.

References

Adams, N., Hitomi, M., & Moody, C. (2017). 'Varied Reports of Adult Transgender Suicidality: Synthesizing and Describing the Peer-reviewed and Gray Literature'. *Transgender Health*, 2 (1): 60–75.

Bauer, G., Pyne, J., Francino, M., & Hammond, R. (2013). 'Suicidality Among Trans People in Ontario: Implications for Social Work and Social Justice/La suicidabilité parmi les personnes trans en Ontario: implications en travail social et en justice sociale'. *Service Social*, 59 (1): 35–62.

Berger, J. (2004). 'Trauma Without Disability, Disability Without Trauma: A Disciplinary Divide'. *Jac*, 563–82.

Berlant, L. (2007). 'Slow Death (Sovereignty, Obesity, Lateral Agency)'. *Critical inquiry*, 33 (4): 754–80.

Berlant, L. & Warner, M. (1998). 'Sex in public'. *Critical inquiry*, 24 (2): 547–66.

Bornstein, K. (2006). *Hello, Cruel World: 101 Alternatives to Suicide for Teens, Freaks, and Other Outlaws*. New York: Seven Stories Press.

Brown, L. S. (1991). 'Not Outside the Range: One Feminist Perspective on Psychic Trauma'. *American Imago*, 119–33.

Butler, J. (1993). *Bodies That Matter: On the Discursive Limits of Sex*. New York: Routledge.

Butler, J. (2016). *Frames of War: When Is Life Grievable?* London: Verso Books.

Chen, M. Y. (2012). *Animacies: Biopolitics, Racial Mattering, and Queer Affect*. Durham: Duke University Press.

Clements-Nolle, K., Marx, R., & Katz, M. (2006). 'Attempted Suicide Among Transgender Persons: The Influence of Gender-based Discrimination and Victimization'. *Journal of Homosexuality*, 51 (3): 53–69.

Cohen, H., Neumann, L., Haiman, Y., Matar, M. A., Press, J., & Buskila, D. (2002, August). 'Prevalence of Post-traumatic Stress Disorder in Fibromyalgia Patients: Overlapping Syndromes or Post-traumatic Fibromyalgia Syndrome?' *Seminars in Arthritis and Rheumatism*, 32 (1): 38–50. WB Saunders.

Cvetkovich, A. (2003). *An Archive of Feelings: Trauma, Sexuality, and Lesbian Public Cultures*. Durham, NC: Duke University Press.

Cvetkovich, A. (2012). *Depression: A Public Feeling*. Durham: Duke University Press.

Drolma, L. P. (2019). *Love on Every Breath: Tonglen Meditation for Transforming Pain into Joy*. California: New World Library.

Edelman, L. (2004). *No Future: Queer Theory and the Death Drive*. Durham: Duke University Press.

Garland-Thomson, R. (2011). 'Misfits: A Feminist Materialist Disability Concept'. *Hypatia*, 26 (3): 591–609.

Harvey, P. (2012). *An Introduction to Buddhism: Teachings, History and Practices*. Cambridge: Cambridge University Press.

Hatfield, J. E. (2019). 'The Queer Kairotic: Digital Transgender Suicide Memories and Ecological Rhetorical Agency'. *Rhetoric Society Quarterly*, 49 (1): 25–48.

Häuser, W., Galek, A., Erbslöh-Möller, B., Köllner, V., Kühn-Becker, H., Langhorst, J., … & Glaesmer, H. (2013). 'Posttraumatic Stress Disorder in Fibromyalgia Syndrome: Prevalence, Temporal Relationship Between Posttraumatic Stress and Fibromyalgia Symptoms, and Impact on Clinical Outcome'. *PAIN®*, 154 (8): 1216–23.

Hawa, F. (2018, December). 'Lady Gaga's Speech on Elle Women Award: Theme and Stylistic Levels'. *Proceedings of International Conference on English Language Teaching (INACELT)*, 2 (1): 88–99.

Hottes, T. S., Ferlatte, O., & Gesink, D. (2015). 'Suicide and HIV as Leading Causes of Death Among Gay and Bisexual Men: A Comparison of Estimated Mortality and Published Research'. *Critical Public Health*, 25 (5): 513–26.

Kafer, A. (2013). *Feminist, Queer, Crip*. Bloomington: Indiana University Press.

Menzies, R., LeFrançois, B., & Reaume, G. (2013). 'Introducing Mad Studies'. In B. L. LeFrancois, R. Menzies & G. Reaume (eds.) *Mad Matters: A Critical Reader in Canadian Mad Studies*. Toronto: Canadian Scholar's Press, pp. 1–22.

McRuer, Ropert. (2006). *Crip Theory: Cultural Signs of Queerness and Disability*. New York and London: New York University Press.

Morrigan, C. (2017a). 'Failure to Comply: Madness and/as Testimony'. *Canadian Journal of Disability Studies*, 6 (3): 60–91.

Morrigan, C. (2017b). 'Trauma Time: The Queer Temporalities of the Traumatized Mind'. *Somatechnics*, 7 (1): 50–8.

Perreault, Y., Fitton, W., & McGovern, M. (2010). 'The Presence of Absence: Bereavement in Long-term Survivors of Multiple AIDS-related Losses'. *Bereavement Care*, 29 (3): 26–33.

Perreault, Y. (2011). When Grief Comes to Work: Managing Grief and Loss in the Workplace, a Handbook for Managers and Supervisors. Toronto: AIDS Bereavment and Resiliency Program of Ontario.

Piepzna-Samarasinha, L. L. (2018). *Care Work: Dreaming Disability Justice*. Vancouver: Arsenal Pulp Press.

Poole, J. M. & Ward, J. (2013). 'Breaking Open the Bone: Storying, Sanism and Mad Grief'. *Mad Matters: A Critical Reader in Canadian Mad Studies*, 94–104.

Pryor, J. (2017). *Time Slips: Queer Temporalities, Contemporary Performance, and the Hole of History*. Evanston: Northwestern University Press.

Ptsdsafe. (2019). *Traumatized PTSD/LGBT Pride Flages Based off of* the PTSD flag by @your-fave-has-ptsd. Tumblr. https://ptsdsafe.tumblr.com/post/187331785763/traumatizedptsd-lgbt-pride-flags-based-off-of.

Puar, J. K. (2017). *The Right to Maim: Debility, Capacity, Disability*. Durham: Duke University Press.

Reisner, S. L., White Hughto, J. M., Gamarel, K. E., Keuroghlian, A. S., Mizock, L., & Pachankis, J. E. (2016). 'Discriminatory Experiences Associated with Posttraumatic Stress Disorder Symptoms Among Transgender Adults'. *Journal of Counseling Psychology*, 63 (5): 509.

Roberts, A. L., Austin, S. B., Corliss, H. L., Vandermorris, A. K., & Koenen, K. C. (2010). 'Pervasive Trauma Exposure Among US Sexual Orientation Minority Adults and Risk of Posttraumatic Stress Disorder'. *American Journal of Public Health*, 100 (12): 2433–41.

Rood, B. A., Puckett, J. A., Pantalone, D. W., & Bradford, J. B. (2015). 'Predictors of Suicidal Ideation in a Statewide Sample of Transgender Individuals'. *LGBT health*, 2 (3): 270–5.

Savage, D. & Miller, T. (Eds.). (2011). *It Gets Better: Coming Out, Overcoming Bullying, and Creating a Life Worth Living*. New York: Penguin.

Sedgwick, E. K. (1993). *Tendencies*. Duke University Press.

Shipherd, J. C., Maguen, S., Skidmore, W. C., & Abramovitz, S. M. (2011). 'Potentially Traumatic Events in a Transgender Sample: Frequency and Associated Symptoms'. *Traumatology*, 17 (2): 56–67.

Smith, B. C., Armelie, A. P., Boarts, J. M., Brazil, M., & Delahanty, D. L. (2016). 'PTSD, Depression, and Substance Use in Relation to Suicidality Risk Among Traumatized Minority Lesbian, Gay, and Bisexual Youth'. *Archives of Suicide Research*, 20 (1): 80–93.

Sycamore, M. B. (Ed.). (2010). *Nobody Passes: Rejecting the Rules of Gender and Conformity*. Berkeley: Hachette UK.

Tarrier, N. & Gregg, L. (2004). 'Suicide Risk in Civilian PTSD Patients'. *Social Psychiatry and Psychiatric Epidemiology*, 39 (8): 655–61.

The AIDS Memorial Quilt. (n.d.). Retrieved from URL https://www.aidsquilt.org/about/the-aids-memorial-quilt.

Thom, K. C. (2019). *I Hope We Choose Love: A Trans Girl's Notes from the End of the World*. Vancouver: Arsenal Pulp Press.

Westengard, L. (2019). *Gothic Queer Culture: Marginalized Communities and the Ghosts of Insidious Trauma*. Lincoln: University of Nebraska Press.

Chapter 4

WHY ALL THE BLACK WOMEN SIT TOGETHER ON THE U-BAHN?

BLACK FEMME RESISTANCE IN GERMANY

Madeline Bass, Cienna Davis, Nasheeka Nedsreal, Laetitia Walendom

Introduction

The title of this essay, and the seminal educational text it is drawn from, *Why Are All the Black Kids Sitting Together in the Cafeteria*,[1] both pose a question with resounding relevance to Black communities across the (white) world; rephrased one might ask why the rest of the U-Bahn (the German underground train) is so hostile, what about it has made the group of Black girls cluster so closely together. It is with this latter point that we are concerned with here, sitting with the cluster as a way of understanding space-making and resistance practices. In this chapter, drawing from autoethnographic explorations emerging from our Afro-diasporic lives in Germany, we seek to explore both the conditions of unsafety (which prompts the urge to group together at all), and add some clarity to the way we create alterities and sites of strength.

The U-Bahn as a space embodies divergent experiences, since it is frequented by all living in and visiting Berlin. All manner of Berliner converges in the public transit system, constructing a microcosmic entity wherein otherwise anonymous residents and visitors of the capital end up seated side by side. It is, in sum, an essential, confined zone where lives overlap. Inevitably, the U-Bahn produces a representative social space where intersubjective intimacy gives way to unwelcomed stares, where one's outsider status becomes fortified in daily micro-aggression. The U-Bahn, like Tatum's cafeteria, is an emblematic site of a larger problematic: the way sociocultural spaces are built exclude and marginalize non-white Others. Our race, gender and class positionalities further exacerbate these hierarchies, creating additional challenges to the way we move through space. In the metaphoric cafeteria table and train car, the hub that we have created, we are able to breathe a little easier, laugh a little louder, engage with the city around us

---

1. First published by Beverly Daniel Tatum in 1997, reissued by Penguin Books in 2017.

on our own terms. Comprehending these racialized and gendered interactions as spatial processes offers additional insight into structural and societal violence, and forms of resistance.

The data that comprises this paper was collected in 2021, during an intimate gathering on an autumn evening in Berlin. We took advantage of a brief lull in pandemic restrictions, which allowed us to reunite in person after months locked down in different countries. While this was not our first time in space together, it was the first documented as such. We are artists, scholars, professionals and creatives whose paths crossed while living in Berlin. Some of us met online, through friends, or at events. As an informal collective we had met in bits and pieces, pairs and trios, largely in spaces and events targeting Black women. In this particular conversation we are friends and researchers, but beyond this meeting we pursue a range of different career and personal trajectories. Nasheeka hosted the evening, Cienna visited from the United States after having lived in Berlin for six years,[2] and Laetitia and Madeline had spent several months organizing this particular gathering and the research that followed. The first time we had all gathered together was the summer prior, 2020, on a boat trip along a Berlin canal.

The premise from which our conversation began was in opposition to these moments and histories of harm; we came in pursuit of strength, both transnational and sustainable. We wanted to explore how we are understood, described and adjudicated at the intersections of our Blackness and femininity. We focus particularly on Berlin and Germany at large, and in this same geographical context, describe the ways that we write our own narratives, claim our own presence and assert an active sense of self that is freer. We also process these questions following the provocations of Christina Sharpe, as she asks:

> Can I live? Where can I live? How can I live? Can I live and not, just, barely, almost, survive? What is living when that living requires that black girls and women be small, be half-living, be subordinated, be open to condemnation, abuse, and censure? What about the worlds they are making? Can you see them? Do you apprehend them and the beautiful lives that they make in the midst of deprivation and terror?
>
> (2018: 171)

Applying those questions to ourselves, and creating the answers we need is part of our space-making, the spatiality of a 'beautiful life'. Our collective narrative is one which offers insight into forms of movement and relationality employed by Black people in Germany. We utilize autoethnography as our attempt at exploring the

---

2. In 2014, Nasheeka Nedsreal, Cienna Davis and Christine Seraphin founded Soul Sisters Berlin – a diasporic, Black feminist collective that organized workshops, social events and retreats while also providing a digital enclave for over 1.5K Black womxn, femmes and nonbinary people in Berlin to connect, share and exchange around the experience of being a hypervisible minority in Germany.

theoretical and methodological knowledge stemming from our experiences and offering an alternate approach. This chapter thus has two interrelated objectives: to explore methodologies for understanding Black resistance, and, through this autoethnographic process, to make a preliminary offering of these strategies as an answer to those questions posed above, or at least a partial explanation of how we live, beyond survival, in pursuit of these 'beautiful lives'.

Positionalities

While previous generations of Black women activists in Germany shattered the 'symbolic non-existence' of the historic African and Afro-German presence in the nation (Eggers 2011: 191–2), most Black people living in (BPLI) Germany and even Berlin still live in isolation from one another and lack access or awareness of a shared collective memory of the Black presence in Germany. Because of the silencing and active forgetting that occurs around these counter-narratives in Germany, community becomes the most viable historical resource, archive and means of racial uplift and outreach (Davis 2018: 74). The experience of a hypervisible minority is one of being perpetually treated as an outsider, despite the long legacy of the Black presence in Germany and the labour of generations of Black German activists (Florvil 2020).

The lack of racial statistics makes it challenging to quantify structural racism in Germany, but the harms and violences of being a hypervisible racial minority in 'politically raceless' Europe live in the bodies of queer, migrant, Muslim and people of colour minorities who are marked as 'eternal newcomers' rather than 'native minorities' (El-Tayeb 2011: xx–xxi, xxviii). The stares, overt racist comments, insensitivities and fetishization translate into rejected apartment applications, unwanted sexual advances, higher rates of unemployment and general feelings of unease and discomfort navigating public and private space in Germany's lauded multicultural capital.

We position ourselves within a lineage of BPLI who have contributed to the mosaic of Black German identity with insider access to the locally specific diasporic relations and formations in Berlin (Esuruoso & Koepsell 2014: 48). Our relationality to Germany and our shared identities warrants further explanation. We write as Black people in Germany, but not Black Germans. We write as African diasporic peoples whose connections to Africa are both linked to very specific geographies (e.g. born in the Ivory Coast to Chadian parents) and paths of im/ migration and movement that follow in the wake of slave routes. It is also critical to include that our physical movements across Germany and Europe at large are characterized by our physicality as young women living without disabilities,[3] even

---

3. The role of abilities in conceptualizing the oppression of Black women is discussed at length in Bailey and Mobley's 2019 piece 'Work in the Intersections: A Black Feminist Disability Framework' (*Gender & Society*).

though we access juridical frameworks and infrastructural environments built for white, cisgender men. Our experiences of our femininity and femme identities are further complicated by gender and sexuality in ways that exceed the limitations of this paper.

Theoretical model

This paper uses concepts of spatiality and Black geography as a theoretical framework. Blackness and Black femininity unfold and develop in the long afterlives of slavery (after Saidiya Hartman 2007) resulting in distinctive processes of resistance. Black diasporas are not analogous to other transnational groups, and these nuances are further complicated by nation-state, 'post' colonial and settler politics. While we cannot draw direct comparisons between Black diasporas in settler colonies such as the United States and post-empire such as Germany (Campt 2003; Wright 2015), thinking through Black geography as a distinct space-making process provides one mechanism for understanding our resistances. Although larger spatial and structural formations like the nation-state, the colony and the metropole have been built by their 'paradigmatic relation' to the African continent, these oppressions do not foreclose Black people's abilities to reshape their surroundings (Wilderson 2009: 120).

The connection between Black experiences and space-making, with attention to the gendered elements of this process, is a central focus of Katherine McKittrick's 2006 text on the 'cartographies of struggle,' and what she describes as Black geography. *Black geography* is a call to know the world and the 'material, theoretical, and imaginative landscapes we occupy and express' in ways that more fully encompass Black experiences (McKittrick 2006: xxx). The original premise that Black geography presents is a counter to traditional geographic methods, insisting that the map, the archive and other state-sponsored mechanisms for defining space fail to fully describe Black people, and in particular Black women. We are written out of historical texts just as African place names were recast in colonial tongues. The spatial boundaries and subject-knowledges produced by this anti-Blackness, concepts which enforce Black being as out of place, are subverted by Black spatiality (McKittrick 2006: 40). As a resistance practice, thinking through our spatiality makes clear the radical nature of our movement. This is work that makes 'visible social lives which are often displaced, rendered ungeographic' (McKittrick 2006: x). This visibility in part explicates the potential power of Black women despite marginality.

Black diasporas cannot be easily conceptualized within other analytical frames. The shared inheritance of our transatlantic community emerges from the wake as, Sharpe writes, a reverberation that has no regard for borders and nation-states (Sharpe 2016). Reframed, while our participants do not share a historical relation to slavery, the afterlives and aftermath of the system enacts similar forms of harm in our everyday lives (Hartman 2002; Wright 2015). These transatlantic linkages make the modernity of our shared inheritances more peculiar, or at least more vivid. The white supremacist epistemology that we are subjected to is unable to account for these differences, and our subjection, whether resonating from the slave auction block or the brutality of the European migration regime, is in conversation, running in tangent (Saucier & Woods 2014; Wilderson 2009). None of the passport privileges we possess has made for a European life or livingness in which we can breathe easily. The wake of the slave ship, the waters of the boat continue to rise and override us.

Black women's geographies as political formations are clarified further by the work of William C. Anderson, whose notion of a 'nation on no map' encapsulates the Black and Afro diasporic experience of place (2021). He argues that anti-Blackness, legacies of the slave trade and mass incarceration as a consequence of these phenomena are so deeply embedded in the global world order, that moving despite them requires a citizenship unknown by these institutional forms. To be Black in America is to know the 'damage the idea of citizenship can cause', and this white imperial tendency follows the Black diaspora across the global north (2021: xxv). Just as imperial perspectives on African diasporic people have been performed and imprinted into German culture, a sociocultural 'language' that defines Blackness as outside of the national borders underwrite our Berlin experiences, bringing with them a violence indigenous to this city and its fallen empires. In resistance, we stake our own claims and build a community that remains unintelligible to that of the oppressor. This form of resistance is a move towards abolition,[4] in the long era of emancipation (Walcott 2021).

Methodologies

The methodological tools used to develop this paper are derived from the collective self-ethnography used in pieces such as Berihun and Kumsa et al. (2015) and in African diasporic traditions of stories and storytelling. Autoethnography, and reflective and collective ethnographic practice as used by Berihun, allows the researcher to 'generate data that delve into such subtle processes of ongoing construction and reconstruction of Self' (Berihun et al. 2015: 423). These methods are deeply linked to our theoretical framework. Following the work of Linda Tuhiwai Smith, methodologies are both an expression of imperialism and a form of resistance against it (2012). The work of researching ourselves, both

---

4. Abolition as we use it refers to a concept and movement that is broad in scope, confronting the entanglements between institutions and ideologies of violence from antiblackness and settler colonialism to incarceration. As Ruth Wilson Gilmore has succinctly stated, 'Abolition requires that we change one thing: everything.' Discussion on some of these 'things' include William C. Anderson's *The Nation on No Map: Black Anarchism and Abolition* (2021), Angela Davis's *Are Prisons Obsolete* (2003) and Tiffany Lethabo King's article on 'Abolishing Moynihan's Negro Family' (2018).

as individuals and across our shared identities, requires close attention to how we care for each other, and how this care and relationality impacts our ways of learning and collecting data. This praxis is a subversion of methodologies that treat the human as data and employ dehumanizing forms of data collection in pursuit of an unattainable objectivity (Chilisa 2012; McKittrick 2020). Methodologies which centre care, relations and collaboration move beyond these imperial tactics from within the margins. They are attentive to spoken and unspeakable traumas and demand no more than the community wants to give.

As Sharpe describes, 'living … in spaces where we were never meant to survive, or have been punished for surviving and for daring to claim or make spaces of something like freedom, we yet reimagine and transform spaces for and practices of an ethics of care (as in repair, maintenance, attention)' (Sharpe 2016: 130). Sharpe's 'wake work' embodies the larger Black feminist sensibility that underwrites this paper. Wake work helps us 'imagine new ways to live:' informed by past lives of African descendants through and beyond a process of mourning, and towards critiquing the containment and captivity that positions us outside of normative forms of belonging (Sharpe 2016: 130). Placing this practice and care at the fore, we designed a methodology that allowed us to mitigate the harm of reliving past violence. Collective gatherings as a research method decentre the researcher and dismantle hierarchies by empowering all participants to direct the conversation and its end results (Bass, Cordoba, & Teunissen 2020).

Furthermore, adding sensory ethnographic data to the conversation is a way of capturing the meaning beyond the textual. Sensory details speak to the value we as a group placed on the collective nature of the gathering and of our intention to be with each other. Sensory data also serves to amplify and capture that which cannot be easily said, a particularly crucial addition in environments of violence and danger (Duru 2020).

This paper coincided with the second year of the global Covid-19 pandemic, a catastrophe that slowed down the tempo of our relationality as well as our methodological work (a longer reflection on slow philosophy during Covid-19 can be found in Behrisch 2021). Death walked with us. And just as an obituary cannot encapsulate the vibrancy of a life, we in turn included silences and gaps as a data point, as they mark the times of our separation, delayed from gathering by public health and legal frameworks as well as our own traumas.

Conversation analysis

The following section comprises the key data points of the paper, formed as a series of 'vignettes'. These vignettes are either exact quotations from our conversation, sensory notes from the meeting, or further sensory explorations from the recording. A few lines of significant context follow each vignette. The data points in the section that follows are theoretically grounded and cohere into a larger case study. A vignette which should be interred throughout this piece is placed at the beginning as an interlude, the composition of silence.

Interlude: Silence

In writing and speaking and reflecting on our resistances, from the planning of the conversation to the slow process of analysis, the impact of the Covid-19 pandemic is never far from our minds. It haunts us, shades us and leers when we leave the house. Death and dying, fearing death and dying. In this chapter, as a textual form, Covid-19 enters through the silences. Emails left unopened, calls missed, texts unanswered. Rather than signalling disrespect, these silences reflect the larger urgency of our survival. These gaps characterized our writing process, our way of meeting and the timeframes of our conversation. Our collective willingness to wait for a face-to-face meeting required that we carefully study the known risks and precautions of any particular choice, testing and retesting, preparing ourselves as a small pod. We knew that the limitations of the pandemic-induced 'Zoom era' and the conversations emerging in that form would erase something we needed, desperately, to express.

Vignette #1: Sensing the scene

> *We started by sharing dinner: Ethiopian food with spices freshly delivered from Addis Ababa by a friend of a friend, injera from a local Berlin restaurant, a few bottles of wine. Jazz is playing in the background, candles light each shadowy corner. We have arranged ourselves in a loose circle, cuddled up on the couch and stretched on pillows across the floor as the gentle horns of Mulatu Astatke's 'Tezeta' (meaning nostalgia) envelop our surroundings. It took some navigation to bring us all together. Here, there is a sense of easy comfort in our interaction and a softness to the atmosphere, evidence of the way we relate to each other, how much we cherish a moment that was long coming.*

The apartment's materiality (carefully arranged furniture, stacks of well-loved books, Black diasporic art), and its sensuality (the occasional ruffle of the living room curtain from the late summer breeze, our laughter echoing across the courtyard, a lingering smell of roasted vegetables wafting in from the kitchen) reflect Nasheeka's curatorship as well as our larger group presence, and our gathering here suggests a feeling of safety, a respite from the outside. The curation is one of many steps taken by Nasheeka, and by each of us in turn, to build our lives here in Berlin. The time to hang artwork that speaks to the soul, to select music, to add softening elements like blankets and pillows; these steps provide a contrast to the harshness outside.

We have each arrived here by way of Berlin's infamous U-Bahn, a place with some notoriety for exhibiting traits oppositional to our space. The U-Bahn is often dank and musty, a site where huddling in the corner can be a survival strategy, where the cool metal of the walls can offer respite from the heat of an unfamiliar body looming behind. Its cold familiarity is further mirrored in the clinical settings of the academic institutions we have passed through, the straight-backed chairs and mass-produced desks that housed our former sites of data collection. While we recognize the necessity and history of these alternative locations, we have taken strategic steps to undo them here, to an extent.

Vignette #2: The surrounding sounds

> *Soon we begin with the formality of the focus group. The early minutes of audio captured pulse and vibrate with our overlapping chatter and laughter, recalling choice stories from an African music festival that took place the previous weekend.*
>
> *Each of our voices is distinct, easily discernible to us, and there is an easy flow from one point of dialogue to another, side conversations to facilitate our sharing of food and blankets. In the shift we make from participants to self-reflective researchers, listening back to the recording sounds like eavesdropping on any other group of friends in any other Black space. Mentions of race are inevitably sprinkled in (a Black British friend, the festival 'de l'Afrique') and addressed from our mutually understood point of view. The warmth and vibrancy of this conversation reflects the intimacy of the space.*
>
> *There is a distinct shift in tone in the transition from our conversation to the 'Conversation:' our voices pitch downward, becoming softer and less certain. Akin to a code switch, we alter not our words and vocabulary so much as our tone, a solemn, breathy quality affecting all of our voices. There is a thin layer of hesitation, like the difference between the approach of a young reader struggling through a text and their parent narrating the same story. Without needing to discern the exact words, the tonality reveals a disruption to the space we've built.*

Even in a non-academic environment, one that has been carefully curated and filled with food and love, the university haunts us. That Black women have been conditioned to express their emotions only through a static set of societally proscribed norms is well documented and tangible. Our options and modes of expression are confined to the limited scale ranging between Hortense Spillers' 'Brown Sugar' (1987) and Patricia Hill Collins's range of 'controlling images' (mammies, matriarchs, welfare queens, etc.) (2000: 69). To varying extents we imagine and establish ourselves outside of these limitations, asserting our right to thrive in environments that were never meant for us: the academy, the worlds of elite dance, technology and start-ups. This assertion, one that seems at the time to be the screaming surround, is softened as soon as the intentions of our gathering change. This muting hearkens back to a poetic warning given by Warsan Shire, and a subject who 'closed your mouth more/ tried to be softer/ prettier/ less volatile, less awake' (2017). As awake as we are, and as much as our mutuality has absented the question of gendered subjugation from our gathering, we have instinctively softened and silenced ourselves to face the academy. This tonal shift demarcates the particularities of the words that follow.

Vignette #3: Fever dreams of Germany

> *– Returning to Germany from Philly, where everyone is Black and the airport is run by Black people and you got all types of diversity, I realized Berlin is just as white as I thought it was. I didn't just make it up. I felt the eyes darting at me again. It's real, not just a fever dream that was starting to define my experience of being in this place.*

—

> – *When I first moved to Berlin I lived way south in Schlachtensee, the whitest of white places, and people would flat out stare. Meanwhile in Wedding I worked at the archives, and the difference between being seen in those types of ways … I don't know which one I prefer.*
> – *Which kind of staring is the better one? Which is safer?*

—

The fever dream actualizes in different forms throughout the conversation. It is the Frankfurt airport, Kreuzberg,[5] the sidewalk next to a shisha bar. In each of these spaces there is a surreal element interjected, the feeling of every eye pointing in your direction, a direct affront to any notion you may have of yourself being normal. The open, unblinking eyes and their unabashed stares make it known that you are Other rendered outside of society. These experiences are more sharply delineated in our individual comparisons to the world outside; home neighbourhoods, an African community centre in Northern Berlin, the city of Philadelphia, a list of places where the nightmarish dream is over, where we can be in a place without being seen as such.

> – *I was walking from Moritzplatz in Kreuzkolln[6] when this older Black man smiled and I reciprocated. Five minutes later he was pulling up on his bike beside me and I was like, I just thought we had a pleasant exchange! It's not an invitation, and now you're trying to force a conversation on me while that was just a friendly greeting.*

Accompanying our litanies of harm and avoidance are a number of survival strategies, listed both intentionally and grasped by the context, strategies we use to reclaim some autonomy from an unsafe space. We take steps to control conversation, minimize interactions where possible, holding, avoiding and being intentional with our gaze. We discuss the Black diasporic urge to acknowledge each other in these white spaces, the need to make eye contact and nod when we spot each other in the crowd. We dig further into the way that our femininity further dictates even this form of relationality, how men take this as invitation beyond the familial. And even in this alterity, we recount our options for escape, ways we have steered this danger to a safer route.

Vignette #4: Vocalizing defence

Voices rise again, later, in laughter, as we make light of the violence of daily street harassment. The sound of our voices returns to its initial timbre; the warmth is brought back in. We laugh in spite of ourselves, describing the practices of

5. A trendy neighbourhood in Berlin known for small boutiques, fancy restaurants and other classic signifiers of wealth and gentrification.
6. Portemanteau for Neukolln and Kreuzberg, central Berlin locale that straddles the historical east and west of the city.

avoidance used in the face of gendered attacks: looking at your bag, faking a phone call, headphones on full blast.

- *That's why I've always liked Moabit, though it's out of the way it's regular working class. I don't feel like I have to show out, or have those negative encounters like I did in Kreuzberg or Neukolln.*
- *I feel like Moabit/Wedding is the place to be! People don't really spot you out … well ok mild sexual harassment, but not every day, and to be fair I always have headphones in, so it may be every day.*
- *I wonder all the time, if I weren't wearing these headphones what would I hear?*
- *Neukolln is very stare-y. I regularly have the awkward direct eye contact moment with men sitting outside the shisha bars along Karl Marx Strasse.*
- *When I walk past I just don't look at them, I look straight ahead.*
- *Eyes on the prize, we're heading to the station baby.*
- *Deflection is the strategy for most of my encounters.*

–

In its textual form, the conversation has taken a grim turn, the inevitability of this violence is one with consequences beyond the aural (rates of violence against women, and especially Black women are egregious, even as they are widely underreported). In a sensory reading of the moment, one without language, we have reclaimed our earlier joy, laughing, voices stacked and singing in unison. Making space for joy, unconsciously and in defence of the virulently un-joyful conversation we engage in, reflects the praxis of our politics, the community with which we are working.

Vignette #5: Finding anywhere

- *I was walking around and thought man, all these white people are everywhere, I want to go out to these restaurants and bars! I want to do this stuff! Looking at these really beautiful apartments, I wanted to live there. But now I realize actually no, those were never the best times, entering those spaces never felt really good to me and never matched what I wanted them to.*

—

- *I managed to survive here but I think it's because I have Louisiana there. I need to just feel like I can go anywhere. With COVID I've been craving feelings of mobility and accessibility, and I need to be in a space where I can go anywhere and have a good experience, and just be chill. But I'm faring in Berlin, I'm giving it less power … The whole irony is that it's not our problem but we spend the most time thinking about it and experiencing it and being confronted by it.*

—

Although we are each passported and documented according to the arbitrary standards of Europe, we are denied full access and the privileges of this movement. These are restrictions preceding (but admittedly exacerbated by) the global Covid-19 pandemic. Though technically we *can* go freely around the city and country where we live, the sense of hostility which characterizes these spaces has placed a (legally) unintelligible limitation. In these moments we frame our movements as a form of survival rather than an expression of leisure or desire. We have moved to Berlin on worker's visas, seeking employment, to advance academic pursuits. Despite the benefits of healthcare or accessible public transportation that accompany our documentation, the sense of being out of place and in the wrong space follows us.

Vignette #6: Shrinking selves

– *Berlin is a particular place, with its Berliner schnauzer, that rudeness for no reason, where of course you put up your guard …. I'd made myself so small living here just to be able to make it livable. The only place I could feel big and like I could do something was in community. It's liberating but sad to know what comfort and anonymity exist in not being visible everywhere I am. It's shocking, realizing 'wow, you've put yourself through a lot.'*

–

– *The first time I experienced something racist the only thing I could say was 'no,' and even then with all the emotion [I couldn't respond in German.] Since I don't see myself leaving anytime soon, my perspective has changed on needing to find other strategies outside of isolating myself and trying to find a likeness of people. Being with Black people and women is important, but I want to be here and I want to make my presence known on my terms.*

–

A testament to the inability of the purely physical to capture the lived experience of a place. Materiality (shrinking physically back away from another person) comes secondary, in this sense to relationality. The ways in which we are silenced and choose to silence ourselves. This reflection was made in the context of sociocultural practices unique in some ways to Berlin, and the way language intersects with race to prevent feelings of inclusion and relationality. We shared experiences of blatant rudeness dismissed as a local quirk, discrimination passed off as a reflection of our varied, and for some limited, access to the German language. Shrinking in response to this daily violence is a survival strategy. The harm that has led up to this point may have been small moments or brief interactions, but the frequency of the attacks and the need to survive each additional assault leads to this inevitable outcome.

Reflections: The no/where or resistance

In the sensual and textual composition of our conversation, a few central themes emerge. The first might be understood as the spatiality of resistance practices, and the way spatial formations set conditions of hostility, influence our methods of coping and are altered by our counter-struggles. We discussed strategies of resistance directly, as we came to understand each other's tactics of movements across Berlin, Germany and Europe at large, but they also revealed themselves in more subtle ways. The apartment building where we gathered was rendered a type of Black geographic that McKittrick (reading Sylvia Wynter) calls a 'demonic ground', a space that has been fundamentally altered by the lives and livingness of Black women (2006). More than just alteration, this was also a carefully cultivated space wherein Black womanhood could unfold in ways less burdened by the pressure of white social life. Insisting this space into being, and tending to intimate sensory and aesthetic details, is a way of creating conditions that allow us, finally to breathe.[7] This material resistance was paired with our performed resistance practices, actions tailored to particular street corners and neighbourhoods. The changes in tone and voice throughout the conversation reflect in some ways what Patricia Williams describes as 'word bondage', the direct result of Black women's socialization which has encouraged our silencing and suppression (1991: 147).[8]

The ability to go 'anywhere,' as described in Vignette #5, must be read in a Black geographic lens with the idea of a nation that cannot be placed on a map. Though passports have determined access to a set list of nation-states, these legally accessible places are not necessarily safe, nor are they welcoming. Even in the city we call home, in this case Berlin, where mobility was largely unrestricted during the first years of Covid-19 pandemic, we discussed the shared understanding that mobility was not synonymous with an easy route. Legal distinctions determining our freedom of movement are not interchangeable with the lived experience of being and living in these places. Although imperial geography has offered us visa functions, the Black geography informs us of real and implicit limitations and routes that we should stay away from. Hostility is un-bordered.

Conclusion

As an exploration of both our challenges and paths of resistance, our conversation and subsequent analysis point to the importance of finding alternative approaches to understanding Black women's practices of resistance.[9] In an academic research

---

7. Referring here to Frantz Fanon's notion that the colonized revolted because 'it was, in more than one way, becoming impossible for him to breathe' (*Black Skin, White Masks* 1986).

8. For more work on Black resistance in the academy, see Melody Hawse 2019.

9. Resistance movements by Black women have been studied as forms of pedagogy (Perlow, Wheeler, Bethea, Scott 2018), as a militant practice (Jones 1949), as an archive and resource (Davis 2018), among countless other examples.

context where harm is overrepresented, our collective data collection and reflection practice provides a way of learning and addressing difficult topics that mitigates this violence. We have made a case for sensory ethnography as a counterpart to textual interviews and analysis, as a methodological experiment and new way of learning for us all. The sensory shifts enabled us to fully capture the nature of our conversation. Further, embedding sensory elements and sensuality is a form of expression that better fits the depths of our ethnographic work. By placing ourselves fully into the scene-as-data, we draw attention to the value that space-making has for Black women in a tangible, sensed way. The labour of curating a space is a necessary praxis (Bacchetta, El-Tayeb, Haritaworn 2015; McKittrick 2006), and its value is reflected in the sensory data. The spatiality of our meeting served as an intentional reflection of the methods we set out to employ, a way of mitigating some of the harms that inevitably follow (from the train ride across town to the structural harms that surround them). We cannot prevent larger forms of violence in the immediate, but steps were taken at that moment to create an atmosphere that was careful and caring. The ethnographic notes on our sensory experiences and the tonal shifts we make call to mind that making space is more than just the material, as our experiences of being out of space/place are visceral and violent.

As a statement on the various forms of resistance employed by Black women, common themes included the role of spatiality, space-making and understanding the surrounding beyond a singular static geographic formation. Our arsenal of resistance practices is diverse and ever-changing as it works against a white supremacist world in its own evolving harm. Our expansive experiences across Berlin are a clear indication of these variants, as they ranged from the safety of our gathering to the potential violence of the next neighbourhood. In terms of a political praxis, the communal basis from where we began represents a significant contribution to politics-at-large, a politics of the commons, of the We and the Us, a politics which reaches into each marginal and subjected place to generate itself. As we sit together on the U-Bahn, at the café, in the parliament, in the heart of the riots that sweep our world, we plot and create the conditions for a world that may one day actually open itself up to us.

References

Anderson, William C. (2021). *The Nation of No Map: Black Anarchism and Abolition*. Chico, CA: AK Press.

Bacchetta, P., El-Tayeb, F., & Haritaworn, J. (2015). 'Queer of Colour Formations and Translocal Spaces in Europe'. *Environment and Planning D: Society and Space*, 33 (5): 769–78. https://doi.org/10.1177/0263775815608712.

Bass, Madeline, Cordoba, Daniel, & Teunissen, Peter. (2020). '(Re)Searching with Imperial Eyes: Collective Self-Inquiry as a Tool for Transformative Migration Studies'. *Social Inclusion*, 8 (4): 147–56.

Behrisch, Tanya J. (2021). 'Cooking a Pot of Beef Stew: Navigating Through Difficult Times Through Slow Philosophy'. *Qualitative Inquiry*, 27 (6): 667–76.

Berihun, Gebrehiwot, Kumsa, Martha Kuwee, Hussein, Abdullahi, Jackson, Jemila, Baksh, Amilah, Crutchley, Jenany, Ellis, Shani, & Ma, Yunfei. (2015). 'Reflections on Using Physical Objects as Data Generation Strategies'. *Qualitative Social Work*, 14 (3): 338–55.

Byrd, Jodi. (2010). *The Transit of Empire*. Minneapolis, MN: University of Minnesota Press.

Campt, Tina. (2003). 'Reading the Black German Experience: An Introduction'. *Callaloo*, 26 (2): 288–194.

Chilisa, Bagele. (2012). *Indigenous Research Methodologies*. Thousand Oaks, CA: Sage Publications.

Collins, Patricia Hill. (2000). *Black Feminist Thought 10th Anniversary Edition*. New York and London: Routledge.

Davis, Angela. (2003). *Are Prisons Obsolete?* New York: Seven Stories Press.

Davis, C. (2018). 'Community als historische Resource und Archiv'. In M. Bauche & S. D. Otoo (eds.), Neue Rundschau: Geschicte schrieben. Frankfurt: S. Fischer, pp. 71–4.

Duru, Asli. (2020). 'A Walk Down the Shore'. *Cultural Geographies*, 27 (1): 157–61.

Eggers, Maureen Maisha. (2011). 'Knowledges of (Un)Belonging: Epistemic Change as a Defining Mode for Black Women's Activism in Germany'. Hybrid Cultures – Nervous States, 187–202. https://doi.org/10.1163/9789042032293_011.

El-Tayeb, Fatima. (2011). *European Others: Queering Ethnicity in Postnational Europe*. Minneapolis: University of Minnesota Press.

Esuruoso, A. & Koepsell, P. K. (2014). *Arriving in the Future: Stories of Home and Exile* (2 edition). Berlin: epubli.

Florvil, Tiffany. (2020). *Mobilizing Black Germany*. Champaign: University of Illinois Press.

Goeman, Mishuana. (2014). 'Disrupting a Settler-Colonial Grammar of Place'. In A. Simpson and A. Smith (ed.), *Theorizing Native Studies*. Durham: Duke University Press, pp. 235–65.

Hartman, Saidiya. (2002). 'The Time of Slavery'. *South Atlantic Quarterly*, 101 (4): 757–77.

Hartman, Saidiya. (2007). *Lose Your Mother: A Journey Along the Atlantic Slave Route*. New York: Farrar, Straus, and Giroux.

Hawse, Melody. (2019). 'Creating a Space Within the German Academy'. In A. Emejulu and F. Sobande (eds.), *To Exist Is to Resist: Black Feminism in Europe*. London: Pluto Press.

Jones, Claudia. (1949). 'An End to the Neglect of the Problems of the Negro Woman!' *Political Affairs. PRISM: Political & Rights Issues & Social Movements*. 467, 1–19. https://stars.library.ucf.edu/prism/467.

King, Tiffany Lethabo. (2018). 'Black "Feminisms" and Pessimism: Abolishing Moynihan's Negro Family'. *Theory and Event*, 21 (1): 68–87.

McKittrick, Katherine. (2006). *Demonic Grounds: Black Women and the Cartography of Struggle*. Minneapolis, MN: University of Minnesota Press.

McKittrick, Katherine. (2020). *Dear Science and Other Stories*. Durham, NC: Duke University Press.

Perlow, O. N., Wheeler, D. I., Bethea, S. L., & Scott, B. M. (2018). *Black Women's Liberatory Pedagogies*. Cham, CH: Palgrave Macmillan.

Saucier, P. Khalil & Woods, Tryon P. (2014). 'Ex Aqua: The Mediterranean Basin, Africans on the Move and the Politics of Policing'. *Theoria: A Journal of Social and Political Theory*, 61 (141): 55–75.

Sharpe, Christina. (2016). *In the Wake: On Blackness and Being*. Durham, NC: Duke University Press.

Sharpe, Christina. (2018). 'And to Survive'. *Small Axe*, 22 (3): 171–80.

Shire, Warsan. (2017). 'For Women Who Are "Difficult" to Love'.

Smith, Linda Tuhiwai. (2012). *Decolonizing Methodologies 2nd Edition*. New York, NY: Zed Books.

Spillers, Hortense. (1987). *Black, White, and in Color: Essays on American Literature and Culture*. Chicago: University of Chicago Press.

Walcott, Rinaldo. (2021). *The Long Emancipation*. Durham, NC: Duke University Press.

Wilderson, Frank B. (2009). 'Grammar & Ghosts: The Performative Limits of African Freedom'. *Theatre Survey*, 50 (1): 119–25.

Williams, Patricia J. (1991). *The Alchemy of Race and Rights*. Cambridge: Harvard University Press.

Wright, Michelle. (2015). *Physics of Blackness: Beyond the Middle Passage Epistemology*. Minneapolis: University of Minnesota Press.

Chapter 5

FEMINIST PRACTICES IN ARCHITECTURE: HOW WOMEN DEVELOP RESISTANCE THROUGH CRITICISM AND ACTION

Maria Silvia D'Avolio

Introduction

During my twelve-year-long journey as a student in higher education, I have cultivated an interdisciplinary educational and professional background obtained from a full qualification in architecture followed by training and experience in social sciences. After a short working experience in an architectural firm in Italy, I realized that I was not enjoying the job and attributed this outcome to being 'unfit' for the profession. I then decided to leave architecture practice and pursue a PhD in sociology to understand the extent of my problem by exploring more broadly the material, cultural and social reasons why also many other women were leaving this profession. I developed a study that compares Italy and the UK as two case studies, where I conducted thirty-nine individual interviews and two focus groups with women in architecture or who left the profession at different stages of their careers.

Despite women representing 50 per cent of the total students enrolled in architecture courses, there is a considerable lack of retention and progression of women in the industry all over Europe and the presence of women represents only 42 per cent of the total (ACE 2021). Architecture is still considered a white-male-dominated profession that lacks diversity, with the organizational habitus of architecture, understood as the set of class- and gender-based perceptions and dispositions commonly recognized in an organizational culture (McDonough 1997), reproducing male dominance. Investigating the reasons behind the phenomenon of women leaving architecture helped me understand how my 'dropping out' of this male-dominated profession was the outcome of a broader social defeat rather than a personal failure. Concurrently, I soon recognized that most of the women did stay in the field. This different approach at considering the issue was unusual in both academic and general audience literature, although, while reaching this point in my research, I considered it very comforting to discover. Therefore, in this chapter, rather than illustrating the barriers that women face, I decided to explore the informal system of resistance that lets them withstand the push-out.

Drawing upon data from my study and an interdisciplinary pool of feminist authors and theories from various disciplines, I employ an autoethnographic approach to reflect on how feminist praxis in the architecture workplace goes beyond an individual attempt at addressing and adapting to a hegemonic working culture. In fact, feminist praxis can be considered as a collective action aimed at exposing and challenging structural barriers affecting women and minorities in the field. In particular, in the three main sections of the chapter I explore feminist principles of developing networks of support, challenging gendered interactions, and questioning hegemonic language as forms of everyday resistance within and beyond the workplace.

My experience as both a feminist researcher and an ex-architect has been fundamental in identifying these practices of resistance. The attempt to interpret and give shared meanings to individual phenomena in order to connect the personal to the cultural (Ellis and Bochner 2000) is a key element of autoethnography as a method. In my case, hearing other people's stories helped me become aware of the challenges that I also faced when I was in architectural education and practice. It created the feeling of 'I am not alone', which led me to consider our common struggles as a broader outcome of discrimination that needed to be challenged. The key aspect of this challenge is that it is one that cannot be fought alone. Hence the potential of autoethnography to share my process of understanding, which was aided by my participants' life stories. This facilitates readers to empathize with the narrative that I am presenting and reflect on their own situated position on the topic. The desired outcome of this process is to spread awareness of a broader issue and suggest that there is a wide net of people experiencing the same problems, to which solidarity and activism can be effective solutions. In addition, this is a feminist issue because it strives for social justice and stems from the need to deconstruct the 'status quo' and reflect on how culture is based on hegemonic meanings and socialization is reproduced by dominant culture (Ghabra 2015; Allen and Piercy 2005). Both feminist standpoint theory (Hartsock 1983) and Black feminist thought (Hill Collins 1990) consider feminist resistance as an instrument aimed at challenging hierarchies of power. Both employ autoethnography and reflexivity as methods able to make the personal political (Griffin 2012), as clearly illustrated by Crawley (2012: 154): 'I write autoethnography because I am commonplace; my lived experience is interesting because my social location is likely shared by many others and informative to a broader project of understanding power in everyday lives.' Feminist methodology transforms the commonplace into a project of consciousness raising, able to create networks of solidarity and offer ground for diverse forms of resistance.

Feminist praxis in architecture: Everyday resistance

In architecture, women are the 'other' (de Beauvoir 1949), and they do not usually challenge this condition of 'othering' because they perceive it as natural and innate (Powell and Sang 2015). Men, instead, hold symbolic power, which represents the ability to impose one's own definitions, meanings, values and rules on a situation.

This power affects women's access, in particular to knowledge, capitals and movement, which, in turn, affects their ability to hold institutional power, which is crucial in the reproduction of the norm. *Normalcy* is reproduced not only on the institutional and cultural level of the organizational habitus of architecture, but it is also reproduced in everyday interactions. Since the 1980s, awareness of this otherness led women in the profession to reflect on dominant practices and institutions and criticize them. A diverse group of authors, mainly from the UK, the United States and Australia, focused on women's resistance towards the *status quo* in architecture and questioned normalized practices and identities. The catalyst of this interest can be inscribed in the seminal text *Making space: Women and the Man-made Environment* by Matrix (1984), a collective organization of women architects in the UK. The essays collected in the text covered a broad range of topics with a gendered scope, from working in women-only spaces to female approaches to design and the built environment. The body of literature focussed on the topic of women in architecture can be divided into three timeframes: in the 1990s authors such as Agrest (1996), Coleman (1996) and Hughes (1996) collected a variety of writings including theoretical critiques of issues such as identity and gendered dualism between the private/public spheres. Literature in the early 2000, instead, illustrated material impacts of the profession's habitus on women in the construction industry by presenting original empirical data (De Graft-Johnson et al. 2003; Fowler and Wilson 2004). Work produced and edited after 2010 by authors such as Lori Brown (2011), Jane Rendell (2011), Naomi Stead (2014) and Doina Petrescu and Kim Trogal (2017) merged theory and practice in developing an interdisciplinary analysis of critical feminist practices in architecture. Across these three timeframes, many authors used autoethnography to explore various architectural and urban issues, for example Despina Statigakos (2016), who uses her reflexive journey around the design of Architect Barbie to make a point about the generational divide between women in architecture. Or Francesca Hughes, who invited the authors of her edited book (1996) to write autoethnographical essays in which practice is both the site and the vehicle for change: or, more recently, Leslie Kern (2020), who dragged her readers with her on the streets to exemplify urban and social theories through activism and situated positionality.

In accordance with some of the main criticisms of the profession identified in literature, my participants raised similar negative opinions focussed mainly on *institutions*, which reproduce traditional norms; the *StarArchitects system*, which fosters individuality over collectivity; a *lack of diversity*, not just in terms of gender but also ethnicity and economic background; the use of gendered *language*; and *elitism*, *hereditariness* and the *work ethic* typical of this profession. These criticisms highlight the need for women to discover and create alternative practices, and their interest in a redefinition of the concept of being a successful architect. My insider position as an ex-architect enabled me to read my participants' accounts through my specific positionality and identify these themes of criticism. Through my education and profession, I developed scepticism towards a variety of cultural and material elements connected with the profession. This suggests how significant my own experience has been in the analysis of the data. The way a dataset is gathered and analysed is inherently connected to the researcher's standpoint, which aids the interpretation and assignment of certain meanings to phenomena. These meanings, in fact, are not created in a void but are a consequence of the reflexive journey of the researcher. In my experience, for example, I noticed that the coding that I was employing in my initial pilot study was tangibly different from the one I implemented in the final draft of my thesis. I found that the more literature I was reading, the more interviews I was conducting, and the more I was discovering that feminism did not represent a single approach to increasing gender equality but carried incompatible perspectives, the more I was reorienting my interests and understanding of the issue. My own feminist stance was shifting, and my focus moved from material aspects of discrimination (which could be read as neoliberal feminist concerns) to intersectional issues of resistance that had more to do with the actors involved in architecture than the profession itself. My autoethnographic journey enabled me to ask reflexive questions about the nature of the research process itself, about its aims and what I expected to achieve with the discussion of the results. In feminist autoethnography these reflections help think beyond the mainstream approaches to research and allow the researcher to tailor their methodology and the way they interpret the data in a way that is specific to their research and their standpoint as a researcher (Allen and Piercy 2005).

One of the main issues on which I shared criticism with most of my participants was towards institutions, intended as both professional bodies and the educational system, and the consequent lack of diversity they reproduce. For example, this was clearly expressed in an interview with Kathleen (UK) when she defined the Royal Institution of British Architects (RIBA) as a 'gentleman's club', which re-valorizes sexism by perpetuating the image of the white wealthy man as the norm, through outdated images still exposed in its representation halls. 'Do not ever mistake the institution for yourself. The institution's interests are not yours,' warns Patricia Hill Collins (1990: 209). The reference to 'white men' is recurrent in many accounts and highlights the lack of diversity which is deeply ingrained in the profession. The lack of diversity, in terms of not only gender but also ethnicity and class, is one of the aspects more problematic of the profession, as it both carries material consequences on education and practice and replicates standardized professional identity, thus inherently reproducing structural exclusion. While analysing the transcripts of the discussions I had with my participants, the concept of standardized professional identity resonated with my discomfort in perceiving myself as 'not fitting'. I then looked back at the notes that I took in my research journal to see if there were any overlaps with my participants in the way I described my feelings. I spent time reading how my past-self formulated my 'constant feeling of inadequacy' as a result of a lack of cultural and social capital compared to other students who had architects or professional figures in their family, and the subtle sexism that I experienced during exams and in the office. This process led me to develop a heightened awareness of episodes of discomfort in my personal experience. I switched from considering it a result of my inability to fit into the profession to a consequence of subtle exclusion experienced throughout my educational and occupational pathway. The more I read my journal entries and found similarities of feelings with many of my participants, the more I became invested in investigating how they experienced and dealt with these issues. I did not feel sorry for them or myself. Instead, I needed stories of resistance. This enabled me to identify three key areas in which women were informally adopting resistance strategies to challenge hegemonic professional practices and identities. These strategies consist of developing networks of support, challenging gender expectations in workplace interactions and questioning hegemonic language. The potential of autoethnography resides in its ability to transform empathy into an instrument aimed at addressing change and fostering social justice (Grant 2021).

Developing networks of support

During my fieldwork, what struck me immediately was that most women lamented a lack of support in their professional lives, from bosses, co-workers or family members. The surprise came from the fact that I initially assumed that participants would not be so open about admitting vulnerability and having a clear awareness of their needs, as it happened in my own experience. In fact, it took my family and everyone close to me by surprise when I expressed my intention to leave the architectural profession to pursue an academic career in another discipline. Another example from my participants is Shirley, who is currently employed in academia and remembers her time spent in a non-supportive workplace as extremely challenging.

> There were all sorts of challenges that I felt could be attributed to the fact that I was a female architect. Ways in which the office was not supportive enough. […] But at the time I just felt I should be able to handle it. That I should be able to deal with it on my own.
>
> (Shirley, UK)

Shirley's account illustrates a recurrent feeling that matches the effects of the lack of support: isolation. The reason why this aspect is particularly relevant for women can be exemplified by one of the keywords utilized by many women in this regard: 'nurturing'. Men, according to participants, do not have to 'handle things on their own' but have infrastructures around them; they are looked after by their superiors. Women, instead, tend to question their self-worth instead of acknowledging the lack of support as the main problem. This mechanism has been theorized through the concept of *homosocial behaviour* which refers to the attitude of the majority to reproduce itself in a social setting by directly or indirectly favouring people who appear similar to those who hold power in that social setting (Kanter 1977). Homosocial behaviour reproduces gendered and racial inequalities in organizations (Acker 2006), as it is recurrent in various aspects of working practices: from hiring attitudes (Pinto et al. 2017), to access to networks (for example the gendered pub gatherings as described by Sang et al. 2014), and promotions. The main hiring and promotion requirements considered by employers are age, post-entry qualifications, geographical and occupational mobility, and long unbroken service (Crompton and Jones 1984). It is easy to notice that women usually lack the possibility to acquire promotable qualities, mainly due to caring jobs, and found themselves in what Whittock et al. (2002) call 'the tender trap' – getting left behind in terms of career development. One of the main strategies employed by women to overcome this structural and cultural discrimination is to develop *networks of support*, an instrument already theorized in feminist literature (Ahmed 2017; Macoun and Miller 2014), which foster women's well-being and progression at work by accruing their own forms of social capital. Men in architecture do not need this system of support because their existence is normalized and institutionalized: 'architecture is a boys' club', as candidly put by Carrie. The absence of an equivalent of the boys' club for women carries many material gendered consequences: in terms of networking, women lack the social capital which would allow them to reach clients and better job opportunities (Sheerin and Hughes 2018). In terms of sexism, women feel isolated and discouraged to challenge sexist behaviours. In terms of working arrangements, a more supportive environment would allow them the flexibility needed to carry out caring duties in their personal lives. Hence the extreme importance that women themselves place on the lack of a network of support in their working environments and the need to actively develop their own networks:

> I think the girls' club is a good idea, we should get better at doing clubs like boys do.
> (Carrie, UK)

The creation of a girls' club would offer that sort of support that some female bosses are already offering, which can be mainly summarized as having 'consideration to people's individual circumstances' as argued by Amanda (UK), the founder of her practice which she is very proud to define 'family friendly'.

In the last fifteen years various organizations created groups of networks for women in architecture, or in construction at large, both informal and institutionalized, such as UK-based WIA – Women in Architecture, NAWIC – National Association of Women in Construction, and FLUID Diversity Mentoring Programme, or Australian Parlour and Italian RebelArchitette. Among recurrent initiatives offered by these groups there are 'meet-ups', workshops and mentoring. The idea behind the role of the mentor is not only to offer an example to follow, but also to have someone more experienced able to offer tailored suggestions for career development, or for alternative pathways maybe not familiar to the mentee. The group Black Females in Architecture (BFA), for example, stresses the importance of these initiatives in offering 'a space to experience creative opportunities and networks' to minority groups, such as women of colour or non-binary architects, who experience additional and intersecting mechanisms of exclusion from dominant professional practice and identity.

Support systems can also take the form of alternative organization of practice, such as architectural cooperatives, which was one of the fundamental principles that the Matrix collective extensively applied and discussed in their praxis. Both Barbara McFarlane and Frances Bradshaw discuss the potential of architectural cooperatives, arguing that 'this type of practice is probably more responsive to the needs of many women workers than the conventionally organised office' (1984: 24), as it challenges hierarchies and power relations typical of the office structure (Rendell 2000). However, the Matrix authors warn that, to work efficiently, women need to be conscious of the discourses and strategies they employ to be able to challenge dominant practices and working relations.

Challenging gendered interactions

'Work is not an isolated relationship between actor and activity,' argues Rosabeth Moss Kanter (1977: 250); instead, it is set within organized systems. This is particularly relevant to gender relations in organizational settings, where gender is not just a factor to add to pre-existing processes, but it is ingrained in them (Acker 1990). From the conversations that I had with participants in various countries, specializations and stages of their career, I realized that women have a different awareness and understanding of the concept of sexism and discrimination, with specific consequences on their identity and their employment. Therefore, they engage in a variety of performances to address gendered expectations at work. In this section I illustrate how women respond to discrimination in two of the sites of performativity typical of the architectural field, namely the office and the construction site, and how they develop tailored coping strategies.

Gender performances at work The workplace is the site where everyday working interactions happen, power relations are negotiated and gender stereotypes reiterated. This is organized in hierarchical order, where the increase in seniority is usually paired with an increase in symbolic power. As argued by Bradley: 'power [is] the capacity to control patterns of social interaction' (Bradley 1999: 33), and it does not take long after entering an architectural practice to realize that it is a heavily gendered environment, where these interactions run along the lines of gendered expected and performed behaviours. For example, some of my British participants mentioned that they were implicitly requested to perform tasks that required more care than professional duties. For example, Allison clearly sums up this request:

> [My boss] said that I was going to deal with conflict because I was a woman, so any problems in the office [...] they'd always put to me to deal with them.
>
> (Allison, UK)

Caring is a recurrent concept in the life of women: from an early age they learn how to internalize this labour that is essentialized and constructed as feminine. Men are not expected, as much as women, to express caring attitudes other than for the tasks required in their working life (Kan and Laurie 2018; Lyonette and Crompton 2015). For women, caring must be displayed as a performance of moral value, and they end up becoming dependent on the needs of others (Skeggs 1997).

Therefore, in working environments the performance of stereotypically feminine characteristics (such as dealing with conflict or managing aspects external to work duties – e.g. making coffee) requires women to perform extra unpaid labour, in the form of care work and *emotional labour* (Hochschild 1983). This dynamic reproduces the difference between women and men in terms of expected everyday tasks: suggesting that emotional labour can be perceived in terms of performance while hiding further material and structural inequalities. Doing work-related tasks specifically assumed as female jobs not only segregates women in those specific tasks, but also influences and shapes the gendered perception of their work-identity, therefore their own doing gender (Gherardi 1994). While typing these observations I realize that a reader might be getting a picture of a clear gender distinction between the actors participating in these interactions, with men imparting tasks to women. However, I recall an episode from an internship I did while studying where my boss, who was a woman, asked my colleague, who was also a woman, to help her daughter write an exam paper necessary to obtain her high school diploma. Although my colleague was mortified and incredulous, she agreed to 'volunteer' for the task. This episode led me to question the straightforwardness of the formula man/imparting and woman/executing orders. Instead, it makes this an intersectional issue that needs to be critically analysed in terms of power rather than merely gender. In most architectural practices, it is typically men who are on the side of imparting orders, but a more nuanced assessment requires taking into account other aspects of their identities (white, wealthy, citizen) and of the identity of those at the bottom of the pyramid (e.g. gender, ethnicity, nationality, economic background).

This reflection is in line with a difficulty that I encountered during the whole research journey, where I struggled to find a framework of analysis able to discuss a gendered topic and make the most of participants' accounts while, at the same time, being critical of binary and essentialist discourses. Although I was being cautious in generalizing findings based on differences between women and men, because further intersecting characteristics clearly suggests that neither 'woman' or 'man' are homogeneous social groups, I did not want to undermine participants' examples or interpretations, despite these often relied on essentialist arguments. After all, as Jane Rendell (2011) points out, binary thinking is a social construction, meaning that this can change according to our positioning and experiences. Various literature on the topic of women in architecture often relied on essentialist views as well. Therefore, to incorporate this into the analysis of participants' accounts I employed both a materialist and a constructionist approach in order to understand the implications of binary thinking in the profession. For example, criticisms of the work values are often essentialized on the ground that women are more interested in the social and collective, whereas men are more individualistic (Woodfield 2007). This view is heavily reproduced because of the many confirmations in the reality of the labour market, where women tend to create and work in alternative working arrangements such as co-operatives, whereas men continue to be overwhelmingly present and celebrated in architecture panels and awards. However, this view lacks a wider understanding that architecture is a male-dominated profession where many women struggle to fit-in, therefore they are more likely to think and create alternatives. Thus, women are more critical of the organizational habitus of architecture and its working ethic not because they are inherently different and more 'social', but because of the need to create something different which does not carry centuries of male domination and reproduction of men as the norm.

Italian participants described a further way in which they feel their working behaviours are indirectly controlled by the masculine attitude dominant in architecture. Many of them admitted feeling they need to work harder by both challenging stereotypes and constantly proving themselves. Tonia (IT) claims that 'if you want to work you need to put more effort than a man. This is a thing', as a taken-for-granted statement of which everyone working in the field is aware of. I have been able to grasp this reference because it echoed my own experience, for example when I had to convince one of the contractors that my all-women practice was able to produce an electrical system plan for a project despite not having a *male* engineer in the team. In both countries, women are conscious of different performances required from men and women in working environments, and some of them mentioned the need they felt to perform masculinity in certain situations as a way of dealing with specific behaviours. Useful in theorizing these mechanisms is the gender performativity approach, which suggests that there are a multitude of gender performances required for different jobs, in the double meaning of *gendering practices* and *practicing of gender*, as outlined by Martin (2003). Angela exemplifies the concept of gendered performance through this account:

> I've encountered many women who act as men. Because they ended up exacerbating aspects of themselves in order to limit jokes and other things from the people surrounding them.
>
> (Angela, IT)

Or Kathleen (UK), who described an episode about competition with a male colleague. After months of indirect challenge, she felt the need 'to move from a kind of relational working way to the male model' in order to settle the competition. She refers to the 'male model' as something individual rather than relational, voicing an essentialist assumption that I observed in accounts from both countries. I found this essentialist view one of the only few aspects on which I was in contrast with my participants. I was trying to discover the ways in which women would and were imagining and creating alternative working patterns and professional identities, thus reinventing a more inclusive practice of architecture. Instead, listening to how most women where actively employing dominant behaviours to be able to stay in the field made me aware of the determinism of the profession, which risks reproducing itself the way it is.

However, after a more in-depth reading of their accounts, I started to realize that participants considered gender essentialism as a mere way to play with gender roles and resist them, rather than accepting the fate of fitting in a male-dominated profession. This becomes clear while considering these performances as *coping strategies*, which are often narrated by women with a playfulness that suggest their agency behind the performance.

Coping strategies One of the most recurrent keywords identified in the analysis of the Italian dataset is coping strategies, intended as resistance actions put in place by women architects when working, especially in construction sites. From the participants' accounts it was easy to observe how women tend to modify both their appearance and their behaviour when interacting with other actors on site. This is clearly exemplified in Giada's account:

> I firstly learnt that you need to go on the construction site dressed anonymously … otherwise you'll lose authority. Because it's a man's world out there. Then, you need to pretend you're angry, so they listen to you, you'll instil fear. It's a team job so you need to socialise, but at the same time you need to be aware of not sending feminine messages. You need to learn to make male jokes.
>
> (Giada, IT)

Giada pointed out the need to amend both her appearance and her attitude, a consideration shared also by other participants, such as Angela (IT): 'on the construction site I'm not myself. A man can be whatever he wants. There are double standards'.

Differently, British architects illustrated other ways not linked to their gender performance to actively overcome tensions in the workplace. Shirley, for example, put attention on building effective *alliances*. Jen, Kim and Anna employed a strategy aimed at gaining skills, and they all undertook building workshops. Anna's motivation was that she

> wanted to be a woman who could go onto a site, talk to the bricklayer and say 'I know about laying bricks, I know about mixing water, how to place a timber'. And I was jealous about the young men that already had that experience in college.
>
> (Anna, UK)

Few other participants denounced a structural limitation in their possibilities to have experiences in building sites during school and university, compared to their fellow male students. The aspect of practical building skills has been also argued in Matrix's text, highlighting how this mechanism is important to consider in its wider consequences as it leads to a lack of experience for female students which inevitably affects their confidence in the job.

Considering the examples from the two contexts, it is clear that Italian and British women discuss these issues from different awareness of discrimination. My living and professional experience in both countries offers me a vantage point in recognizing possible reasons behind these differences. My understanding of architecture practice in Italy is that it is still based in various ways on biological essentialism, and this can be a result of the structure of society in Italy which relies on more traditional norms and family roles. These inevitably affect women's presence in the labour market and their employment. Whereas in my experience in the British labour market I perceived society being more aware of gender inequality, to the point that institutional initiatives such as Athena Swan are heavily criticized as meaningless box-ticking activities that do not challenge structural barriers that reproduce inequality. Overall, even if Italian women put more emphasis on their coping strategies and in the need to alter their gender performance, British architects seem to be more reflexive about wider implications of gender discrimination on the construction industry. This might be a direct consequence of the historical critique of the architectural value system from a gendered perspective, already initiated in the 1980s by groups such as Matrix. Therefore, they implement coping strategies without naming them as such.

Questioning hegemonic language

Language can be sexist, and this is particularly true for the Italian language since every noun is gendered, including names of professions (Menegatti and Rubini 2017). The historical gendered division of labour is reflected in contemporary language, and architecture is one of the historical male-dominated professions that carry sexist language. However, in the last five years there has been a rise of awareness about this limit, and Italian women architects are reclaiming their word, *Architetta*. For example, the activist collective *RebelArchitette*, formed in 2018, is fighting to normalize the noun Architetta and to support female representation in peculiar professional settings, such as awards juries and conferences. However, this language change is not welcomed by everyone, and various objections have been made on the grounds of language integrity, reverse sexism and mere cacophony. In a research journal entry from 2017 I tried to address each of these oppositions by retracing my own path that led me from being sceptical about the use of this linguistic implementation to being a fierce advocate. My overall argument was that language has an impact on collective imagination and disrupting hegemonic language stirs debates about representation able to raise awareness on issues of equality.

It is interesting to notice how the trend for English-speaking architects is exactly the opposite. Practitioners and theorists mostly agree on their dislike in defining themselves as female architects, because this implicitly genders the term and naturalizes it as masculine. Karen Burns (2012: 238) suggests that by using the pair architect/woman architect 'we reinforce the visible and invisible patterns of gender production', and supports her position by mentioning examples of like-minded authors, such as Hughes (1996), who uses longer synonyms to avoid the use of the dichotomy in the introduction of her edited book. More recently, an article on Dezeen titled after the straightforward words pronounced by practitioner Dorte Mandrup, 'I am not a female architect. I am an architect' (Dezeen 2017), has been widely shared among groups aimed at promoting women and diversity in architecture. Highlighting through language the difference between women and the norm also fosters in many women the fear of being labelled and confined to practices and ideas considered as 'female areas'.

The striking difference between Italian and English-speaking women's preferences of use can be explained in terms of previous uses of the language itself, and in the disruption that the reclaiming of a non-existent term would make. While for English speakers the expression 'woman architect' can be perceived as emphasizing a defective architect in a denigrating tone; for Italian speakers 'architetta' is a term made up from themselves to represent themselves, as a form of reclaiming their own identity, which does not need an extra generic term (woman/ female) to be complete.

Language reproduces the dominant culture and, therefore, discrimination of whoever does not fit the mainstream indicators of that culture. Challenging the language means to actively challenge discrimination and also the value system of the profession and the industry, as exemplified by Rendell when discussing the innovative approach of Matrix's work in the 1980s: 'such work tends to use the more inclusive, less hierarchical term "built environment" rather than "architecture". It defines the role of the architect as an enabler, rather than a genius' (2000: 230).

Conclusions

The overall argument emerging from this chapter is that communities of resistance in architecture are counteracting hegemonic power relations. Practices of resistance can be either spontaneous, organized, unintentional or performative, but they all stem from the intention to disrupt the organizational habitus of the profession. I have been able to identify forms of this resistance by employing autoethnography as a research method through which I explored my own experiences and cultural understandings of the profession while navigating the voices and accounts of my participants. At the same time, I employed autoethnography to reflect on the development of my research project, including its aims, research questions and methodology. Autoethnography recognizes how personal experience influences the research process (Adams et al. 2014). During my research journey, it became clear that both the reflexive and the autoethnographical effort had a clear aim in mind: I needed to witness solidarity and resistance in a profession that made me feel like an outsider. My standpoint as a researcher, comprising my personal experience and my feminist politics, offered a specific lens to analyse the data obtained from my research project: I was thrilled to see that many women were challenging those feelings of otherness and I wanted to know *how*. In an effort to reassure the 20-something 'othered' me, I looked at the intricacies of the networks of support and resistance women were constructing. I wanted to shift the narrative about women in architecture: move on from the decades-long focus on how the profession was failing women and minorities and celebrate, instead, the collaborative and individual ways in which the 'others' in the construction industry are fighting to carve a space for themselves. The fight begins with building networks of support, challenging gender expectations in workplace interactions and questioning hegemonic language. But this is not all: resistance is spreading both in numbers and in methods.

References

ACE (Architects' Council of Europe). (2021). *The Architectural Profession in Europe 2020. A Sector Study.* [Accessed on April 2021 at: https://www.ace-cae.eu/fileadmin/user_upload/2020ACESECTORSTUDY.pdf].

Acker, J. (2006). 'Inequality Regimes: Gender, Class, and Race in Organizations'. *Gender & Society*, 20 (4): 441–64.

Acker, J. (1990). 'Hierarchies, Jobs, Bodies: A Theory of Gendered Organizations'. *Gender & Society*, 4 (2): 139–58.

Adams, T. E., Holman Jones, S., & Ellis, C. (2014). *Autoethnography. Understanding Qualitative Research.* New York, NY: Oxford University Press.

Agrest, D. (1996). *The Sex of Architecture.* New York: Harry N Abrams Inc.

Ahmed, S. (2017). *Living a Feminist Life.* Durham: Duke University Press.

Allen, K. R. & Piercy, F. P. (2005). 'Feminist Autoethnography'. In Sprenkle and Piercy (eds.) *Research Methods in Family Therapy.* New York, NY: Guildford Press.

Bradley, H. (1999). *Gender and Power in the Workplace.* London: Palgrave.

Brown, L. A. (ed.) (2011). *Feminist Practices: Interdisciplinary Approaches to Women in Architecture.* London: Routledge.

Burns, K. (2012). 'The Woman/Architect Distinction'. *Architectural Theory Review*, 17 (2–3): 234–44.

Coleman, D., Danze, E., & Henderson, C. (eds.) 1996. *Architecture and Feminism.* New York: Princeton Architectural Press.

Crawley, S. L. (2012) 'Autoethnography as Feminist Self-interview'. In Gubrium, Holstein, Marvasti and MCKinney (eds.) *The SAGE Handbook of Interview Research: The Complexity of the Craft.* London: Sage.

Crompton, R. & Jones, G. (1984). *White-collar Proletariat: Deskilling and Gender in Clerical Work.* London: Macmillan.

de Beauvoir, S. (1949). *The Second Sex.* Translated by Parshley, H. M., 1953. New York: Vintage books.

De Graft-Johnson, A., Manley, S., & Greed, C. (2003). *Why Do Women Leave Architecture?* RIBA/University of West of England Research Project. London: RIBA.

Dezeen. (2017). *I am Not a Female Architect. I am an Architect* [Accessed on March 2019 at: https://www.dezeen.com/2017/05/25/dorte-mandrup-opinion-column-gender-women-architecture-female-architect/].

Ellis C. & Bochner, A. P. (2000). 'Autoethnography, Personal Narrative, Reflexivity'. In Denzin, N. K. & Lincoln, Y. S. (eds.), *Handbook of Qualitative Research.* 2nd edn. Thousand Oaks: Sage.

Fowler, B. & Wilson, F. (2004). 'Women Architects and Their Discontents'. *Sociology*, 38 (1): 101–19.

Ghabra, H. (2015). 'Disrupting Privileged and Oppressed Spaces: Reflecting Ethically on my Arabness Through Feminist Autoethnography'. *Kaleidoscope: A Graduate Journal of Qualitative Communication Research*, 14 (1): 1–16.

Gherardi, S. (1994). 'The Gender We Think, The Gender We Do in Our Everyday Organizational Lives'. *Human relations*, 47 (6): 591–610.

Grant, J. (2021). 'No, I'm Not Crazy: A Black Feminist Perspective of Gaslighting Within Doctoral Socialization'. *International Journal of Qualitative Studies in Education*, 34 (10): 939–47.

Griffin, R. A. (2012). 'I am an Angry Black Woman: Black Feminist Autoethnography, Voice, and Resistance'. *Women's Studies in Communication*, 35 (2): 138–57.

Hartsock, N. (1983). 'The Feminist Standpoint: Developing the Ground for a Specifically Feminist Historical Materialism'. In: Harding, S. & Hintikka, M. (eds.), 1983. *Discovering Reality: Feminist Perspectives on Epistemology, Metaphysics, Methodology, and Philosophy of Science: Volume 161.* (Synthese Library). Dordrecht: Kluwer Academic Publishers.

Hill Collins, P. (1990). *Black Feminist Thought: Knowledge, Consciousness, and the Politics of Empowerment.* London: Routledge.

Hochschild, A. R. (1983). *The Managed Heart: Commercialization of Human Feeling.* Berkeley, CA: University of California Press.

Hughes, F. (ed.) (1996). The Architect: Reconstructing Her Practice. Massachusetts and London: MIT Press.

Kan, M. Y. & Laurie, H. (2018). 'Who Is Doing the Housework in Multicultural Britain?' *Sociology*, 52 (1): 55–74.

Kanter, M. R. (1977). *Men and Women of the Corporation.* New York: Basic Books.

Kern, L. (2020). *Feminist City: Claiming Space in a Man-made World.* London: Verso Books.

Lyonette, C. & Crompton, R. (2015). 'Sharing the Load? Partners' Relative Earnings and the Division of Domestic Labour'. *Work, Employment and Society*, 29 (1): 23–40.

Macoun, A. & Miller, D. (2014). 'Surviving (thriving) in Academia: Feminist Support Networks and Women ECRs'. *Journal of Gender Studies*, 23 (3): 287–301.

Martin, P. Y. (2003). '"Said and Done" Versus 'Saying and Doing' Gendering Practices, Practicing Gender at Work'. *Gender & society*, 17 (3): 342–66.

Matrix. (1984). *Making Space: Women and the Man-made Environment.* London and Sydney: Pluto Press (UK).

McDonough, P. (1997). *Choosing Colleges: How Social Class and Schools Structure Opportunity.* Albany: State University of New York Press.

Menegatti, M. & Rubini, M. (2017). 'Gender Bias and Sexism in Language'. In *Oxford Research Encyclopedia of Communication.*

Mohanty, C. T. (2003). *Feminism without Borders: Decolonizing Theory, Practicing Solidarity.* Durham, NC: Duke University Press.

Petrescu, D. & Trogal, K. (eds.) (2017). *The Social (re)production of Architecture: Politics, Values and Actions in Contemporary Practice.* London: Routledge.

Pinto, J. K., Patanakul, P. & Pinto, M. B. (2017). '"The Aura of Capability": Gender Bias in Selection for a Project Manager Job'. *International Journal of Project Management*, 35 (3): 420–31.

Powell, A. & Sang, K. J. (2015). 'Everyday Experiences of Sexism in Male-dominated Professions: A Bourdieusian Perspective'. *Sociology*, 49 (5): 919–36.

Rendell, J. (2011). 'Critical Spatial Practices: Setting out a Feminist Approach to Some Modes and What Matters in Architecture'. In: Brown, L. A. (ed.) *Feminist Practices: Interdisciplinary Approaches to Women in Architecture.* London: Routledge, pp. 17–55.

Rendell, J., Penner, B. & Borden, I. (eds.) (2000). *Gender Space Architecture: An Interdisciplinary Introduction.* London: Routledge.

Sang, K. J., Dainty, A. R. & Ison, S. G. (2014). Gender in the UK Architectural Profession: (re)producing and Challenging Hegemonic Masculinity. *Work, Employment and Society*, 28 (2): 247–64.

Schalk, M., Kristiansson, T. & Mazé, R. (2017). *Feminist Futures of Spatial Practice: Materialisms, Activisms, Dialogues, Pedagogies, Projections.* Baunach, Germany: AADR/Spurbuchverlag.

Sheerin, C. & Hughes, C. (2018). Gender-segregated Labour Spaces and Social Capital – Does Context Matter? *European Journal of Training and Development*, 42 (3/4): 226–45.

Skeggs, B. (1997). *Formations of Class and Gender: Becoming Respectable* (Vol. 51). London: Sage.

Stead, N. (ed.) (2014). '*Women, Practice, Architecture: "Resigned Accommodation" and "Usurpatory Practice"*'. London: Routledge.

Stratigakos, Despina. (2016). *Where Are the Women Architects?* New York: Princeton University Press.

Whittock, M., Edwards, C., McLaren, S., & Robinson, O. (2002). '"The Tender Trap": Gender, Part-time Nursing and the Effects of "Family-friendly" Policies on Career Advancement'. *Sociology of health & illness*, 24 (3): 305–26.

Woodfield, R. (2007). *What Women Want from Work: Gender and Occupational Choice in the 21st Century.* Basingstoke: Palgrave Macmillan.

Part II

ANTI-NORMATIVE POSSIBILITIES AND EVERYDAY RESISTANCE

Chapter 6

AGAINST 'THE DEVIL FROM WITHIN': DOING FEMINISM THROUGH RE-MEMBERING THE MULTIPLE SELVES

Po-Han Lee

Introduction

I am not a good storyteller, but I do tell stories. To me, storytelling has the power to put feelings into words (by speaking and writing) and make sense of those words. Storytelling helps me decide whether to remember or forget those feelings and/or related events. When necessary, I always take some notes that help me, at different moments, re-member my present self and connect it to the past one, which is related to, and sustained by, what the world would consider 'trivial' matters. These notes reflect life's vicissitudes, experienced affectively and in an embodied manner. This process reformulates the past through narration and documentation.

Who I feel I am in this moment would like to tell a few stories here, through autoethnography, about the closets where I once hid and some others that I have no idea how to break out of yet. To resituate my-self back in the stories in an effort towards unpacking the generality and particularity of these unpleasant experiences and resist the easiness generated from denying, erasing, silencing and thus forgetting, our life's stories that are an essential element of feminist and queer politics (Stephens 2010). And, acts of remembering enable me to position my own identity in a space where the past is not recalled mechanically; through storytelling, the re-subjectivization process refuses to privilege the future and the present over the past – a past in which injustices were experienced but were not yet describable (Tronto 2003).

My struggles with different closets in life represent a trajectory. They have enabled me to engage with and comprehend diverse versions of feminist thought, even though I have never settled for any version. I understand feminism as a line of flight from a world full of micro-dynamics of violence. When discharging feminist responsibility, I have learned to listen to and care for others and myself. Feminism offers a strategy and a way of critically thinking about 'autonomy and embodiment within a social field saturated with power' (Ahmed 2016: 491), to use Judith Butler's words in an interview with Sara Ahmed. So, feminist remembering and storytelling are simultaneously personal and political and can dismantle hierarchies and subvert the existing order of things.

Therefore, the most urgent task of feminist politics, in my opinion, is to enable one to counter forces that make people remain unheard (who speak but are not listened to) and even silenced (not allowed to speak at all). Indeed, everyone has vulnerability and needs a way to express it. Around 2015, my family experienced a storm because of my younger brother's sudden decision to marry, without 'a proper conversation' with my parents, to quote my dad's words. My parents did not accept my sister-in-law in the first place. She did not fit in much with the Taiwanese stereotypes of a good wife or mother-to-be; she was tough and often disagreed with my parents and her father. Han-Chinese social expectations about a wife to be resourceful (useful for the husband) and reproductive (useful for the family) are not only gendered but also classist and, of course, ableist. Coming from a middle-class background and having a daughter gives her more leverage to say no, yet the gender norms are less easy to negotiate. My parents are not traditional in many ways but prefer obedience in familial matters.

I called my brother, who knows me the best and has been supportive and helped me cope with many ups and downs in life. 'I don't want to disappoint anyone, but I am so tired, really tired,' he said. It was probably the first time I heard his voice filled with doubt, fear and uncertainty. He had always looked firm, so I was surprised when he showed his vulnerability to me. I was also shocked by my negligence, 'Sorry, I've been running away from home for years, leaving the burden of meeting their expectations of being a "real son" to you.' We both cried during the call. That was the first time I saw the wall between us: I'm the son in exile who regards himself as unwelcome, and he is the one who, hence, needs to be reliable and wanted.

Although silence and powerlessness go hand-in-hand, silence can be powerful if we pay closer attention. Around a year of my brother's marriage, my brother and sister-in-law had a big argument with my mum, again. This time, it was about having a baby. In that fight, my dad stepped aside, taking up the role of a mediator who *appeared* liberal and carefree. That made me wonder why my mum always stands at the front line against us. Does she believe that 'fighting "the good fights" for the family in a traditional sense' is her responsibility? This incident also made me realize that my mother is lonely in these fights, representing a *good parent*, giving a larger space for negotiation and leveraging power for my father – who dominates in terms of open-mindedness, leaving my mum to do power brokering to be a stereotypical wife.

My brother and I have thrown arguments based on the many social and critical theories we have learned against her – striving to force her to accept our challenges. By doing so, we have forgotten to locate the debate in the greater social context where my mother grew up, married and learned to be a 'good woman'. Instead, we intentionally or unconsciously reduced familial contradictions and complexities into a confrontation between individuals, generations and ideologies. In short, our attack was directed at someone who could be a victim herself due to a loss of freedom of choice. 'Can I say no? Did I ever get to choose?' she once yelled at me.

My mother broke her silence by not repeating what she had learned about being a daughter, a helpful sister, a wife, a daughter-in-law and a mother in Taiwan. The mother–son tension demonstrates the reproduction and variations of gender norms, which entrap people differently. As a queer person, I have been trapped in various closets crafted by my mom, who came from a generation (around the 1960s) where women, including herself, needed to battle gender entrapments for recognition from family, respect from the outside world and liberation from the closets around them. But what did she mean about *choosing*? She said no more.

Eventually, she cried. 'Is everything okay?' I asked. 'I'm fine. Don't worry!' I was speechless, staring at that abstract closet that had blocked her from being free. The closet looks like mine, which has her behaving like a 'good mom' who disciplines their kids and prevents her from showing vulnerability. Gosh – all too similar. What did she mean by *fine*? Or, what do I mean 'okay' when I probed her that? I have been trying to talk to her, not in a face-to-face interactive way but by sending texts. I ask her to reply when she has spare time, 'no rush, and don't feel obligated to reply. It doesn't matter.' I send messages, talk a bit about my day and wait for her to reply when she likes.

The narrating subjects are never immune to undetected interference, which, like a ghost, is already entangled in the choice of our words, tones, volume and even emojis. The interference has its power and needs to be identified, whoever the message receiver is. In Mandarin Chinese, we call such invisible interference *the devil from within* (心魔, *xīn mó*). We usually ignore that it is the most significant barrier that prevents us from freely expressing ourselves and listening. In a class on *Self, Voice and Creativity in Research Writing* at the University of Sussex in February 2016, Dr Kim Lasky mentioned Mikhail Bakhtin's (1986) 'trio theory' in conversational interpretation, according to which 'the devil from within' may come from a desire for ownership over the words as well as how they are being spoken and performed. Bakhtin argues:

> Everything that is said, expressed … cannot be assigned to a single speaker. The author has his own inalienable right to the word, but the listener also has his rights, and those whose voices are heard in the word before the author comes upon it also have their rights (after all, there are no words that belong to no one). The word is a drama in which three characters participate (it is not a duet, but a trio).
>
> (121–2)

Considering this, a feminist sociological approach to observation and analysis enables me to hear more than what a word means and see more than what a person (or an emoji) expresses. The most 'trivial' little things contain several voices – of unequal volume – from the body, our minds, society and the roles we voluntarily or involuntarily subscribe to. However, we tend to ignore and then forget such complexity. However, *forgetting* it requires us first to get and make sense of it before letting it go; we are forced to remember it – even with the least effort. Rather than denying the trivial moments and unimportant signifiers, which might make us recall regret and shame, I would argue for the necessity of facing the closet of memory – to re-read the narratives, not for anyone but ourselves.

The combination of feminist politics and symbolic interactionism – encompassing the macro-political and micro-sociological accounts – has provided me with a tool to interrogate the events that happen to me and others, and undertake self-reflection to interpret the interrogations. In the following sections, I will try to explain what I mean by 'the closet of memory', which is multi-layered, blocking our way to reconciling our present with our past selves. Every showdown is to be addressed, even if between our multiple selves. Perhaps, there will be no answers, but 'the devil from within' will have been exposed and identified. At least, we will have given a voice to many of our past selves who could not find a word to explain their struggles at some point.

Are they mine? The multiple selves

This section and the next were drafted with much emotion, containing old and new stories. Eventually, I decided to share old stories and narrate new ones, starting with how I now understand 'the self'. These lived realities have been influential enough to make me re-evaluate what my own *selves* mean to me. I want to highlight how random events and other people's uninvited involvement in our lives can shape and reshape one's worldview. These events don't need to be immensely tragic. Tiny changes beyond our notice, informed by mundane and everyday affairs, can leave a profound impact (Scott 2018).

There are things we do not pay much attention to, at least not in the moment when they occur. We would not even bother telling others. We think, 'That's nothing. Don't be dramatic.' This inattentiveness is what I hope to emphasize here. I was unsure whether I could describe stories towards which others might not feel sympathetic, yet you, as part of the Bakhtinian 'trio', are forced into my closets when you read this. Therefore, I will go directly to the experiences with closets, which – may not sound heroic or magnificent – have changed me. Looking at my diaries, I realize I have tended to blame myself for being powerless to fight micro-aggressions. 'Spelling out the cruelties may be an alternative way of facing them,' I told myself.

The multi-layered and interconnected closets have shaped how and what one can see in the world. I ask, are they mine – those closets, the layers of the world that penetrate me, and in which I look after myself – and the multiple 'selves' that emerge from time to time through coming-out processes? Weirdly enough, performing the role of an activist, who seems capable of making it easier for people to come out of closets, is very different from what I have learned through my own experiences of un-closeting. Of course, life has no guidebook. As an abstract concept, the self is just a reflexive pronoun, intersecting the experiential and the ontological; it is a product contingent on the dispositioning of social relations (Braidotti 2011). The self is simultaneously subjective and objective. When 'I' say *myself*, what is the essence that constitutes that piece of the self? Do I know that part of the self, and how have I approached it? Asking these questions implies that no singular self represents the whole me, yet the whole 'I' is mysterious and constantly transforming. The Deleuzian concept of becoming – instead of being – forms the ontology of the self (Biehl and Locke 2010). More precisely, the Deleuzian becoming is, according to Rosi Braidotti (1993: 44), 'the affirmation of the positivity of difference, meant as a multiple and constant process of transformation'. Indeed, this is where I start exploring the various possible ways of reflecting on *who I am (becoming)*.

The 'me' spoken of by others, seen from their eyes, projected by myself, with or without a nickname, in a crowd or alone, can be very different. I began to have the language to describe these observations when I started learning about feminism. Feminist inquiries can be about the body, appearance, a sexual partner or an intimate encounter. I would wonder which part of me was present and dealing with that observation. Through which closet am I looking and learning to speak and behave? I would not notice this if I never felt the nuances between the more vulnerable and the stronger selves I embody in different scenarios. As Eve Sedgwick (1990: 59) writes, 'the paths of allo-identification are likely to be strange and recalcitrant. So are the paths of auto-identification.'

All the F-words: Faggot, fat, foreign

Sexuality had never been a thing until they shamed him

I will now try to explain the strange feeling of mapping out the self with some small stories – in a third-person voice, which displays autoethnographic storytelling by keeping a distance between now and then as a method of strategic *re-membering* (Dillard 2008). He is not the kind of person who can easily express his feelings, except in a diary. Recently he read a news article containing gay people's coming-out stories in Taiwan,[1] which evoked many memories from his adolescent past – vivid but fragmented. He turned to look into the notes from his private blog site, in which specific names of people had been erased. The story began with the day his parents found out about his sexual orientation in 2011 after his ex-boyfriend broke up with him. He cried a lot the night before when he viewed the old photos. He fell asleep when the sun was rising, forgetting to turn off the laptop. Maybe he could not care less. It was a lovelorn night.

'Get out of here! I can't live under the same roof as you anymore. I don't want to breathe the same air as you.' That sentence, word by word, until today, still comes back to him. His relationship with his parents somehow recovered – mysteriously, after nearly a year of losing contact – under circumstances in which no one mentions that particular day and that unfinished conversation. Today, he and his

---

1. The news article was about the publication of an anthology of essay, *A Gay Man Living Downstairs* (樓下住個GAY, *lóu xià zhù gè gay*), by an ophthalmologist, Dr Ke-Hua Chen, in 2016.

parents can sometimes joke about his new relationships as if he were never driven away from the family due to his queerness. That day is still taboo. He often wonders why he has resisted looking back at himself – so much denial and embarrassment. He does not feel less guilty about not defending himself at that moment, even now.

However, he also wonders whether things would have been easier if he had talked back and argued. Then he remembered an evening in 2009. Some friends had chased him on campus, asking him if he liked boys: 'Hey, I won't look down on you because you're gay.' He did not know how to respond but kept running away and escaped from the crowd. He was unsure why he did not want to speak out since he was already out to close friends. What concerned him more was 'what to say' than 'not to say anything'. 'Should I come out to someone when I don't feel like doing it?' he wondered, but at the same time, he asked, 'does it mean I am ashamed of myself if I can't be honest about it?' Is it an obligation to come out? This question has haunted him for years.

Moreover, there was a love confession in 2004. It was the first time he left Taipei for college to live alone. He took things too simply, following the dominant discourse that 'for love, you have to say it out loud'. In return, he got a cold response from the boy: 'I think it's kinda disgusting to me,' handwritten on a small Post-it. They never talked again. He recalled that he was anxious some years earlier than that confession and felt the whole world would explode. He rushed to the school counsellor and asked, 'have I become like *this* because it is a school for boys?' Vaguely, he remembers the teacher telling him, 'Don't worry, *that* is not a big deal.' He naively thought *it* was nothing until he was made fun of by schoolmates and thrown into the streets by his parents. The gesture of forgetting – to let go, acquiescently, by people involved, including the hurters and the hurt – renders the feelings suppressed and leaves the violence unspoken, enabling the emergence of *the devil from within*.

The gay world is not for everybody unless you can fit in

Nearly graduating from college, he finally felt 'settled' in the gay world – they call it 'the circle' (圈子, *quān zi*) in Taiwan. He could leave behind everything *in real life* (outside the circle), go out with friends partying every weekend, stay late in cruising parks, spend nights at gay saunas and feel no fear. He learned how to be gay. He did not expect that he also had to learn, even sceptically, all the unwritten rules of the gay world. These rules include the judgement of body types, subcultural practices, sexual encounters, age prejudice/preference and the subtlety of biases in the 'imbalanced' relationships embodied by people assuming different sexual roles that reflect the power of masculinity over femininity. He once truly believed that the circle was all about freedom; he was wrong.

'What made you think you could just come here? You're too chubby for this place,' he clearly remembers when the butch lesbian bouncer stopped him at the entrance. 'Nah, I'm just kidding. Of course, you can come in but won't have any fun there.' It was the most popular gay club in Taipei, *Funky*. It would be packed every weekend until the nightlife was replaced with house parties and dating apps – shutting the club down in 2017. Back then, he did not realize that there were many small *circles* within the larger gay circle in the city. One day, someone told him that he belonged to the bear group. It was around 2005 when the bear culture had just emerged in Taiwan. Gradually the bear culture has become dominant, thanks to its members' (relatively) muscular bodies and (presumably) masculine image, along with the rising trend of gym culture in urban Taiwan.

Everyone wants to become and be with a 'classy bear', who has the 'right' body type, 'moderate' amount of body hair and looks 'just' (not toxic) masculine (Lin 2009) as what Adam Green (2008) defines as sexual capital in the field. The bear *circle* has thus been divided into 'real bear' versus 'piggy' (or 'chub' in gay slang). The *boy*, who was infantilized and made to feel 'emasculated', was reclassified into the latter. He had not thought hard enough about the phenomenon until another factor intervened when he moved to Brighton, England, in 2014. The strange English culture had barred him from approaching and exploring the gay world there. He could not find any 'circle' based on his experience back in Taiwan. 'You are an otter, or at best, a *panda* (he thought it was a joke before a friend mentioned it could be a racist comment).' On his first night out in a bar flying the bear flag, the 'International Bear Brotherhood Flag', 'you are in no way a bear', someone told him. Again, such brotherhood applies only to men with beefy bodies and facial hair, which a typical East Asian man tends not to have. The hierarchy between body shapes and appearances is unquestionably racial, both colonial and orientalist.

After all, he discovered that he could have been categorized as 'Asian' – a group for all East and Southeast Asians regardless of their nationality, language and body type. Not many English gay men find members of this group attractive.[2] Asians seem preassigned, by default, to a given sexual role – bottom, the penetrated and the subordinated – since they are (considered) generally shy, petite, slim, smooth and sexually passive, just as Tan Hoang Nguyen (2014) notes. According to a Thai friend of his, all of these characteristics – or stereotypes, he thinks – justify Asian gay men's effeminacy 'in those blue or green eyes'. For *rice queens* (Caucasian men attracted to East Asian men in gay slang), 'you, such a chubby Asian guy, just don't fit their type', his Japanese friend told him in a trying-to-be-polite tone. The chubby boy found love after all, but he had never felt part of a gay community before he left England. Classification creates classes and territories, designating and positioning people to 'their' places through spatial and social segregation. Refusers of exclusion get punishment by losing not only attention but also belongingness.

Everyone is hiding something. Learn how to deal with it

While pursuing a research degree in Taipei, he experienced different on-and-off romantic lives, sometimes with a married man. He was waiting for his lover, a

---

2. Thanks to Sohini's, the editor of this book, introduction to an excellent roundtable discussion on the way in which racialized gay men are forced to leave bars soon after they enter because they are not figured as worthy of being desired (Dinshaw et al. 2007).

married man, in a convenience store. When their secret relationship was exposed, his lover's wife yelled at them and called them 'perverts' and 'monsters'. She did not want a divorce because of their daughter. The story here happened a few weeks before things got messy. He had just landed in Taiwan from a trip to the United States in 2009. Nearly an hour later, a man came into the convenience store, 'I'm sorry, too much traffic.' 'Not at all. We don't get to meet much lately. Don't worry.' He then took out lots of stuff from his bag, 'Hey! I've got something for you, and this is for your wife, and the toy is for your daughter.' 'You don't need to.' 'Of course I do. It'd be odd if I only bought you souvenirs.'

They caught up but did not speak much, hugging each other in a buddy-buddy style. After a long pause, the man asked, 'do you want to come over?' 'Now? Are you crazy? It's going to be too suspicious. I don't want to risk it.' 'Yes, of course, exactly … I know. I'm *sorry*.' After that day, they lost contact because the man's wife forbade them from seeing each other too often. They had never looked like 'just good old friends', especially with a ten-year age difference. The next time they met, the man asked for a 'cool down'. Neither of them knew what that meant. Suddenly they apologized to each other. 'Sorry for messing up your life!' 'I can't be selfish; I have a family. Sorry, I am a coward.' He could not afford to come out as he was a middle-aged man, even though their relationship seemed no secret anymore. In Taiwan, getting older means stopping 'fooling around' (e.g. frivolous gay life) and assuming family responsibility, which is inherently heteronormative before the debate over marriage equality became heated in Taiwan.

That was a decade before Taiwan legalized same-sex marriage in 2019. After all these years, sometimes the boy still thinks of the man. He wonders whether the story could have ended differently if, in Taiwan, coming out was not considered an irresponsible life choice and divorce was not a resolution that usually harmed the woman more than the man. All of them, the many he-s I mentioned above, form an integral but distinct part of my present *self*. The boys in the stories once suffered from family rejection, peer pressure, unspoken social codes, the burden of sexual identity and categories, and their own and others' closets and messy relationships. Each of them tries not to hate anyone but, for sure, struggles a lot. Have we all had other options? Could there be a second chance to be or not be free of particular gender/sexual/ethnic identities, normative relationships or social norms?

Every encounter with others generates a conversation between my multiple selves – the rational and the emotional one, the sensitive and the indifferent one. Some events may seem unimportant and uninteresting, but they all leave a mark on one's life, in response to which our multiple selves emerge. These memories (including our conversations with others, the existence and absence of actions, and how they are imprinted on us) are inscribed on, and sometimes reinforced in, our performative negotiations with hostilities, exclusions and prejudices (Butler 1990). Feminist teachings have empowered me to feel and face, bravely and critically, the power dynamics between others and me concerning our different subject positions (Mouffe 1992). To borrow Liz Stanley's (1990) words, the 'moments of writing' have allowed me to ruminate over these events and resist heteronormativity and the sizeism and racism embedded in the 'liberal' Taiwanese and English gay worlds.

Micro-political resistance practices

You cannot be a feminist. You can only become one. It is a lifelong process
in which you start with observing the world around you, and you feel, ask
questions, think, and try to make sense of it – justify or resist, love or dissent,
uncertainly. Then, the whole process runs again. You observe, feel, question,
think, hesitate, and get angry, over and over again!

That was the first time I learned about feminist thinking in a class on *Gender and
Law* at National Chung Hsing University, Taiwan, in 2007. There were few module
options regarding gender or sexuality issues in law, at least when I did my first
degree. Indeed, law schools do not pay much attention to gender and feminist
studies in Taiwan, even though Taiwan has experienced robust sexual rights and
gender equality social movements since the 1980s when the Martial Law was lifted
(Lee 2017). Most legal professionals do not consider gender a 'useful category'
(Scott 1986) of social relations. More specifically, they usually take 'the question
of women' only from a binary perspective in a dominant/subordinate relational
framework, which assumes womanhood as well as femininity to always correspond
to a female body, fixing normative gender roles in the legal history of Taiwan
(Wang 2004). This variety of legal scholars might not see the fundamental problem
of patriarchy and the power asymmetries it induces, including the problem with
the men/women gender binary and heterosexism. The sociolegal and educational
context in which cis-heterosexism is legitimized through discursive and
pedagogical practices and 'hidden curriculum', in Cheng and Yang's (2015) words,
has, however, provoked my critical consciousness regarding gender/sexual norms
and facilitated my multiple selves to evolve in everyday interpersonal encounters.

That was the context in which I became interested in a series of gender questions
that I had taken for granted. Thanks to Prof Wang Hsiao-Tan's inspiration, though
not systematically, I eventually detected the power of feminism. Gender has
become a helpful lens to identify and analyse problems and make sense of the world,
especially in recognizing discomforts with the expectations of family and society
associated with how I express myself. It was not enough, nonetheless. Much later,
in 2012, through the lectures of Mr Chang Hong-Cheng, I learned about sexuality
as another category of social relations in which a set of legal and social discourses
is maintained as a truth (Rubin 1984). It is not merely a question of discrimination
on a case-by-case basis. Instead, it presents another series of questions regarding
one's body, emotions and intimacies, subject to problematization and hence
unaddressable simply by law. Therefore, the question starting with 'am I ... ?' is an
oxymoron. Could *I* know who *I* am without others' recognition?

In addition to intellectual enlightenment, feminist thinking also empowers. The
moments of feeling feminist are like undertaking many small adventures of self-
understanding and self-help along a journey of subscribing to different roles from
a relatively vulnerable position. I sense feminism diversely, to stand up against
various enemies and shout aloud. As Eugene Gendlin (1992) would say, it is the
feminist *felt sense* – a non-verbal, impulsive and not always readily comprehended
moment in which you encounter the need of the self. It is the point of departure to

approach empowerment with or without a proper word to describe the situation. Feminism, in this light, offers the ground from which I have access to liberation and a reconciliation process between me and others who have expected me to be someone else – someone who is more masculine, fit and straight-acting. All interrelated expectations require me to think and behave like a proper man, an obedient son, a beautiful lover and a good citizen.

Feminist sensitivity, countering the social roles assigned by these expectations embodied in my encounters with others, has allowed me to pause, reflect on how these expectations have moulded and worked on me, and, what's more, has given me tools to fight, not just to survive but also to thrive. Sensing and questioning the territorialization of a 'closet' that prevents you from freely living and expressing makes you wonder what has led such prevention to happen – a crucial step towards critically interrogating how the world sees (or wants to see) me and how I respond to their way of seeing: at home, on campus, from Taiwan to England, within and outside the gay/bear circles. When I can analyse and speak about it, I know how to assert better my existence and the right to exist in all my complexities.

I appreciate the tensions and confrontations at the micropolitical level, which I had avoided for a long time. These moments occur to me along with a desire to manage better how I perform my multiple selves and how I interact with others and even resist their illegitimate projections upon me and my body. When it comes to a fight against oppression, the struggle requires a name, such as those regarding my sexual orientation, gender expression, body image and family and cultural background. Feminist sensitivity has helped me expose the repertoire of norms imposed on my social selves. Moreover, it pushes me to initiate communication with those who have forced me to be who I am not, to let them see the power in their hands and how they are also governed by the social norms that give them power in exchange for their freedom and agency.

Conclusion

Applying the indigenous concept of 'devil from within', in this chapter, I have considered the construct and operationalization of closets in everyday life, such as the incidents with my parents, brother and sister-in-law, as well as the autoethnographic accounts of fat-phobia and casual racism in the mainstream gay world. The autoethnographic reflections on nonbelonging are tied to the generation and complexity of multiple selves. To reconcile these selves requires critical thinking and alliance building as a resistance strategy against structural violence. Before concluding this reflection process, I would like to use a final example to illustrate the increasing difficulty in countering queerphobia in Taiwan and worldwide.

At an academic conference on *Towards Gender Equality: Clashes in Law*, organized by myself and two colleagues in mid-2018, we were fortunate to have many inspiring presentations. At that gathering, feminism was presented theoretically and empirically in very diverse ways. However, not only could we not come up with a universal strategy to achieve gender equality, but we also could not entirely make sense of the globalization of the anti-gender movement, which has mobilized the crisis discourse (regarding masculinity, 'traditional family values' and social reproduction) (Hemmings 2021; Guney et al. 2022). The tension between the so-called *silent majority* and social justice initiatives has made most governments reluctant to stand with human rights advocates. 'The desire for peace (absence of conflict) curtails all other hopes for justice,' one participant asserted at the conference.

Meanwhile, a final note would be, taking on board what we've learnt from critical theories as I did within and beyond my family, our awareness of not to over-romanticize and/or generalize personalized effort and triumph in negotiating social norms. Such an awareness, however, should not cancel our celebration for ourselves of the bravery and excessive care work one has to offer in everyday life either. So-lived everydayness involves, in a dramaturgical sense (Goffman 1956), navigating – sometimes ridiculously exhaustingly – complex interpersonal relationships, all the 'roles' we identify, counteridentify, dis-identify (Muñoz 1999) and even, not purposefully, non-identify (Lee 2022), and 'dramas' we have to engage and disengage, on front stage and back stages (Scott 2018). Our selves emerge and inhabit in these imposed, chosen and unchosen roles in the daily dramas where conflicts and reconciliations occur.

References

Ahmed, Sara. (2016). 'Interview with Judith Butler'. *Sexualities*, 19 (4): 482–92.

Bakhtin, Mikhail. (1986). 'The Problem of the Text in Linguistics, Philology, and the Human Sciences: An Experiment in Philosophical Analysis'. In Emerson, Caryl & Holquist, Michael (eds.), *Speech Genres and Other Late Essays*. Austin, Texas: University of Texas Press, pp. 103–31.

Biehl, João & Locke, Peter. (2010). 'Deleuze and the Anthropology of Becoming'. *Current Anthropology*, 51 (3): 317–51.

Braidotti, Rosi. (1993). 'Discontinuous Becomings. Deleuze on the Becoming-Woman of Philosophy'. *Journal of the British Society for Phenomenology*, 24 (1): 44–55.

Braidotti, Rosi. (2011). *Nomadic Subjects: Embodiment and Sexual Difference in Contemporary Feminist Theory, Second Edition*. New York: Columbia University Press.

Butler, Judith. (1990). *Gender Trouble: Feminism and the Subversion of Identity*. New York: Routledge.

Cheng, Ling-Fang & Yang, Hsing-Chen. (2015). 'Learning About Gender on Campus: An Analysis of the Hidden Curriculum for Medical Students'. *Medical Education*, 49 (3): 321–31.

Dillard, Cynthia B. (2008). 'Re-membering Culture: Bearing Witness to the Spirit of Identity in Research'. *Race Ethnicity and Education*, 11 (1): 87–93.

Dinshaw, Carolyn, et al. (2007). 'Theorizing Queer Temporalities: A Roundtable Discussion'. *GLQ: A Journal of Lesbian and Gay Studies*, 13 (2): 177–95.

Gendlin, Eugene. (1992). 'The Wider Role of Bodily Sense in Thought and Language'. In Sheets-Johnstone, Maxine (ed.), *Giving the Body Its Due*. Albany: State University of New York Press.

Goffman, Erving. (1956). *The Presentation of Self in Everyday Life*. New York: Doubleday.

Green, Adam Isaiah. (2008). 'The Social Organization of Desire: The Sexual Fields Approach'. *Sociological Theory*, 26 (1): 25–50.

Guney, Gizem, Davies, David & Lee, Po-Han Lee. (eds.) (2022). *Towards Gender Equality in Law: An Analysis of State Failures from a Global Perspective*. Berlin: Springer.

Hemmings, Clare. (2021). 'Unnatural Feelings. The Affective Life of "Anti-gender" Mobilisations'. *Radical Philosophy*, 2 (9): 27–39.

Laclau, Ernesto & Mouffe, Chantal. (2001). *Hegemony and Socialist Strategy: Towards a Radical Democratic Politics*. London: Verso.

Lee, Po-Han. (2017). 'Queer Activism in Taiwan: An Emergent Rainbow Coalition from the Assemblage Perspective'. *The Sociological Review*, 65 (4): 682–98.

Lee, Po-Han. (2022). 'Struggle for Recognition: Theorising Sexual/Gender Minorities as Rights-Holders in International Law'. Feminist Legal Studies, 30: 73–95.

Lin, Dennis C. (2009). 'Becoming a "Bear": Identity Formation and Sexual/Gender/ Bodily Performativity among the Taiwanese Gay Bear Community'. *Taiwan: A Radical Quarterly in Social Studies*, 76: 57–117.

Mouffe, Chantal. (1992). 'Feminism, Citizenship, and Radical Democratic Politics'. In Butler, Judith, and Scott, Joan (eds.) *Feminists Theorise the Political*. New York: Routledge, pp. 369–84.

Muñoz, José Esteban. (1999). *Disidentifications Queers of Color and the Performance of Politics*. Minneapolis: University of Minnesota Press.

Nguyen, Tan Hoang. (2014). *A View from the Bottom: Asian American Masculinity and Sexual Representation*. Durham: Duke University Press.

Rubin, Gayle. (1984). 'Thinking Sex: Notes for a Radical Theory of the Politics of Sexuality'. In Carole Vance (ed.). *Pleasure and Danger: Exploring Female Sexuality*. Boston: Routledge and Kegan Paul, pp. 267–93.

Schulman, Sarah. (2016). *Conflict Is Not Abuse: Overstating Harm, Community Responsibility, and the Duty of Repair*. Vancouver: Arsenal Pulp Press.

Scott, Joan. (1986). 'Gender: A Useful Category of Historical Analysis'. *The American Historical Review*, 91 (5): 1053–75.

Scott, Susie. (2018). 'A Sociology of Nothing: Understanding the Unmarked'. *Sociology*, 52 (1): 3–19.

Scott, Susie. (2019). *The Social Life of Nothing: Silence, Invisibility and Emptiness in Tales of Lost Experience*. London: Routledge.

Sedgwick, Eve Kosofsky. (1990). *Epistemology of the Closet*. Berkeley: University of California Press.

Stanley, Liz. (1990). 'Moments of Writing: Is There a Feminist Auto/biography?' *Gender & History*, 2 (1): 58–67.

Stephens, Julie. (2010). 'Our Remembered Selves: Oral History and Feminist Memory'. *Oral History*, 38 (1): 81–90.

Tronto, Joan. (2003). 'Time's Place'. *Feminist Theory*, 4 (2): 119–38.

Wang, Hsiao-Tan. (2004). 'What Can Legal Feminism Do? The Theoretical Explorations on Gender, Law and Social Transformation'. *EurAmerica*, 34 (4): 627–73.

Chapter 7

NEOLIBERAL PRECARITY AND NEUROQUEER POSSIBILITY: EXPLORING CARE, KINSHIP AND RELATIONAL BECOMING AS RESISTANCE

Sohini Chatterjee

Journeying into neuroqueer possibilities

In September 2021, I move to a new city again (I have been on the move since 2015, affectively anchorless and drifting into directions barely known, with a naïve conviction I no longer recognize as my own). My move to London, Ontario, in 2021 was, in part, informed and prompted by my own repeated resistance against compulsory, neurotypical, cisheteronormative ways of relating and being, and quotidian dissidence against sanist, heteropatriarchal demands of middle-class, dominant-caste, monogamous heteronormative futurity placed on my bodymind. However, as much as this migration was an enactment of resistance it was also limned with many losses. The loss most intimately felt was the loss of embodied access to familiar sites beckoning queer, lesbian possibility and potentiality in multiple spaces and places in India – which I inhabited variously throughout my twenties and which facilitated, multiply, my own queer becoming. Transnational migration – in my case from eastern India to southwestern Ontario – brought with it the threat of loss of familiar caring queer community networks while opening up different possibilities as well as challenges of relating and caring queerly, sometimes in defiance of normative time and stabilized space. This intimate fear of loss is certainly not unique to my experience but is felt viscerally by many of us who partake in privileged transnational mobilities in the hope of a queer(er) future that participation in 'progressive' and 'developmental' temporality (Weber 2016) associated with the West (particularly North America) seems to promise from afar – even if many multiply marginalized queer and trans people come to be marked by it as 'underdeveloped' and 'underdevelopable' (Weber 2016). Your affective experience of loss is magnified further when you have to attune yourself anew to different vocabularies of desire, and unlearn and relearn multiple modes of desiring, being and resisting on the daily – having been confronted with a new queer adolescence (if not infancy) all over again, brought on by complexities of transnational migration. Such queer becoming is indicative of a life structured by migrant mobility and queer temporality where migration informs how you inhabit and embrace both migrant temporality and 'queer time' (Freeman 2010). Life can only happen in phases because neoliberal precarity ensures you are never not a migrant – you are always on the move and in the unending process of beginning anew.

As migrant mobility and queer temporality structures your life, you also have to learn to understand the ways in which you are perceived in a different sociocultural and economic context with codes of queer sociality and intimacy firmly in place that demand a different embodied, gestural language and sensibility for comprehension as well as subcultural articulation. Your personhood is now subjected to quotidian forms of cultural regulation and surveillance which is insidious and hence cannot quite be figured as regulatory at all. Given the inevitable complexity of context, how do you seek anti-normative kinship – while resisting 'kinship idealism' (Butler 2022: 40) – when hetero/homonormativity continues to be prioritized and privileged over neuroqueer relationality? How do you prevent casteist logics of purity and impurity from seeping into your neuroqueer kinships and care work as a dominant-caste person? How do you resist your 'own colonizing tendency of making the Other an enemy' (Mayer 2007: 38) (as you begin recognizing the possibility of kinship with them)? How do you resist carceral logics – or logics of 'carceral sanism' (Ben-Moshe 2020) – of punishment, regulation, surveillance and ostracization from claiming space in your most intimate and affective realms of being, knowing, loving, desiring, and caring without abandoning the needs of your bodymind as well as your commitment to yourself to affirm its complex history? This chapter – brought into being by autoethnography recognized as neuroqueer methodology – explores complexities of relating both queerly and neurodiver/gently through care work, reflects on kinships that emerge quietly in the midst of hetero/homonormative ways of relating, and tries to understand how structural violence continues to threaten marginalized forms of neuroqueer relationalities in the everyday. I also attempt to articulate how care labour, when released from carceral, casteist, colonial logics, can be reimagined in the context of neoliberalism and racial and casteist capitalism to prevent us from falling apart, or how care-ful kinships can facilitate repair and reconnection, and enable us to survive and live in our wholeness after many instances of falling apart. As Thenmozhi Soundararajan writes, violence of caste and Brahminism (and casteist logics) seek to wire multiply marginalized people to 'replicate separation, polarization, violence, and hate' and facilitate the creation of policies (and indeed relationalities) that are 'artifacts of this wiring' (Soundararajan 2022: 47). Caste is founded upon hatred. How do we resist this impulse as well as casteist logics of ensuring 'inclusivity through gatekeeping' (Borisa 2020: 92) while seeking care and doing care work? How can neurodivergent people ensure we stop being governed by oppressive logics to obtain care? This story – with all the limitations of space, time and language that keep us from 'writing [ourselves] in' (Kafai 2021: 26) – is committed to centring my 'embodiminded' (Acevedo 2020) knowledge and experience, felt sensations and affective complexity, and could not have been told without autoethnography – a methodology that facilitates the work of journeying into the self while listening to, and honouring, my neurodivergent 'bodymind' (Price 2015; Schalk 2018) – or the intimate entanglement of the body and mind.

Autoethnography is neuroqueer methodology. I am writing this chapter while living with complex trauma (or what is referred to as 'Complex Post-Traumatic Stress Disorder', or 'C-PTSD' in therapeutic and psychiatric parlance, which I distance myself from because I do not identify my mind as disordered in a world that continues to produce, and traffic in, disorders of various kinds), ADHD (or Attention Deficit Hyperactivity 'Disorder') and its attendant insomnia. Needless to say, my writing, among other things, is affected. Writing is as important and necessary to me as breathing (as hyperbolic as it may sound), it has saved me from myself countless times, and owing to bouts of reactive depression, I have gradually become conscious of my need to write in order to stay and feel alive. However, with recognition and understanding of the complexities of my neurodiversity, I am beginning to challenge and unlearn ruthless commands of neoliberal sanism over my life as I write this chapter in 'crip time' (Kafer 2013) and honour my bodymind and its demands of slowness during the process of writing. 'Crip Time is broken time', writes Ellen Samules (2020: 192). 'It forces us to take breaks, even when we don't want to, when we want to keep going, to move ahead. It insists that we listen to our bodyminds *so* closely, *so* attentively, in a culture that tells us to divide the two' (Samuels 2020: 192). Crip temporality, by offering relief from capitalist temporality, provides 'exultance, solidarity, grace, the simple rhythm of the breath' (Price 2011; Samuels and Freeman 2021: 249), and I allow its tenderness to flow through me. As I write in broken time, I accept the fact that my racing, intrusive thoughts will interfere with my writing and thinking, executive dysfunction will ensure other aspects of my daily life cannot merit attention as much or at all (and I know it affects my body), and I will have to write without putting myself through a rigid schedule that may very well be compatible with neoliberal compulsions of productivity, and capitalist demands of discipline, but will not be compatible with quotidian needs of my bodymind or the complexities associated with the 'disabled [or neurodivergent] quotidian' (Piepzna-Samarasinha 2022: 92). I also develop during this process 'an ethics of pace' which challenges capitalist stipulation of producing more and producing fast in ways that prioritize profit over people (Bailey 2021) – especially those caste-oppressed, Black, indigenous, Muslim, poor, working-class disabled and neurodivergent people who have historically been oppressed and excluded by the authority of the capital and continue to be failed by its norms of social organization and regulation, as well as its obligations of rapid, sustained and profitable production.

This chapter has taken me a year to write. Crip temporality is also 'crip methodological intervention' and has been recognized for being 'unruly' (Hickman and Serlin 2018: 136) throughout the process of writing. Autoethnography has validated my need for isolation – the kind of agential isolation that lets me experience relative emotional safety as someone with attachment trauma, as and when required, and makes it possible for each word to find its place in this document. Methodological innovation is resistance for many neurodivergent and disabled people whose stories might not get written otherwise – especially when both resource and mobility are limited and restricted. Exploring one's embodiminded histories can offer up insights about structures, structural violence and the resistances they generate. Even though I am located in a resource-rich context in the North American academy, and do not claim to occupy an absolute marginalized positionality, I honour and validate autoethnography as neuroqueer (and crip) methodology because of the subversive research possibilities it holds for marginalized disabled and/ or neurodivergent trans and queer people. Inaccessibility and ableist and sanist inequity in knowledge production ensures that multiply marginalized disabled and neurodivergent people are excluded from practices, systems and institutions that facilitate knowledge production. Autoethnography becomes resistance against dominant modes and exclusionary forms of knowledge building as it empowers marginalized people to 'embrace subjectivity, engage critical self-reflexivity, speak rather than being spoken for, interrogate power, and resist oppression' (Griffin 2012: 142), even if it is denigrated too often for collapsing binary distinctions of subject/object and researcher/ researched – binaries which uphold methodological hierarchies and gravely disadvantage multiply marginalized disabled and neurodivergent people. Autoethnography can invite possibilities of healing, knowledge production and community building – slowly and through disorganized organization neurodivergent people feel comfortable with. I would also like to state here, following Smilges, that even though this chapter makes mention of trauma, it explores and foregrounds more than just my embodiminded experiences of living with complex trauma – especially since 'trauma' is 'regularly taken up metaphorically or pathologically', without attention to the fact that it is 'both deeply embodiminded and culturally produced' (Smilges 2020). I explore, in this chapter, possibilities of care and neuroqueer kinship that cannot be reduced to my embodiminded experiences of living with complex trauma even though my lived experience of trauma heavily informs my engagement with care, innovation as well as imagination of kinship, and resistance, and, hence, 'carries the potential to facilitate togetherness, to offer new kinds of community and coalition' (Smilges 2020). Neuroqueer autoethnography produced by my Traumatized bodymind leads me to identify a whole universe constituted by intimate anti-normative relationalities where moments of care are deeply valued – ensuring that the absence of imagination or possibility of normative futures in specific relational contexts do not diminish the significance of moments and acts of caring.

Autoethnography is revolutionary in a neoliberal, capitalist world that expects we present ourselves as nothing but productive workers, and which demands we privilege and solidify our identity as workers (and hide those stigmatized aspects of our identities that are incompatible with it) first and foremost to remain competitive in a market whose longevity must be preserved at all costs – including the (casteist, racist, ableist, sanist, classist) human cost it produces. We are expected to abandon our sensations, our relational knowledges and our political wisdom for the sustenance and prosperity of the market and remain committed to being efficient, loyal, unassuming and compliant cog in the wheel, offering only the kind of intellectual and affective labour the market wants, needs and demands. Autoethnography infused with crip and neuroqueer ethics of being dissents against such oppressive, exclusionary and marginalizing diktats of the market and can be embraced in anti-capitalist ways to reveal subversive knowledges our bodyminds offer up when we are subjected to the dehumanization wrought by violent structures. It also makes prominent the imaginative and political potential of the relational when we practice care as resistance and seek relational joy as a political commitment to ourselves and our communities of neuroqueer becoming. Autoethnography can also generate critical consciousness emerging from, and evolving with, anti-normative neuroqueerkinships – and makes it possible for us to reimagine caring, living, loving and surviving on the daily that often defy neoliberal market logics – helping us make the journey from 'unconscious unhappiness' to 'unhappy consciousness', facilitating struggles towards the abolition of capitalism (Pross cited in Adler-Bolton and Vierkant 2022: 236).

Owing to its critical vitality, autoethnography as neuroqueer methodology can be cathartic for many neurodivergent people living with life-defining trauma. McMillan and Ramirez observe, 'approaching trauma from a traditional clinical modality represents a false boundary by severing off the social/cultural/ political contexts that inform how an individual interprets their experience' (McMillan and Ramirez 2016: 454). The authors contend that autoethnography as therapeutic method allows for a deeper and more meaningful exploration of trauma that is informed by an understanding of structural factors and is not myopically focused on the clinical. Autoethnography welcomes possibilities of healing as well as resistance and offers 'active demonstration of the personal as political' (Ritchie 2019: 72) by making the field not a 'faraway space' but a space 'within past and current experiences, memory, and body' which invites 'risk, extreme vulnerability, and perhaps even danger' (Ritchie 2019: 72). It creates knowledge about quotidian enactment of resistance by people who inhabit and embrace marginalized, stigmatized identities and unstable, anti-normative relationalities. Autoethnography helps us honour our subversive relational knowledges – and life-affirming anti-capitalist, anti-casteist and anti-carceral possibilities emerging therein – and share it as resource and neuroqueer bequeathment to those of us who are sustained by dissident wisdom we make in community. It demands the engagement of reflexivity as methodological priority. As a neurodivergent queer femme who is also dominant-caste, autoethnography allows me to reflect on the simultaneous presence of privilege and penalty in my life and in my everyday. Autoethnography is methodologically vacuous and unreliable without reflexivity. 'Reflexivity in autoethnography includes reflexivity in both acknowledging and critiquing our place and privilege in society and using the stories we tell to *break long-held silences* on power, relationships, cultural taboos, and forgotten and/or suppressed experiences' (Adams et al. 2019: 103). In this chapter, I also respond to the call of 'queering autoethnography' which is 'an offer to difference, to disorienting and disrupting, to impermanence and change, to expansion, to disruption and to new ontologies' (Jones and Harris 2018: 7). Queering autoethnography entails having 'an intersectional, disruptive and disorienting intervention into normativity, precariousness and death-making politics and actions through the always already political project of autoethnography' (Jones and Harris 2018: 7) and 'embraces fluidity, resists definitional and conceptual fixity, looks to self and structures as relational accomplishments and takes seriously the need to create more livable, equitable and just ways of living' (Jones and Adams 2010: 211) – and bears witness to neuroqueer autoethnographic intentionality. Naming autoethnography as a queer method 'means taking a stand on a poetics of change' (Jones and Adams 2010: 212), and it facilitates disabled, neurodivergent storytelling (even though autoethnography despite being constituted by storytelling, exceeds it) whereby we have a 'chance to know ourselves better, to really question who we are, where we've been, and who we want to be' (Wong 2022: 225). Neuroqueer and crip storytelling through autoethnography has the potential to exist with other 'disabled narratives, pushing back at the status quo' (Wong 2022: 225), making it possible for the latter to offer 'cripistemology' or 'crip epistemology' (Johnson and McRuer 2014). And it can affirm a 'politics of difference' (Young 1990) within crip and neuroqueer communities of resistance, instead of looking for homogeneity to solidify alliances.

Care is political, care in (neuro)queer

A few months after I arrived in London, Ontario, in 2021, I experienced – what is colloquially referred to as – a Covid 'scare'. My body started exhibiting, what I thought were, symptoms of Covid-19, and I had no choice but to rely on the care provided by another neurodivergent, racialized, queer person. Owing to our interpersonal history of extending and receiving care, and in the context of relating neuroqueerly and romantically with each other, it was an expectation that had relational legitimacy. As I struggled to move my body and it kept burning with high fever that day, they came over and cooked, cleaned after, and took me out to do groceries the next day. However, they seemed unusually, uncharacteristically quiet on our way home. I could sense fear but I could not identify its nature. And perhaps, for the first time, there was an uncomfortable, impenetrable silence between us. As they dropped me off hurriedly – and rather unceremoniously – at my place, I recognized their hesitation. It was a kind of hesitation that originates in fear. I sensed that they were struggling to be there and perform the care labour that was expected of them – even though I could not articulate that need in so many words (but perhaps did communicate it in more embodied, gestural ways). I could not bring myself to discard this feeling as Sara Ahmed had taught me to embrace sensation by contending that 'feminism begins with sensation: with a sense of things' (Ahmed 2017: 21). I sensed that they wanted to provide care but were hesitant to continue offering it if it meant putting their own bodymind at risk. At the same time, they were unable to refuse it because of our affective investment in each other. They were perhaps afraid of the consequences physical proximity with me might result in as Covid-19 had laid bare the necropolitical workings of power and they were aware of their own disposability in this context (complicated by precarious employment status). Sensing their fear, I offered them a way out, even though, in all honesty, I felt betrayed. And my sense of betrayal came with insurmountable grief. I had felt alone many times over in this new city, but, in that moment, I felt lonelier than the loneliest I had felt thus far. I read their hurried departure as withdrawal of care. But then it occurred to me – slowly but surely – that perhaps my sense of betrayal, grief and entitlement to care was misplaced. Carceral and colonial logics at play in neuroqueer relationalities mislead and lead us astray by exacerbating our hypervigilance, stand in the way of community-building and dissident ways of relating, and contribute to our insularity. My fear of abandonment as well as relational trauma and attachment wounds, in that moment, was speaking louder than my own relational ethic of inhabiting relationalities neuroqueerly where we honour each other's need for self-preservation; sometimes give more than we expect in return (especially if we are in a position of power in a specific relational context); leave room for reflection, renegotiation and open communication; ensure that terms of care work are carefully and consistently negotiated (and invented anew, as and when required); and affirm giving and receiving on terms that sustain generative mutuality and equity. However, carceral, colonial and casteist logics teach us to be hostile towards multiply marginalized people for having (and prioritizing) survival instincts and demand that they barter it to ensure the survival of those more powerful and privileged (Nadasen 2021).

When multiply marginalized people demonstrate their need to survive, live and thrive, they are figured as perfidious, since structures invested in their decay and death demand their martyrdom on the daily and do not easily accept non-compliance from them. Unlearning carceral, casteist and colonial logics is resistance. Upon care-ful reflection, I came to realize that they had in effect, not withdrawn care, and the feeling of betrayal I had been experiencing thus far emanated from my own dominant-caste and oppositional (and agonizing) entitlement to care. Their act of preservation was just and needful. They did not have the life-affirming supports they needed to survive in a world as a neurodivergent queer person and were, hence, multiply marginalized. Care is heavily dependent on dehumanizing structures that render it inaccessible and spurious. I refused to feel betrayed by them, I felt betrayed by the world that makes providing and receiving care difficult.

Capitalism triggers our relational trauma on the daily and makes neurodivergent queer people feel that we are undeserving of care in our vulnerable moments. However, not giving myself the permission to believe this narrative was my resistance against structures that threaten to alienate variously marginalized people from one another, make and keep us lonely in a world of 'organized loneliness' (The Care Collective, 72), stabilize our precarity and inflict relational wounds on us. I convinced myself cognitively to not hold a grudge (even though affectively I wanted to); could not allow myself to nurture hostility towards them; resisted the pull of carceral, colonial and casteist logics to withdraw my affection in that moment; and refused to privilege transaction (which is very different from reciprocity) over queer, neurodivergent relationality. This was my resistance against structural violence and inequity which threaten to disintegrate our neuroqueer kinships on the daily. As the threat of Covid-19 slowly dissipated from my body, we did move through life and navigated this city with as much life as we could muster – having gradually moved past feelings of betrayal and grief. And we continued to offer, provide and receive care at different times between each other for a long time after (especially when I got Covid-19 a few months later) that fateful day, as long as we could. However, the gravity of that vulnerable moment made me realize that resistance can be enacted by extending anti-capitalist forms of care and by recognizing their will to live and survive and not misrecognizing their need for preservation as a moral failing, limitation or abdication of responsibility towards me. Resistance has meant undoing dominant-caste, colonial, capitalist and carceral logics of wanting care without wholly acknowledging its complexity even if it has left me overwhelmed with a sense of grief at times – which was also my responsibility to question in order to subvert relational harms such affect could cause. Resistance has meant not mimicking the violence of hierarchies and learning to believe that we do not have to perform care sacrificially to be figured as worthy carers. Resistance has meant honouring care as and when it is received, receiving wholeheartedly what is given, not grudging the limits placed on caring, accepting withdrawal of care without conflict, and learning to innovate in its wake. Kinships, Butler argues, are 'striated with unlived futurities' as they are constantly in the process of being made (Butler 2022: 40). To resist dominant, exclusionary, oppressive logics is to honour that process and move towards a world where we become 'ungovernable' (Stanley 2021) – where we can no longer be governed by oppressive and alienating logics of becoming. 'Abolition feminism reminds us that getting rid of police and prisons means nothing if we do not abolish the ideologies, practices, and affective economies of policing in our interpersonal relationships and communities' (Spira et al. 2022: 27). Regulatory practices put people under surveillance at all times and facilitate policing governed by dominant logics of relating – where multiply marginalized people always find themselves having to perform quiet compliance, unstinting loyalty, obedience, and have to keep their difference at bay to keep communities together. Abolishing carceral logics in neuroqueer relationalities can help us cultivate 'networks of care that are rooted in support and self-determination rather than surveillance, punishment, criminalization' (Spira et al. 2022: 28). Imagined from the margins, abolition can help us sustain anti-exclusionary practices of care, offering us, in the process, 'a roadmap for an otherwise' (Spira 2022 et al. 46).

Caring against carceral, casteist, colonial logics

In the lives of variously marginalized, neurodivergent queer femmes, crisis of care is normalized. We are supposed to be doing the caring without wanting any of it in return. Its denial is normalized and its refusal is more acceptable in our lives than its need is recognized. For crip, neuroqueer people or those who are caste-oppressed Dalit-Bahujan, Adivasi, Black, indigenous, racialized, working class, trans and queer femmes – whose desires, embodyminded knowledge and existence are seen as a threat to non-disabled, neurotypical, cisheteronormative, neoliberal ways of being and relating – care is inaccessible at worst and precarious at best. Care continues to be in crisis. It is rarely offered in ways that affirm the denigrated identities of the marginalized among us and if and when it is offered, it is provided on terms dictated by hetero and homonormativities, ableism and sanism, casteism, racism, racial and casteist capitalism, and classism. And it demands the flattening of disabled, neurodiverse queer and trans complexities. However, multiply marginalized neurodivergent trans and queer people perform care labour as resistance even when caring is difficult and when recipients of our care are moralistically and normatively figured as unworthy of just care. Leah-Lakshmi Piepzna-Samarasinha (2018) writes in *Care Work: Dreaming Disability Justice*,

> I think about the person I was lovers with who was an asshole about thirty percent of that time, who I still send twenty bucks every now and then because they are seriously disabled and can't work. I do this because they are a queer and trans person of colour who grew up working class who's pissed off a lot of people, and they still don't deserve to die alone in their own piss.
>
> (Piepzna-Samarasinha 2018: 132)

Here, the author's racialized, disabled, neurodivergent queer femme care labour is resistance against racial capitalism and its endless demands of productivity placed on variously marginalized disabled and neurodivergent people that render them disposable when their contribution to society and economy can no longer be quantified and used for profit. Care is offered here as resistance against compulsory neoliberal productivity, cultural attunement, homonormative ways of relating and social likeability, defeating capitalist market logics that demand the survival of only the productive among us (despite structural violence making their lives unliveable and productivity improbable). Care can affirm survival beyond norms of productivity, popularity and extroversion. It can be offered through the recognition that 'the archetypal neoliberal subject is the entrepreneurial individual whose only relationship to other people is competitive self-enhancement' (The Care Collective 2020: 13) which disallows 'caring across difference' (The Care Collective 2020: 61). Care humanizes and prioritizes survival and advances self-determination. Intentional acts of equitable caring demonstrate commitment to the survival of reviled, forgotten, forsaken and disposable many who do not meet social expectations of worthiness. Just care – care that is rooted in justice, ethics and equity – resists capitalist logics that demand the diminishment of people and turn them into mere instruments of labour (Dowling 2021). When care is offered in neurodivergent, disabled, crip, trans and queer femme affirming ways, it allows us to embrace our complexities and creates possibilities for our experiential knowledge to be sustained. And it also sustains our neuroqueer knowledges by paying attention to how the Traumatized among us respond to care crises. It prompts us to 'care promiscuously' (The Care Collective 2020: 51). Promiscuous care is 'an ethics that proliferates outwards to redefine caring relations from the most intimate to the most distant. It means caring more and in ways that remain experimental and extensive by current standards' (The Care Collective 2020: 51). It is indiscriminate care which helps us expand our caring imaginaries (The Care Collective 2020: 51). As a queer, neurodivergent femme, receiving care in femme and neurodivergent affirming ways has meant having the liberty to talk about suicidal ideation – with other neurodivergent, queer and trans femmes living with suicidality – without the fear and threat of institutionalization, hospitalization and criminalization. Talking about suicidality has also helped reclaim suicide as 'a queer desire' while 'demedicalizing and re-politicizing it' (Krebs 2022: 168). It has helped me understand why every single neurodivergent queer person I have ever been in a relationship with has, at some point, expressed the desire to unalive themselves. Inhabiting caring neuroqueer kinships has meant being able to explore the interconnections between suicidality, sanism and ableism, capitalism, and xenophobia. Femme-centric care has also taught me that care being reciprocal and purposive does not make it 'impure' but the need to sanctify care is oppressive. The oppressive pure/impure binary through which we interrogate intention is sustained by casteist logics. Even if care work is being done in the hope of receiving care and/or material supports in return, this is not a moral failing but just reciprocity in a world where queer, trans, neurodivergent, disabled people only have each other. This is especially true for neurodivergent people among us with relational trauma – those of us who live with the fear, threat or memory of abuse, harassment, bullying and abandonment – whose need for support outside of neuroqueer and neurotrans communities is not met and is perceived with derision and judgement. We provide care and supports to each other in ways non-disabled, neurotypical people cannot. It is also important, however, to remember that the care needs of resourceful people (who have emotional and material supports to offer, or at least, are considered capable of offering both) are more likely to have their care needs met than those multiply marginalized and stigmatized people, who cannot similarly be benefitted from in the transactional economy guiding our everyday existences. I know why I manage to access care in certain vulnerable moments but others without my privileges (and with my penalties) do not. However, this is not to discount the fact that reciprocity is vital – and exceeds terms of transaction which are more rigid – and is at the heart of care as mutual aid.

Neuroqueer and neurotrans relationalities can make us experience affirming care. My trans and queer, disabled, neurodivergent friend who would comfort me through attentive listening and affirmations while I cried for hours almost every time they came over to my place – sometimes staying as late as 3 am – never stopped being my friend because I was 'too much' or 'too emotionally dysregulated'. They stayed with me for 12 hours at a stretch and helped me move out of a house (merely two months after my arrival in London, Ont.) – where I was subjected to relentless xenophobic abuse – despite being in physical pain. They told me repeatedly that they would never think less of me because of what I was going through, or because I lacked the necessary coping skills to self-regulate. They never opted out of our neuroqueer kinship. I also think about my queer friend back in West Bengal who calls me regularly and keeps checking up on me despite the constraints of time and space between us. We have seen each other through many crises – coming to the realisation that we understand each other in ways our closest heterosexual friends and natal families do not. We found each other at a time when we had both either lost, or were losing, lovers and close friends to heteronormative domesticity and its normative prioritization of relationships. My discerning, wise, caring friend defied – and continues to defty – the constraints of time and space to extend care, always reminding me that this is not a favour but an act of reciprocity and affective commitment. And I remind them that we will continue to be friends for the rest of our lives because we helped each other live at a time when both of us did not know how to carry on. Neuro/queer relationalities can make us want to live a little longer.

In a world where the most marginalized among us lack access to care, mutual aid as just reciprocity is equitable. Care work when seen as efforts towards equity and community-centred justice can help us let go of feelings of betrayal, disappointment, grief and anger emerging from oppressive notions of purity of purpose and casteist, colonial, carceral demands of self-effacement that is placed aggressively and disproportionately on variously and multiply marginalized and historically excluded peoples. In a world where marginalized people are asked to constantly outperform, outwit, outsmart, outdo each other for security and relevance, care does not end competition but it keeps us from distancing ourselves from one another instead of being consumed by rivalry, hostility and opposition. Moreover, because disabled and neurodivergent trans and queer knowledge, labour, wisdom, expertise, interests are more often than not questioned and invalidated, care enables our subversive knowledges to be sustained, shared and offered within communities and with the world in transformative ways. Because my neuroqueer/trans kinships has kept me alive (quite literally), the knowledge I want to offer the world has also survived with my bodymind. When I accept and offer care, I am aware that this is the work that ensures the survival of marginalized people and knowledges and hence is transformative.

Caring validates our difference and cultivates heterogeneous possibilities of care-ful, equitable worlds where the uncool, unheard, unsuccessful, misunderstood and maladjusted among us can hope to survive and even dare to live. Neurodivergent queer and trans femmes are marginalized in a world that stigmatizes both femininity and neurodiversity, devalues it and is threatened by it. If and when care is offered and its need is affirmed, the promise of disruption is rendered prominent in profoundly political ways. For the Traumatized, socially avoidant and anxious, the socially neglected, reviled and rejected, staying in community requires immense trust and constant questioning of our internalized carceral, colonial and casteist logics. Staying is revolutionary when breakage is normalized in the lives of the most marginalized among us. Acts of care can make us stay, hold our communities together and make neuroqueer kinships and friendships possible. Care can also help us leave spaces where we are treated as disposable for being who we are and when care is not extended in trauma-informed but sanist ways, disregarding ethical queer, neurodivergent, or disabled ways of relating. If necessary supports and care are available to us during moments of crises – when multiply stigmatized identities are no longer affirmed or during periods when a false sense of normalcy prevail – care can facilitate leaving and keep us from being dehumanized in the face of structural and/or interpersonal violence. Care labour by and for neurodivergent queer people can make both staying and leaving powerful political and affective decisions. If care work done for, by and with neuroqueer and neurotrans people can make us stay, it can create possibilities of sustained political activism and organizing and also make living and thriving possible beyond politics and activism. It can also make complex care practices endure and advance for the sustenance of neurodivergent trans and queer care itself. If care work affirms breakage for people living with relational trauma, from the remnants left behind by those very acts of leaving, we can help ourselves relearn how to build and sustain communities of resistance in trauma-informed ways and do better by ourselves.

Care is disruption. Care is revolutionary. Just care does not demand the deification of neurodivergent queer and trans people who provide care and the demonization of those who do not or cannot. An act of care is an act of justice. And it entails learning each other's care languages (Piepzna-Samarasinha 2022: 94). Neuroqueer care languages might begin to be understood when words of affirmation are uttered but go beyond affirmation to open up a universe constituted by difference and quotidian, subversive, relational knowing. Disabled and/or neurodivergent, and/or D/deaf trans and queer people often find ourselves not being consulted on how we would like to give and receive care because the devaluation of our knowledge and personhood is normalized. Learning our care languages is resistance against a world that is not invested in knowing and meeting our needs in trauma-informed neurotrans or neuroqueer ways. Variously marginalized people perform care as intergenerational knowledge sharing and invite the past, present and future to acquire new meanings and significance by assuming anti-ableist, anti-sanist, anti-carceral, anti-casteist, anti-capitalist ethos in our care labour. Care for and by neurodivergent people resists the erasure of our desire, care and access needs, as well as our material, cultural and political needs, wants and aspirations. By doing the equitable work of care as resistance, variously marginalized neurodivergent people do survival work (Piepzna-Samarasinha 2018) for each other and resist necropolitical (Membe 2003) – including queer (Haritaworn et al 2014) and trans (Snorton and Haritaworn 2022) necropolitical –

forces that push the most marginalized among us towards death on the daily. Care creates neuroqueer worlds and makes kinship in the present imaginable and very possible.

In lieu of a conclusion

I learned last year that Sarah Hegazi – who was jailed for waving a pride flag at a concert in Cairo, who sought and secured asylum in Canada, and died by suicide in Toronto on 14 June 2020 – was queer and neurodivergent. Hegazi was autistic (Lannon 2020). I first learned about Hegazi's suicide while in Kolkata, through mainstream inter/national media, which largely foregrounded her queer 'asylee' identity, made mention of her trauma/PTSD but rendered invisible her neurodiversity. The media narrative surrounding her trauma and suicide was widely attributed to the torture and incarceration she was subjected to in Egypt, conveniently erasing the precarity, loneliness and complexities of life in one of the most expensive cities in Canada in the middle of the Covid-19 pandemic – at a time when many multiply marginalized racialized, neurodivergent, queer people, out of jobs and with no savings, could no longer afford Toronto's high cost of living. Thinly veiled Islamophobia that guided media narratives in the wake of her death could not hold accountable structures that made Hegazi die by suicide. While I render visible my own trauma, neurodiversity and suicidality in the pages of this book, I think about people to whom care, affirmation, catharsis remain inaccessible, and who die despite having had the will to live. I also think about many who are named and not named in narratives about trauma and suicide because of political reasons. My resistance began with wanting to be in community with neurodivergent trans and queer people but our communities are fixated on homogeneity and remain uneasy with difference, ensuring that many multiply marginalized, caste-oppressed Dalit, Bahujan, Adivasi, Black, racialized, Muslim indigenous, disabled, neurodivergent, D/deaf, poor and working class trans and queer people will not have access to the kind of just care they deserve. And such crises of care are caused by the fact that we understand and support difference in ways that serve the relatively privileged at the cost of many disposable Others.

My dearest friend told me, many years ago, without a moment's hesitation, 'I'd do anything to keep you alive' after I had told her I was suicidal. I have vivid memories of that day and her voice still rings in my ears. Because these moments are vital but fleeting – and so are the commitments demonstrated through them – our friendships, kinships, queer, trans, neurodivergent, D/deaf and disabled relationalities can only keep us alive if we have material supports needed to move through life, which can also make us honour and recognize the vitality of these moments and the nostalgia associated with them. If people who wanted to live but had to die could have access to life through care and non-normative relationality, they could also secure an affirming relational purpose to live – and not feel as if they deserved to die because of the lack of normative relationships in their lives. But then those of us who keep living get to write what it means to not die so we might never know the embodiminded violence that the crises of care inflict on people who are now physically, socially and culturally dead. If my trauma, in part, originates from watching my father die after living with terminal illness after five years of being rendered disposable structurally, institutionally and socially, it also gave me a keen understanding of the transformative work of care that is needed to keep disabled, D/deaf and neurodivergent people alive in ways that make them want to live – because I know my father wanted to die not because of his disability but because he was made to feel unworthy of life on the daily, while he was disabled. Care work is the work of justice and 'holds potentials for cripping neo-liberalism' (Dasgupta 2014). Neuroqueer autoethnography has allowed me to tell stories of care as resistance and resistance as neuroqueer relationality in fragments. In this moment, I am thinking about the stories that will never be written and the ones that are waiting to be told. Care and resistance have transformed my politics, my pedagogy, my personhood, the neuroqueer relationalities I sustain, the care I cherish and provide, and the sense of justice I nurture. 'Because the world is still ending and care is not simple and we deserve to hear the stories of how we are caring for each other anyway' (Piepzna-Samarasinha 2022: 79).

Even though feminism has never not been contested by those it has excluded – Dalit, Bahujan, Adivasi women by dominant-caste feminists, trans women by trans-exclusionary feminists, Black, indigenous and racialized women by white feminists, queer women by cishet feminists, disabled, D/deaf, hard of hearing and neurodivergent women by non-disabled, hearing and neurotypical feminists – many of us, including myself, came to an understanding of what it means to question hierarchies and the oppressive hold of power over our lives through feminisms and its political evolution. Feminisms also alerted us to the need for justice and activism, made us aware of structures and practices of domination-subordination (and what guides its logics), and made it possible for us, slowly but surely, to think about transformative care and anti-normative relationality – which included developing different frameworks of justice, identity and ethics that 'feminism' could not adequately capture. As feminist scholar Sharmila Rege, who was terminally ill prior to her death in 2013, argued, 'It is imperative for feminist politics that "difference" be historically located in the real struggles of marginalized [Dalit] women' (Rege 1998: 39). To understand difference, we need to honour lived struggles of multiply marginalized Dalit, Bahujan, Adivasi, Muslim, queer and trans, disabled, D/eaf and hard of hearing, and neurodivergent, poor and low-income, Black and indigenous people and also understand the revolutionary potential of the care that they offer one another in the midst of very necessary struggles – because there can be no struggle without just, tender, self-aware, negotiated, ethical care. I end with the declaration that 'any form of crip knowledge production, like any form of crip sociality or crip temporality, must always be understood as an incomplete project – a project that is always in a state of becoming, always unfolding, and which never attains a stature of completion' (Hickman and Serlin 2018: 139). My story, and our stories, that are always in the process of being written and re-written, cannot be so easily concluded. They become a part of a universe of resistance I want to see existing and proliferating.

References

Acevedo, Sara M. (2020). '"Effective Schooling' in the Age of Capital: Critical Insights from Advocacy Anthropology, Anthropology of Education, and Critical Disability Studies'. *Canadian Journal of Disability Studies*, 9 (5): 265–301.

Adams, Tony E., Jones, Stacy Holman & Ellis, Caroline. (2019). *Autoethnography: Understanding Qualitative Research*. New York, NY: Oxford University Press.

Adler-Bolton, Beatrice & Vierkant, Artie. (2022). *Health Communism: A Surplus Manifesto*. London and New York: Verso.

Ahmed, Sara. (2017). *Living a Feminist Life*. New Delhi: Zubaan.

Bailey, Moya. (2021). 'The Ethics of Pace'. *South Atlantic Quarterly*, 120 (2): 285–300.

Ben-Moshe, Liat. (2020). *Decarcerating Disability: Deinstitutionalization and Prison Abolition*. Minneapolis: Minnesota University Press.

Borisa, Dhiren. (2020). 'Hopeful Rantings of a Dalit-Queer Person'. *Jindal Law & Humanities Review*, 1: 91–5.

Butler, Judith. (2022). 'Kinship Beyond the Bloodline'. In Tyler Bradway & Elizabeth Freeman (eds.), *Queer Kinship: Race, Sex, Belonging, Form*. Durham, NC: Duke University Press.

Dasgupta, Debanuj. (2014). 'Cartographies of Friendship, Desire, and Home; Notes on Surviving Neoliberal Security Regimes'. *Disability Studies Quarterly*, 34 (4). https://dsq-sds.org/index.php/dsq/article/view/3994/3789

Dowling, Emma. (2021). *The Care Crisis*. London and New York: Verso.

Freeman, Elizabeth. (2010). *Time Binds: Queer Temporalities, Queer Histories*. Durham, NC: Duke University Press.

Griffin, Rachel Alicia. (2012). 'I am an Angry Black Woman: Black Feminist Autoethnography, Voice, and Resistance'. *Women's Studies in Communication*, 35 (2): 138–57.

Haritaworn, Jin, Kuntsman, Adi, & Posocco, Silvia. (2014). *Queer Necropolitics*. Abingdon, Oxon: Routledge.

Hickman, Louise & Serlin, David. (2018). 'Towards a Crip Methodology for Critical Disability Studies'. In Katie Ellis, Rosemarie Garland-Thomson, Mike Kent, & Rachel Robertson (eds.), *Interdisciplinary Approaches to Disability: Looking Towards the Future: Volume 2*. Abingdon, Oxon and New York: Routledge.

Johnson, Merri Lisa & McRuer, Robert. (2014). 'Cripistemologies: Introduction'. *Journal of Literary & Cultura Disability Studies*, 8 (2): 127–48.

Jones, Stacy Holman & Harris, Anne M. (2018). *Queering Autoethnography*. New York: Routledge.

Jones, Stacy Holman & Adams, Tony E. (2010). 'Autoethnography Is a Queer Method'. In Kath Browne & Catherine J. Nash (eds.), *Queer Methods and Methodologies*. London: Routledge.

Kafai, Shayda. (2021). *Crip Kinship*. Vancouver: Arsenal Pulp Press.

Kafer, Alison. (2013). *Feminist, Queer, Crip*. Bloomington: Indiana University Press.

Krebs, Emily. (2022). 'Queering the Desire to Die: Access Intimacy as Worldmaking for Survival'. *Journal of Homosexuality*, 70 (1): 168–91.

Lannon, Valerie. (2020). 'Our tribute to comrade/rafeqa Sarah Hegazi'. *Spring*. June 14. Available at: https://springmag.ca/our-tribute-to-comrade-rafeqa-sarah-hegazi.

Mayer, Lorraine F. (2007). 'A Return to Reciprocity'. *Hypatia*, 22 (3): 22–42.

McMillan, Colleen & Ramirez, Helen Eaton. (2016). 'Autoethnography as Therapy for Trauma'. *Women & Therapy*, 39 (3–4): 432–58.

Membe, Achille. (2003). 'Necropolitics'. *Public Culture*, 15 (1): 11–40.

Membe, Achille. (2019). *Necropolitics*. Durham, NC: Duke University Press.

Nadasen, Premilla. (2021). 'Rethinking Care Work: (Dis)Affection and the Politics of Caring'. *Feminist Formations*, 33 (1): 165–88.

Piepzna-Samarasinha, Leah-Lakshmi. (2018). *Care Work: Dreaming Disability Justice*. Vancouver: Arsenal Pulp Press.

Piepzna-Samarasinha, Leah-Lakshmi. (2022). *The Future Is Disabled: Prophecies, Love Notes, and Mourning Songs*. Vancouver: Arsenal Pulp Press.

Price, Margaret. (2011). *Mad at School: Rhetorics of Mental Disability and Academic Life*. Ann Arbor: University of Michigan Press.

Price, Margaret. (2015). 'The Bodymind Problem and the Possibilities of Pain'. *Hypatia*. 30 (1): 268–84.

Pross, Christian. (2016). 'Revolution and Madness: The "Socialist Patients" Collective of Heidelberg (SPK)': An Episode in the History of Antipsychiatry and the 1960s Student Rebellion in West Germany'. English synopsis of '*Wir wollten ins Verderben rennen*': *Die Geschichte des Sozialistischen Patientenkollektivs Heidelberg*.

Rege, Sharmila. (1998). 'Dalit Women Talk Differently: A Critique of 'Difference' and Towards a Dalit Feminist Standpoint Position'. *Economic and Political Weekly*, 33 (44): WS39–WS46.

Ritchie, Michelle. (2019). 'An Autoethnography on the Geography of PTSD'. *Journal of Loss and Trauma*, 24 (1): 69–83.

Samuels, Ellen & Freeman, Elizabeth. (2021). 'Introduction: Crip Temporalities'. *South Atlantic Quarterly*, 120 (2): 245–54.

Samuels, Ellen. (2020). 'Six Ways of Looking at Crip Time'. In Alice Wong (ed.), *Disability Visibility: First-Person Stories from the Twenty-First Century*. New York: Vintage Books.

Schalk, Sami. (2018). *Bodyminds Reimagined: (Dis)ability, Race, and Gender in Black Women's Speculative Fiction*. Durham, NC: Duke University Press.

Smilges, Logan J. (2020). 'Trauma Sex: A Queercrip Erotic'. *Disability Studies Quarterly*, 40 (3). https://dsq-sds.org/index.php/dsq/article/view/6847/5701

Snorton, C. Riley & Haritaworn, Jin. (2022). 'Trans Necropolitics: A Transnational Reflection on Violence, Death, and the Trans of Colour Afterlife'. In Susan Stryker & Dylan McCarthy Blackston (eds.), *The Transgender Studies Reader Remix*. New York: Routledge.

Soundararajan, Thenmozhi. (2022). *The Trauma of Caste: A Dalit Feminist Mediation on Survivorship, Healing, and Abolition*. Berkely, California: North Atlantic Books.

Spira, Tamara Lea, McMillan, Dayjha, Stapleton, Madi, & Vélez, Verónica N. (2022). 'ACAB Means Abolishing the Cop in Our Heads, Hearts, and Homes: An Intergenerational Demand for Family Abolition'. In Alisa Bierra, Jakeya Caruthers, & Brooke Lober (eds.), *Abolition Feminisms: Feminist Ruptures Against the Carceral State*. Chicago, IL: Haymarket Books.

Stanley, Eric A. (2021). *Atmospheres of Violence: Structuring Antagonism and the Trans/Queer Ungovernable*. Durham, NC: Duke University Press.

The Care Collective. (2020). *The Care Manifesto: The Politics of Interdependence*. London: Verso.

Weber, Cynthia. (2016). *Queer International Relations: Sovereignty, Sexuality and the Will to Knowledge*. New York, NY: Oxford University Press.

Wong, Alice. (2022). *Year of the Tiger*. New York: Vintage Books.

Young, Iris Marion. (1990). *Justice and the Politics of Difference*. Princeton, NJ: Princeton University Press.

Chapter 8

AAZHAWIGAMIG (THE SPACE BETWEEN TWO LODGES): AN INDIGENOUS MATRICENTRIC FEMINIST PERSPECTIVE ON MOTHERING AND RESISTANCE AS EVERYDAY PRAXIS

Renée E. Mazinegiizhigo-kwe Bédard

Introduction

In this chapter, I intend to outline the conceptual basis of an emerging Indigenous-matricentric feminist praxis that I call aazhawigamig anchored in the Anishinaabeg and French-Canadian cultures I have been raised in. In the first section of the chapter, I will offer the philosophy of aazhawigamig to provide cultural relevance and context for readings. Secondly, I will explore my rationale for utilizing an Indigenous feminist matricentric framework based around the concept of aazhawigamig. Next, I offer the specific maternal teachings of madjimadzuin kwewag to anchor my feminist praxis within aazhawigamig to position my process of decolonization within the Indian Act (1876). Finally, in this chapter, I intend to outline the three principles of aazhawigamig as Indigenous matricentric feminist praxis and articulate how I apply these principles of aazhawigamig to matricentric feminist praxis in relation to maternal resistance as decolonization, maternal resiliency and, lastly, maternal cultural reclamation and resurgence.

Boozhoo! Greetings in the language of my mother's people. I am an Indigenous (Anishinaabeg/Kanien'kehá:ka) woman, a mother, a traditional and a feminist. My Indigenous feminist praxis is articulated through an Anishinaabeg lens and the Anishinaabeg teachings of aazhawigamig ('Aazhawigamig' Translate Ojibwe Online 2021). Aazhawigamig translates to the space between two lodges. I have spent my entire life living in the between space amongst the lodges of Indigenous and French-Canadian cultures (which I will discuss further in the following sections). My Indigenous feminist praxis is anchored in my Indigenous identity and in my use of feminism as praxis to decolonize my own Indigenous women's rights under the Indian Act. I am a feminist because the many Indigenous women feminist role models that showed me the path were picking up feminist frameworks and strategies did not mean that I had to compromise or colonize my identity as an Indigenous woman.[1] Additionally, I am a feminist because of the Indigenous women activists who fought to have amendments to the Indian Act to remove sections with gender-based discrimination and inequalities.[2] These Indigenous feminist scholars and women activists are the ground upon which I stand, along with the Indigenous women who continue to survive and thrive under the mantle of the Indian Act. All of them have helped shape my Indigenized feminist praxis, particularly as I seek to counter the colonial narratives of gender discrimination embedded in the Indian Act and work to gain Indian Status for my two daughters under Bill S-3 (2017) amendment to the Indian Act.

In Canada, Indigenous people of mixed Indian/First Nations[3] and Euro-Canadian heritage understand that they exist between two worldviews and cultures. For many of us of Indian/First Nations descent, our identities are greatly defined by either having or not having Indian Status. Indian Status comes with specific legal rights. Further, the Indian Act punishes many of us for having mixed heritage and continues to prevent individuals from registering for Indian Status under the Indian Act based on strict criteria on blood quantum ratios, thus, removing large segments of the Indigenous population from access to treaty rights, territory, resources, community, family, culture, language and legal protections. My maternal grandmother, my mother, myself and my daughters have suffered under this system, which simultaneously measures and classifies our blood quantum that controls our access to both our treaty rights and inherent rights. Decolonizing our positionality within this system requires an examination of gender inequalities and Anishinaabeg agency from a framework utilizing a bi-cultural or hybrid worldview. In this chapter, I use the Anishinaabeg teachings

---

1. Women like Lee Maracle (Stoh:lo), Paula Gunn Allen (Keres Pueblo/Sioux), Leanne Simpson (Michi Saagiig Nishnaabeg), Audra Simpson (Mohawk), Maile Arvin (Hawaiian, Kanaka Maoli) (AnishinaabekweMétis-Nehiowé), Eve Tuck (Unangax) and Angie Morrill (Klamath).

2. Mary Two-Axe Earley, Yvonne Bédard, Jeannette Corbiere Lavell and Lovelace Nicholas who were all instrumental in getting the Bill C-31(1985) amendment to the Indian Act. Then there is Sharon McIvor, who was instrumental in achieving the Bill C-3 (2011) amendment to the Indian Act. Lastly, there is Stéphane Descheneaux, as well as Susan and Tammy Yantha who got additional amendments to Bill C-3 (2017). Lastly, I would add to the list my own mother Shirley Ida Bédard-*ba* who worked tirelessly to gain her Indian Status and band membership with Dokis First Nation.

3. The term 'Indian' is considered outdated and offensive in everyday language, but it has been used historically to identify Indigenous peoples in North, South and Central America. In Canada, the term 'Indian' also has legal significance. In both the Indian Act (1876) and Section 35 (1) and (2) of the Canadian Constitution refer to legally defined identities. Historically and legally, Indian refers to and is used interchangeably with the term 'First Nations people'. Additionally, both 'Indian' and 'First Nations' are used alongside 'Aboriginal'. 'Aboriginal' is a constitutionally and legally defined term to include all Indigenous peoples in Canada: Indian or First Nations, Métis and Inuit.

of aazhawigamig to guide my praxis in life, living, being, knowing, seeing and relating to all of Creation.

As I decolonize my gendered and cultural identity as a Status Indian, through the lens of matricentric feminist theories and philosophies, I also employ an Anishinaabeg paradigm, in which I situate the Indian Act within my Indigenous sense of womanhood and motherhood. In Anishinaabemowin (Anishinaabeg language), we describe the struggle I have with the Indian Act, identity, gender inequalities as aazhawigamig: sitting between two lodges intersecting because of the impacts of colonization, treaty responsibilities, bi-racial identity and the pathway towards cultural resurgence. My family, my children and I were all thrust into aazhawigamig, which is that between space that has come to exist for peoples in Canada that have mixed Indigenous and non-Indigenous heritage, who have lost their status and, sometimes, their cultural traditions.

In this chapter, aazhawigamig represents hybrid praxis of principal teachings of decolonizing gender inequities and traditional Indigenous maternal knowledge that I carry as part of my sacred bundle[4] as a mother and Anishinaabeg woman. As a hybrid Indigenous feminist positionality, I am able to explore the path of intersectionality between Indigenous worldview and the colonizer's Eurocentric worldview, the loss and return of my Indian Status and Treaty rights, but also led to my journey through aazhawigamig to return to my two daughters' their Indian Status and Treaty rights. That journey through aazhawigamig as maternal feminist praxis is what I will discuss here in this chapter and the ways Indigenous feminist praxis has aided me as a tool of resistance, decolonization and cultural resurgence.

Aazhawigamig: A philosophy of living

Aazhawigamig teachings are rooted in the historically and geographically located epistemologies, ontologies and axiologies of Anishinaabeg people of the Great Lakes Region of both Canada and the United States. Aazhawigamig translates to the space between two lodges or houses, but it is not a space; instead, it holds a sense of movement and fluidity. Philosophically, aazhawigamig is a great deal more than empty space, a gap or a pause in the flow or movement. Aazhawigamig does not actually mean an actual description of a physical space created by objects, people, boundaries or structures. Aazhawigamig asks us to evolve and move on. In Anishinaabeg culture, everything is connected and related to everything else in the universe; therefore, nothing is separated from anything else, but between everything is unseen connections. Anishinaabeg believe that power lies in what manifests in those connections found in the space in between. In those spaces it is all about relationships – relationships that exist between people, things, situations,

---

4. An Anishinaabeg bundle refers to a literal bundle of sacred items that we carry for ceremonial sake, but it also refers to the spiritual teachings, knowledge, songs and stories we carry as individuals.

ideas, beliefs, philosophies and so much more. Further, it can also represent a clear path or a life path, way between and the distance between two places or things.

The essence of the word is the connecting power, an intersectionality or a confluence between two things, spaces, energies or even times. For instance, the space between two places is a space for opportunity, an opening for the possibility of an entirely new way of moving, viewing, thinking or interacting with the world, spaces or people. Walking in the space between the two lodges – objects or people – causes a physical, mental and emotional sensation and evokes a sense of being that has a tangible presence that anyone can feel once they enter that space. Therefore, what you are experiencing is the identity of that space – the energy of what is going on – how it feels to be there in between is aazhawe. In Anishinaabemowin, aazhawe means to go across.[5] Aazhawigamig is not just a space; it is also the feeling of entering a fluid sense of time and reality generated by the movement of going somewhere; a space sitting between one place of being and the next. Such a space allows unique opportunities to view everything and be connected to multiple perspectives, places, directions, ways of knowing and being.

In the traditional teachings of aazhawigamig, the *spaces between* offer opportunities to choose find consensus and negotiate. As mothers we are taught these teachings about the act of breastfeeding. In breastfeeding there are two nations: you, your baby and the space between you two that is your relationship and kinship in your mutual breastfeeding journey. The *between-space* of that journey is often confusing, difficult, fluid and requires purposeful engagement by both parties for mutual benefit. Leanne Simpson describes this relationship as the foundation for conceiving nationhood, strategies for successful nation building and treaty making between multiple parties (Simpson 2011: 106). Aazhawigamig teaches us that this relationship will move forward, evolve and is going to be paramount to our knowledge of each other. There are two perspectives that are very different, and they come from very different contexts, but together, they embody aazhawigamig. Aazhawigamig is the intersection and engagement between both mother and child for mutual benefit in the breastfeeding journey, but it is simultaneously a maternal praxis for creating a healthy life for both ourselves and our children. After the moment of birth, when we put the infant gently to our breast, introduce ourselves and allow the infant to take the first sips of our milk, our life sustaining water and energy, we are taking up the praxis, the work, of leading not only ourselves, but now, a new life down the path of life: Anishinaabe mino-miikana bimaadiziwin. There are many life lessons in these teachings.

5. The word 'aazhawe' can have a variety of spellings due to multiple dialects, writing systems and preferences or pronunciations of language speakers. For example, see 'aazhaw-', in *The Ojibwe People's Online*. Viewed 22 July 2021 https://ojibwe.lib.umn.edu/word-part/aazhaw-initial. There is also another example, 'aazhawa`o', in *Translate Ojibwe Online*. Viewed 22 July 2021 https://www.translateojibwe.com/en/dictionary-english-ojibwe/go%20across.

As Indigenous peoples, aazhawigamig, walking between the lodges is a reality for most of us, whether of mixed ancestry or not, we live under the mantle of colonial policies and in a society not of our choosing: Canadian, American, European and Australian, and so on around the world. Blackfoot Elder Leroy Little Bear describes this as fragmentary worldviews resulting from colonization, which he coined 'jagged worldviews colliding' (Little Bear 2000: 84). We are all forced into the aazhawigamig space in the Canadian context because the goal of colonization is to control every person worldview. Aazhawigamig is also the path, a life path, between the two lodges, the place and the space of potential decolonization because it is fluid, evolving and changeable. As an Anishinaabeg mother, the cultural praxis of aazhawigamig makes it possible to make conscious decolonized decisions along the life path, mino-bimaadizi, which positively impacts or create new opportunities for living a good life as an Anishinaabeg woman and mother.

Aazhawigamig: Rationale of Anishinaabeg matricentric feminist praxis

Aazhawigamig as Anishinaabeg matricentric feminist praxis prioritizes my Anishinaabeg maternal knowledge, contextualizes my life lived inside the policies of the Indian Act and Canadian society, and aids me to decolonize the gender inequalities of Indian Status that negatively impact my life, so that I can move forward on the path of life in a holistic way as an Indigenous mother. Through me, my children gain their Indigenous inherent cultural rights and treaty rights to land, natural resources, language, knowledge and cultural customs. I protect it fiercely as a mother!

As a feminist, I align with Andrea O'Reilly's term 'matricentric feminism', which she coined in the 1990s, 'to denote a mother-centred standpoint and emphasis to designate it as particular, long overdue and urgently needed mode of feminism' (O'Reilly 2014: 2). O'Reilly says that it is different than maternal feminism that combines maternalism and feminism, which is rooted in early feminism; but like Elaine Showalter's term 'gynocentric' (O'Reilly 2014: 3). O'Reilly explains that she uses the term 'matricentric feminism', 'to denote a mother-centred standpoint and emphasis to designate it as particular, long overdue and urgently needed mode of feminism' (O'Reilly 2014: 3). She says that it doesn't replace traditional maternalism or maternal feminism; instead:

> it is to remind and emphasize that the category of mother is distinct from the category of woman, and that many of the problems mothers face – socially, economically, politically, culturally, psychologically and so forth – are specific to women's role and identity as mothers. Indeed, mothers are oppressed under patriarchy as women and as mothers. Consequently, mothers need a mother-centred or matricentric mode of feminism organized from and for their particular identity and work as mothers. I would argue further that a mother-

centred feminism is urgently needed and long overdue because mothers, arguably more so than women in general, remain disempowered despite forty years of feminism.

(O'Reilly 2014: 3)

O'Reilly's matricentric feminism as mother-centred feminism is most aligned with my stage of life that is focused primarily on my roles, responsibilities and duties as an Anishinaabeg parent and mother.

I need matricentric feminism, because I need my role as a mother in the decolonization process to be recognized not just through an Indigenous-centric lens, but through a Euro-Canadian lens that is self-evaluating. I mother through both worldviews that I live. O'Reilly states that 'mothering matters and is central to the lives of women who are mothers' (O'Reilly 2019: 14). Matricentric feminism offers a unique mothering centred space within feminism that acts as a niche for feminist mothers, motherhood and mothering ways of living, knowing and relating to the world that is aligned from a worldview that is mother-centric. Additionally, matricentric feminism offers potential spatial freedom for decolonized zones of resistance, cultural resurgence and gendered activism that goes beyond the perspectives of Eurocentric worldview. As Seneca feminist scholar, Mishuana Goeman testifies that

> locating a Native feminism's spatial dialogue that conceives of space as not bounded by geo-politics, but storied and continuous, is necessary in developing a discourse that allows Native nation building its fullest potential and members of nations its fullest protection. A Native feminist spatial discourse will converge to form different functions: (1) present alternative methods of reading space, race, gender, and nation and thus assert a political practice that razes ongoing ideologies of colonialism; (2) unmoor 'truth' maps from knowledge based on imperialist projects and assert Native ways of knowing that incorporate Native women's knowledges into the project of decolonization; (3) provide paths and routes to heal the rifts and borders that maps of difference (such as men's/ women's space, Rez/urban) continue to construct in the wake of colonialism.
>
> (Goeman 2009: 184)

Matricentric Indigenous-centred feminist praxis has the potential to a self-creating and self-generating space for maternal action aligned towards the needs Indigenous mothers. O'Reilly asserts that 'Matricentric feminism seeks to make motherhood the business of feminism by positioning mothers' needs and concerns as the starting point for a theory and politics on and for women's empowerment' (O'Reilly 2019: 14). As Indigenous and non-Indigenous mothers, we all live under and inside spaces of colonialism, but matricentric feminist praxis offers a new site for decolonization as a space of refuge, mutuality, discourse and rebuilding for all mothers.

When challenged with why I chose to align with any feminism instead of utilizing just Indigenous methodologies, I explain it using a simple analogy. For example, I am a traditional beader and use European glass beads in the same way I ancestors did after they acquired them from fur traders. I use those beads because they do not jeopardize my cultural ways of knowing; instead, those beads protect it, foster it and even enhance its growth. My ancestors were not afraid to adopt specific European ways that allowed their own cultural ways to survive and thrive. For me, matricentric feminism is like beading with European glass beads; it aids me in allowing my culture to thrive, while simultaneously enabling me to identify, challenge, dismantle and later repair the sites where colonization has negatively impacted on Anishinaabeg maternal ways of being. Afterwards, I utilize my Anishinaabeg cultural ways to build, rebuild and foster a resurgence of maternal culture in areas that need to be nurtured within an Anishinaabeg maternal paradigm, ontology, cosmology, philosophies and axiology. Beading embodies aazhawigamig by taking from both cultures to create a space and a thing that allows the beader to live life in a good way and thrive as an Anishinaabeg. Aazhawigamig is how I articulate my engagement with maternal feminist praxis. It embodies as beading does, a between space where both Indigenous and non-Indigenous mothers can come together in purposeful work to facilitate the hard work of mothering, decolonizing, resisting and building strong nations through our children, and ourselves.

Aazhawigamig and madjimadzuin kwewag

Kwewag in Anishinaabemowin means women or adult female. To be an Anishinaabe-kwe or Anishinaabeg woman, means you must find your mino-miikana-bimaadiziwin (living well by upholding the teachings as we walk the good path in life as a human beings) in a way that honours the mothers and grandmothers that came before you, those that birthed and raised you, those women that support you in your mothering, and also, those women that act to be role models for those yet to come. We learn to follow the teachings of our maternal ancestors as we walk the mino-miikana-bimaadizi: good path of life. As women who stand among aazhawigamig, we must still maintain the maternal ancestral teachings for mothering in a good way, even if we stand between those two lodges. As a recognized Anishinaabe-kwe by my family and community, I live to uphold those teachings and ways of living shared with me by those mothers and grandmothers that came before me. On the pathway of aazhawigamig, I uphold the maternal teachings and maintain the unseen connections of Anishinaabeg refer to as 'madjimadzuin' (Jenness 90) or madjimadzuin kwewag, which means our chain of relations connecting us to all women that came before, those with us now and those yet to come. Further, madjimadzuin is a spiritual energy or connection to all the women, the mothers, grandmothers, aunties, and to the Earth Aki, as First-Mother-in-Creation, but also to the plants, animals, birds, insects, air and waters. We are all connected through time and space by way of the madjimadzuin. While walking the pathway of aazhawigamig as an Anishinaabeg woman, I recognize this cultural legacy of madjimadzuin and I am aware of those women as the anchor for my cultural identity and praxis as an Indigenous feminist. Parts of my feminist praxis are devoted to my madjimadzuin as vital to my journey through my aazhawigamig and down the path of life.

Three principles form the conceptual basis of aazhawigamig as my matricentric Indigenous feminist praxis of how I holistically get through the process of decolonizing my positionality within the Indian Act and how I decolonize the process of enrolling my daughters in the Indian Act to affirm their Indian Status and treaty rights. These are: (1) aazhawigamig as an act of maternal resistance; (2) aazhawigamig as act of maternal resiliency and, lastly, (3) aazhawigamig as an act of maternal cultural reclamation and resurgence. These principles are interconnected and interrelated but are anchored in the concept of madjimadzuin and the chain of maternal and female relations that go far into the past, present and future yet to come. It is this chain of relations between women that forms the framework of my feminist praxis in this specific process but is also rooted in how I approach life as a human being dwelling in the aazhawigamig!

Aazhawigamig as maternal resistance as decolonization

Madjimadzuin inspires me to talk about the experiences of my maternal grandmother Roseanne Dokis Sheppard-*ba*[6] and my mother Shirley Ida Bédard-*ba*, who lived under the policies of the Indian Act and subsequent amendments to the Indian Act. Their experiences and stories are a catalyst for where I am today on my journey to reclaim the Indian Status and treaty rights of my two daughters. Born an Anishinaabe-kwe (Ojibwe/Nipissing) and registered Indian and band member with Dokis First Nation, Roseanne (Dokis) Shephard-*ba* is the great-great-great-granddaughter of Chief Michel Eagle Dokis-*ba* (1818–1906), known by either Migisi Dokis or his Anishinaabeg name as Petawachuan (I hear the Rapids Far Away). He was one of the signatories of the Robinson-Huron Treaty of 1850 and established the First Nation reserve community of Dokis, on the island of Okikendawt (Island of the Cauldrons or Kettle Pots). For thousands of years, Okikendawt had long been a sacred site containing various sacred ceremonial locations, sacred sites of pilgrimage and familial settlements, along with hunting, fishing and trading grounds of the Nipissing, Ojibwe and Algonquin peoples of the region. By moving a group of families there to form a permanent reserve settlement, Migisi Dokis protected that site, his people, and protected the territory around it from logging and mining. His great-granddaughter Rosanne grew up living at Dokis until she was a young woman, but everything changed on 8 October 1929. On that date she married my maternal Kanien'kehá:ka grandfather Edward Laurent Shephard-*ba*, whose mother was an enrolled member at Wahta

6. -*Ba* is the Anishinaabeg (Ojibwe and Nipissing) ways of acknowledging our relations who have passed away. We write it at the end of names as a marker that honours their life and tells others they are now in the realm of the Spirits.

First Nation, but he was not enrolled and was not a Status-Indian. However, the Indian Act shaped his life and that of his descendants.

Long before both my grandparents were born, the Indian Act of 1876, along with the many treaties, became a key aspect of the architecture Canada to secure valuable Indigenous land and resources. The Indian Act as law would endure as the legal extinguishment of Indigenous rights, forcing many off their lands, including my grandmother. The ongoing trauma of the Indian Act on my family, particularly the women, began first with the policies encoded in the '1850: An Act for the better protection of the lands and property of the Indians in Lower Canada'. This act was the first law to define who could be considered an 'Indian'. The requirements for being a legal Indian, which can be seen as a precursor for Indian Status, were defined through blood relations, and essentially stated that people 'shall be considered as Indians' if they were of 'Indian blood' and were members of a 'Body or Tribe of Indians' (Government of Canada, 2018). According to the Government of Canada, the act also defined who was an 'Indian' in terms of marriage. It stated that an individual could only retain their status if 'all persons married to such Indians and residing amongst them, and their descendants' and all children must include 'all persons residing among such Indians, whose parents on either side were or are Indians of such body or tribe or entitled to be considered as such' (Government of Canada, 2018).

Then, in 1869, additional legal modifications were added to state that, 'Indian women who married non-Indians are no longer considered Indians and children of the marriage are also not considered Indians under the act' (Government of Canada, 2018). In 1876, the Indian Act updated the legal definition of 'Indian' as:

– any male person of Indian blood reputed to belong to a particular band
– any child of such person
– any woman who is or was lawfully married to such person.

(Government of Canada, 2018)

Under these colonial laws, the maternal women and men on my mother's side of the family lived under those definitions and restrictions of the Indian Act; in addition, to the treaties their ancestors signed to remain on and protect their traditional territory. Anishinaabeg women's agency, sovereignty and cultural legacy were eroded, eradicated and lost almost entirely through the definitions and policies of the Indian Act.

In 1929, my grandmother Roseanne who was a member of Dokis First Nation would have been told by the Indian Agent administrator for Dokis First Nation that she and her new husband would have to leave and live off the reserve. They could visit, but not live there. Her family rallied to their aid upon the news of her loss of Indian Status and rights to land on the reserve. The family helped the couple purchase a small parcel of Crown or government land just off the reserve, and a short boat ride down the French River. There they raised twelve children. By the mid-1980s, many of their children would regain Indian Status, band membership and the lands that their parents had lost.

In 1985, the Indian Act was amended through Bill C-31 as a response to growing national and international concerns over the lack of gender equality in the Indian Act, particularly for First Nations women. To maintain compliance with the Canadian Charter of Rights and Freedoms and eliminate discriminatory provisions in the Indian Act, Bill C-31 enacted various amendments to address inequalities. The amendment that specifically impacts my grandmother, mother and myself is this:

> Indian women who married a non-Indian man no longer lost their Indian status ... Indian women who had previously lost their status through marriage to a non-Indian man became eligible to apply for reinstatement, as did their children ... the process of enfranchisement was eliminated altogether as was the authority of the Indian Registrar to remove individuals from the Indian Register who were entitled to registration.
>
> (Government of Canada, 2018)

Bill C-31 allowed many women to apply for and regain Indian Status. After 1985, my mother, aunts and uncles worked diligently until the mid-1990s collecting the necessary documents (e.g. birth certificates, death certificates, marriage certificates) that charted their mother and father's family histories. Upon submission of their file, they regained their Indian Status; however, there were many issues around rating exact blood quantum ratios, band membership and acquiring land to build upon. The trauma of that period still haunts me to this day. Many might not see what they did as resistance or decolonization, but for me they resisted the loss of their rights, their mother's rights, land, resources, culture and community. My mother modelled Anishinaabeg maternal resistance to me from a young age, asserting, her agency, her rights and her womanhood. She was the first feminist I knew!

However, despite these amendments, despite our regained status, there remained continued residual sex-based along with other inequalities embedded in the Indian Act that continued to negatively impact my siblings, myself and cousins. We could not pass on our Indian Status and band membership to our children. These inequalities caused challenges to Bill C-31, by Bill C-3 and Bill S-3. In 1987, *McIvor vs. Canada* resulted in the 2011's Bill C-3, 'Gender Equity in Indian Registration Act'. Bill C-3 created an amendment that specifically includes the 'grandchildren of women who lost status due to marrying a non-Indian man prior to 1985 become entitled to registration for the first time' (Government of Canada, 2018). This bill would directly impact my children. Previously, grandchildren of individuals with Indian Status were only eligible if both grandparents held Status Indians. Then, in 2017, the Indian act under Bill S-3 was again amended because of the case *Descheneaux c. Canada*. Bill S-3 addresses known sex-based inequities in the registration provisions of the Indian Act for multiple situations, particularly with respect to

> the cousins issue (December 2017): differential treatment of first cousins whose grandmother lost her entitlement to registration due to a marriage with a non-entitled man before 17 April 1985 ... [and] the removal of the 1951 cut-off

date (August 2019): ensuring the entitlement of all descendants of women who lost status or whose names were removed from band lists for marrying a non-entitled man going back to 1869, which recognizes descendants of women who married non-entitled men the same as descendants of men who married non-entitled women.

(Government of Canada, 2018)

The amendments include additional provision, but these two specifically impacted my own family with regard to the level of Indian Status we held as descendants of my maternal grandmother Roseanne, who married an unregistered First Nations man. To this Bill S-3 includes:

the removal of the 1951 cut-off date (August 2019): ensuring the entitlement of all descendants of women who lost status or whose names were removed from band lists for marrying a non-entitled man going back to 1869, which recognizes descendants of women who married non-entitled men the same as descendants of men who married non-entitled women.

(Government of Canada, 2018)

Thus, my siblings, cousins and myself had our Indian Status changed (we call it upgraded!), thus allowing all our children to apply for registration as Status Indians. However, the bill was not fully implemented until 11 December 2020 (Government of Canada, 2018).

In the winter of 2020, I completed the paperwork for my children to obtain their Indian Status. Recently, in the fall of 2021, they were properly registered as Status Indians under the Indian Act and received band membership with Dokis First Nation. The process weighed heavily on my heart because I know the dark legacy of the Indian Act. Yet, I am also relieved I could also do it. There is a sense of resiliency attached to the process and outcome that I needed to see through to the end.

Aazhawigamig as maternal resiliency

Why is this important to me as an Indigenous woman/maternal feminist to have my Indian Status and that of my daughters secured, and how does it embody my Indigenous feminist praxis? First, as a feminist, I see the history of gender-based inequalities against women embedded in the Indian Act laid out there like a roadmap of oppression. I see the entrenched colonial patriarchy that values women over men. I recognized that these colonial-settlers, descendants of Europeans that came from a continent far across the ocean, brought with them their entrenched cultural disdain of female power, leadership and agency. To me, I recognize my Indian Status as part of that foreign and colonizing system, but I also recognize that not fighting for that Indian Status makes it easier for the government to take away our Indigenous-First Nations lands and resources if the overall population of my nation and community dwindles. If we resist and keep fighting through the between space that the Indian Act represents; eventually, there may come a time where our lands are returned outright to us without conditions, but if we do nothing, we lose everything. As a mother, as an Anishinaabeg/Kanien'kehá woman, I cannot let that happen!

Additionally, as a feminist, I cannot let stand that while Anishinaabeg men in our families and communities were permitted to hold on to their Indian Status when they married non-Indigenous women, women like my grandmother and mother lost their rights to status ever so rapidly under the Indian Act. The amendments up until the amendment under Bill S-3 returned the traditional and legal rights back to our women. Our women were always leaders, caretakers of our families and communities, and voices for our people; thus, removing them from the community as legal citizens was a great trauma. I witnessed first-hand as my own mother fought to regain her status. I remember the tears, yelling and crying out in frustration. Also, I remember the rejection by those relatives who sought to prevent her from becoming a band member with Dokis, a place where she grew up going to school, church and spending time with relatives. My feminist praxis and philosophies are rooted in witnessing these inequalities because my mother was first a non-Status Indian, then a registered Status Indian, next a non-band member and then, lastly, a band member of Dokis First Nation. My road to feminist praxis starts with my grandmother's ejection from her band and mother's struggle to regain membership within her band. This evolved into my own anger at the loss of my own two daughters' inability to have Indian Status and connection to their traditional First Nation community, lands and resources that their ancestor fought so hard for them to have one day. All this loss originated from the fact that they descended from women and the Indian Act saw our removal of Indian women's Status as a vehicle of colonization!

As an Indigenous feminist, I have learned to walk and navigate the between space and use the teachings of aazhawigamig to guide me forward to repair some of trauma my grandmother, mother and myself have carried.

Aazhawigamig as maternal cultural reclamation and resurgence

Regaining Indian Status does not repair the loss of culture, language, land or identity. That comes through decolonization of your mind and doing the hard work of regaining cultural experience and knowledge. I learned very young that our family had very few Anishinaabeg culture traditions left due to the dislocation from our family's reserve, conversion to the Catholic Faith, the loss of language, deeper connections to the Dokis community or to my Kanien'kehá:ka cultural heritage. I looked like my mother, dark black/brown hair, brown eyes and olive skin that tans like crazy in the summer but is white like my father's in the winter. My friends were fellow Indigenous kids, and I could assimilate well into most circles of Indigenous people, but that does not provide culture or an identity. So, my life path became reclamation: repairing, gathering and learning what it meant to be Indigenous, an Anishinaabe-kwe (woman) and slowly, I will begin to learn more about my Kanien'kehá:ka heritage. Today, I know that I do this so that my daughters have a cultural inheritance to build identities where they know they are Indigenous and do not have to wonder who they are as human beings on this earth.

Overall, maternal reclamation is the heart of my Indigenous feminist praxis because it is part of the decolonization process ever present and ongoing in my life, but it is also a vital aspect of the cultural resurgence necessary to move past the decolonization phase of life to a place of Indigenized living. I am focused on nurturing the Indigenous worldviews for my daughters and myself, so that we can step off the path of aazhawigamig and into the Indigenous lodge space. There is freedom in dwelling in the space after or post decolonization, and in an Indigenous way of being that comes by delving into Indigenous realities. When I go to ceremony and bring my two daughters to ceremony, we are stepping away from the trauma, joining our ancestors and planning for an Indigenous future. Is this a post-colonial reality? I am not wholly sure that can even exist because I will always return to the colonized world with my academic career, cars, iPhone, Zoom meetings and the lately, the Covid-19 pandemic. I know that I can't escape the colonizer's reality entirely, but the feminist praxis gives me the gift to find moments in time and space where there is Indigenous resurgence back to the maternal Anishinaabeg ontologies, epistemologies, axiologies and cosmologies of my ancestors. The fact that this is even a possibility after so many generations of loss is something I cherish.

Concluding thoughts

My final thoughts are for my daughters' who I fight for and alongside. They will both benefit and be burdened by their new Indian Status and band membership, both of which are colonial constructs, but interwoven is also our inheritance of Anishinaabeg cultural relationality, knowledge systems, kinship to land and people, our cosmologies and our ways of living in a good way as human beings: Anishinaabeg mino-miikana bimaadiziwin. My daughters and I have been walking the path of aazhawigamig since before we were even born to this world. We walked with Rosanne, Shirley and all the women who came before us, and our descendants will likely continue down that pathway for several generations under the mantle of colonial rule. Hopefully, like me who picked up some useful tools along the way, like feminism, they to can find others to help them tear down colonialism and make space to live as Indigenous peoples. Matricentric feminist praxis with an Indigenous centre to guide the way, like my Anishinaabeg beadwork, created from beads made by the colonizer, is a valuable vehicle to continue to allow my daughters and me to decolonize, thrive, resist and built spaces of cultural resurgence.

References

'aazhaw-' 2021, in *The Ojibwe People's Online*. Viewed 22 July 2021. https://ojibwe.lib.umn.
    edu/word-part/aazhaw-initial.

'aazhawa`o' 2021, in *Translate Ojibwe Online*. Viewed 22 July 2021. https://www.
    translateojibwe.com/en/dictionary-english-ojibwe/go%20across.

'Aazhawigamig' 2021, in *Translate Ojibwe Online*, viewed 25 July 2021. https://www.
    translateojibwe.com/en/dictionary-ojibwe-english/Aazhawigamig.

Borrows, J. (2010). *Canada's Indigenous Constitution*. Toronto: University of Toronto Press.

Goeman, M. (2009). 'Notes toward a Native Feminism's Spatial Practice'. *Wicazo Sa
    Review*, 24 (2): 169–87.

Jenness, D. (1935). *The Ojibwa Indians of Parry Island, Their Social and Religious Life*.
    Ottawa: National Museum of Canada.

Little Bear, L. (2000). 'Jagged Worldviews Colliding'. In M. Battiste (ed.), *Reclaiming
    Indigenous Voice and Vision*. Vancouver: UBC Press, pp. 77–85.

Marshall, M., Marshall, A., & Bartlett, C. (2015). 'Two-eyed Seeing in Medicine'. In
    M. Greenwood, S. de Leeuw, N. Lindsay, & C. Reading (eds), *Determinants of
    Indigenous Peoples' Healthin Canada: Beyond the Social*. Toronto: Canadian Scholars'
    Press, pp. 16–24.

O'Reilly, A. (2014). '*Ain't I a Feminist?: Matricentric Feminism, Feminist Mamas, and Why
    Mothers Need a Feminist Movement/Theory of Their Own*'. Motherhood Hall of Fame
    at the Museum of Motherhood, viewed 14 June 2021. https://mommuseum.org/wp-
    content/uploads/2015/05/procreate_andrea_oreilly_july_1_2015.pdf.

O'Reilly, A. (2019). 'Matricentric Feminism: A Feminism for Mothers'. *Journal of
    Motherhood Initiative*, 10 (1 & 2): 13–26.

Simpson, L. (2011). *Dancing on our Turtle's Back: Stories of Nishnaabeg Re-creation,
    Resurgence, and a New Emergence*. Winnipeg: Arbeiter Ring Publishers.

Chapter 9

SETTLER THEORY AND FEMINISMS BEYOND COMPULSORY RELATING: A POLYQUEER AUTOETHNOGRAPHY

Rowan J. Quirk

Introduction

This is a polyqueer origin story. It is my story, but it does not belong to me. Rather, it is a community tale belonging to anyone who recognizes themselves in the feminist, queer and decolonial acts of resistance detailed throughout. It is a collective coming to being for those, like me, who eschew compulsory relating – especially along gendered lines. Messy and painful, beautiful and intricate, I have tried to follow an honest and chaotic reality which resists being neatly wrapped in a bow. Rather than attempt to organize the disorder, this autoethnographic inquiry espouses genderqueer and non-monogamous values by holding space for multiplicity – for multiple selves, multiple relating and multiple ways of knowing – even in the face of 'very different, or even contradictory, versions' of truth (Barker 2005: 85).

An increasingly prominent area of study, non-/monogamies research seeks to explore the context, constructs and structures of relating. Further, critical non-monogamy theorists embrace – and often combine – a range of theoretical approaches to critique compulsory relating, imagining relationships that transcend prescriptive gender, sexuality and family norms (to name a few). As presented by feminist theorist Sara Ahmed, 'queer orientations are those that put within reach bodies that have been made unreachable by the lines of conventional genealogy' (2006: 107). In this chapter, I engage with my personal intimate networks to produce a participatory account of polyqueer kinship building. In doing so, I seek to expand on Sara's use of 'bodies' to include those collective bodies of intimacy which have been undermined, subjugated and disempowered by hegemonic bio-nuclear family structure. In analysing the autoethnographic data from my networks, I consider the lived tensions of navigating, negotiating, resisting and mobilizing settler sexuality – positioning polyqueer relating as an ongoing process of feminist resistance. In the end, I follow seminal non-/monogamies thinkers, such as Mimi Schippers and Kim TallBear, in storying polyqueer relating as antithetical to settler-colonial organization via its potential for disrupting systems of nation building.

Terminology

This chapter is predicated on an understanding of English as a colonial language which often relies on limiting binaries. As such, all identifiers should be read as culturally constituted, non-static and malleable. I use the term 'colonial' to broadly discuss colonial and imperialist action. Meanwhile, 'settler-colonial' refers here to the colonization of Native and Indigenous Nations in North America by European invaders, as well as the ongoing settler-colonial project and its epistemologies. As Scott Morgensen notes, concepts of race and nation are often conflated, thereby protecting the settler system from scrutiny (2011). With this in mind, I strategically use 'white' to name the racialized social structure which has been scientifically and spatially constituted in the interests of settler-state nation building (e.g. racial segregation; Lipsitz 2007).

Generally, I follow Hammack and colleagues' use of 'queer' to be 'notions that challenge or deviate enough from the normative to historically warrant social or legal condemnation and/or political opposition' (2019: 557). I additionally use 'queer' to evoke a distinct culture and epistemology, which resists assimilation with the conventional. The term 'genderqueer' is used to express my gender as resistant to the man-woman binary. Additionally, I use 'heterosexual' to refer to a normative dogma (independent of sexuality), as well as a personally identifiable sexuality. All other genders and sexualities presented throughout this chapter have been self-identified, and therefore reflect personal meaning. Finally, several relational descriptors are used, including 'non-monogamy', 'polyamory' and 'relationship anarchy'. In general, these terms refer to consensual, egalitarian and secular relationship agreements. While each term has a rich history with unique ideologies, practices and values, they should also be read as flexible and marked by personal significance.

As an emerging intimacies theorist, I often wonder what words to choose when discussing knowledge gained by living non-monogamy. Mimi Schippers has proposed the concept of 'polyqueer sexualities' to denote intimacies that '*through plurality*, open up possibilities to "undo" race and gender hierarchies in ways that would not otherwise arise' (2016, p. 25). In my understanding, Mimi has theorized polyqueer sexualities to politicize non-monogamy and position non-monogamous relationships as expressions of feminist resistance. While I find 'polyqueer' intriguing for its personal/political representation of expansive relationships, I am cautious of the term 'sexualities' as possibly limiting the recursive potential of polyqueer notions. Drawing on Indigenous concepts of relationality,[1] Kim TallBear often says – and, in fact, entitled a book chapter – 'identity is a poor

---

1. Relationality has been described 'as the core organizing principle when it comes to the identification, discernment, creation, and continuation of Indigenous systems of knowledge' (Littletree & Belarde-Lewis 2020, pg. 413). It is often described as beginning with or coming from what might be (poorly) translated to country, land or nation (Tynan 2021). Here, I want to make clear relationality as a foundational concept in Indigenous theory and a seminal feature of Indigenous epistemology, therefore contextualizing Kim TallBear's use of 'relating' as nuanced and beyond the considerations of 'polyqueer relating' presented in this chapter.

substitute for relating' (TallBear 2021: 467). Applied to queer feminism, this may be read as problematizing colonialist epistemologies that imagine sexualities, genders and (eventually) relationships as objects in service of people (TallBear 2022). This exposes the human-centric and hierarchical foundations of queer feminism, thereby truncating the capacity of such theories and epistemologies to confront colonial systems of nation building. Therefore, in this autoethnography, I evoke 'polyqueer relating' to draw on a mutual queer and Indigenous opposition to the state, orienting queer resistance in alliance with Indigenous politics to more thoroughly disrupt the bio-legal and nuclear family pillars of the settler-colonial project (Ertman 2008; TallBear 2018). Doing so invites queer theorizing beyond sexuality to trouble colonial relationship logics (e.g. human-other hierarchies and monogamy-non-monogamy binaries) – looking towards expansive relating among not only humans, but also more-than-humans (e.g. animals, plants, mountains), philosophies and perhaps even selves (see Barker & Langdridge 2010; Finn & Malson 2008; Heckert 2010), to amplify the oppositional potential of polyqueer notions.

Place: Troubling settler constructions

Like many people from the settler-colonial US tradition, I do not have a strong awareness of land and place – often conflating the two and fusing them with concepts of nation. In an investigation of critical place inquiry, Eve Tuck and Marcia McKenzie advocate resisting impressions of 'place as neutral backdrop, or as a bounded and antiquated concept, or as only physical landscape', imploring researchers to 'theorize and practice place more deeply' (2015: 18). Although limiting, the lenses of spatialized power dynamics have been one way for me to deepen my consideration of place (Lipsitz 2007; Tuck & McKenzie 2015). Through these lenses, I have begun to see my own whiteness as facilitating not only physical connection to place (e.g. via disproportionate access), but also a mental connection (e.g. as unburdened by the possibility of prejudice or harm based on the colour of my skin). Likewise, as able-bodied, I experience space with the assurance that the built environment has been constructed with my capabilities and limitations in mind. In these situations, place becomes conscripted as a defining feature of daily normative citizenship. Of course, such power dynamics are not always straightforward. For example, as coming from a middle-class family, my socioeconomic status has frequently been a complex picture of in/accessibility, with saliency of place varying accordingly. Importantly, each of these positionalities has evolved through my life, particularly as I moved beyond a US context. That being said, few dimensions of power have made my relationship with place more apparent – or more dishonest – than queerness.

The suburban neighbourhoods of my younger years were, without a doubt, physical markers of colonial land ownership and racist white-flight – reflections of systems which have simultaneously benefitted me and concealed saliency of place. Moreover, the domestic organization of space functioned as the carrot and the stick in an ongoing genderization project, attempting at every turn to teach me to perform gender appropriately. Cookie-cutter houses, four-door cars and the demands of daily life served as quintessential reminders of my burden to be a *good heterosexual female* and produce the next generation of citizens. As I entered my teenage years, I came to (unfairly) regard place as a hated scapegoat for the daily trauma of gendered performance and untenable heterosexual expectation. In attempt to run away from the prescription, I soon turned to the global stage for belonging. In his book *Spaces between Us*, Scott Morgensen stresses the settler-colonial predictability of my queer trajectory and offers an alternative logic (2011):

> Having questioned desires to belong to the settler state or to possess Native history, non-Native queers can consider the groundlessness that follows critiquing settlement as a condition of their existence ... I invoke groundlessness to invite new theory to displace settler imaginaries among queer non-Natives. By detaching from colonial desires to belong to stolen land, the settler state, *or their projections into global possibilities* [emphasis added], queer non-Natives can release imaginaries of indigeneity that formed to resolve the contradictions of settlers possessing stolen land and Native peoples' pasts and futures.
>
> (p. 310)

In my understanding, 'groundlessness' dispenses settler-colonial notions of ownership, thereby imagining one way of separating land from belonging. Through groundlessness, home and belonging – particularly queer belonging – can be reimagined from citizenship paradigms to the relationships that nourish us. For me, this explicitly confronts homonationalism and provides relief from the heterosexist and cis-normative systems of landownership-driven biological and legal family structures. Moreover, focusing on the ongoing action of *relating* (as opposed to the complacency of *having a relationship*) necessitates continual caretaking with particular attention to systematic power dynamics, which are often (re)produced at the relational level. In this caretaking, I have found greater responsibility for enacting intersectional feminist politics in daily connection, including more honest and intentional relating with place.

For example, in this autoethnography, I attempt to practice intentional relating with place by identifying place as a unique actor in the memories shared. Many of the following narratives take place on the current and ancestral homes of the Cheyenne, Arapahoe, Ute and Setalcott Nations. As such, I wish to emphasize the ties these nations continue to hold to these places – despite forced division by the settler-colonial project of the United States of America – and acknowledge my participation in a harmful system of settler-colonial land ownership. Further, I would like to recognize this chapter's engagement with feminist and queer thought, which have often (re)produced colonial epistemologies resulting in the dismissal, appropriation, policing and punishment of (especially LGBTQ2S+) Indigenous and First Nations people. I additionally want to make explicit the increasingly polynormative construction of non-monogamous relationships, which recreate hostile environments for Indigenous people by seeking alliance and assimilation with settler-colonial systems of governance (TallBear 2018).

Throughout this research, I have attempted to appreciate the multiple stories of land and it's people by (1) using Native American naming practices whenever possible (e.g. Setauket – as called by the Setalcott Nation) and (2) naming salient landmarks to stress the physical embodiment of place as influential to the autoethnographic data presented (Vasiliev 2004). Ultimately, I wish to make clear the stolen Indigenous lands, practices, identities, knowledge and histories which I exacerbate, navigate, profit from and resist within this polyqueer journey.

Autoethnography as polyqueer

When I first considered autoethnographic methods, I wondered how a polyqueer approach might influence the research process. This led me to contemplate the ways in which memories (a form of autoethnographic data) are relationally constituted and, therefore, a collective entity. At first, I felt disempowered by my sudden lack of memory ownership (attn: settler-colonial values); then, I began to imagine how skills used to navigate non-monogamous relating could facilitate collective memory telling. From a research ethics perspective, I wondered how a polyqueer ethic could bring sensitivity to this unique form of inquiry by clarifying boundaries, holding space for differing experiences and engendering authority within these histories – personal authority for those involved, but also a broader community authority. With this in mind, I applied a feminist approach of community care to data collection, embarking on a mutually constitutive process of storytelling aimed at honouring the multiples of memory. In choosing whom to consult in data collection and analysis, I employed Jamie Heckert's view of relationships as 'organic, living, mortal things which always necessarily involve change including growth, death, decay and rebirth' (2010: 10). Most memories in this research have been collectively authored, some in relationship growth and others, quite unexpectedly, in decay. A few relationships were also better left in memory. In this case, I have still attempted to extend an ethic of care by storying the possibilities, aided by the insights of my collaborators. In this attempt at polyqueer-ing autoethnography, I hope to have presented 'auto' and 'ethnography' in good balance and with strong responsibility to myself, my relations, the stakeholder communities and beyond.

Inherited relational ethic

It's hard to tell exactly when I first realized that my family wasn't held together by the same rules as the nuclear families in my mostly white, mostly Christian, Rocky Mountain hometown. Maybe I had the realization during a school assignment when my non-biologically related uncle (my mom's brother by adoption) had a place on the pre-constructed family tree, while my non-biologically related aunt (my mom's best friend) didn't quite fit. Or perhaps, it was while my godparents shared our home, neighbours peeking out their curtains trying to make sense of the four-parent, two-child family next door. Of course, if these instances didn't tip me off, I was certainly aware by the time terms like 'bonus grandma', 'second mom' and 'found family'² became a household regularity.

Truthfully, the non-biological and queer kinship models of my childhood took root long before I was born. My mom was adopted and raised by a divorced, single mother, during an era when both divorce and being a single working woman were taboo. Without a strong biological family network, my nana turned to kinships beyond the family tree for support, surrounding her children with strong women and a diverse network of care. Through this upbringing, my mom not only learned that family was chosen, but also the power women hold as decision-makers, community builders and caretakers. She brought this same family building ethic to my childhood, where I too was surrounded by non-biologically related kin who served important roles as aunts, uncles, parental figures and teachers. Some of the strongest familial support came from my mom's friend group, playfully called Women in Transition (WIT), which formed to inspire collective growth against gendered expectations and prospects. In my recollection, WIT met in sunny parks, among backyard gardens and around kitchen tables (though, in the research process, I also learned of many adult nights out and weekends away). While not directly involved, I remember being always keenly aware of the connectivity and healing taking place. As I grew older and joined the circle, I came to understand this connectivity as a set of self and mutual care rituals aimed at building precious bonds away from everyday trauma of the patriarchy. Even today, the women in the circle do not always like each other – but their group ethic is an unbreakable code of emotional disclosure, holding space, nonjudgement and supportive action, which resists the patriarchal systems that undermine feminized connectivity and isolate women from one another.

Settler sexuality

To appreciate the significance of such childhood kinship models as fundamental to my current relationship ethic, it is important to contextualize them within the beliefs of my settler colonial cultural heritage. Through this heritage I internalized specific relational values – such as the concept of the core self and the ideal of romantic love – as well as structural philosophies, including the gender binary, heterosexuality and monogamy. One story which perhaps best demonstrates these internalizations is that of the 'relationship escalator'; common elements of this story include *go on a first date, have a first kiss, get engaged, get married, have sex, adopt a pet, have a baby, buy a house, retire* and *grow old together* (Brunning 2018). As Hostetler and Herdt might frame it, the relationship escalator illustrates happiness and fulfilment through a prescriptive 'sexual lifeway' (1998: 251) which

2. Found family often refers to queer kinship networks. Here, it describes both non-biological kindships and the biological family my mother found when she went looking; regardless of bio-legal connection, all chose our family and are equally legitimate relatives.

acts as a moral tale to guide appropriate romantic relating, family building and aging (Carlström & Andersson 2019).

Scott Morgensen (2011) and Kim TallBear (2018) have similarly proposed 'settler sexuality', as the gender, sexuality and relational mythologies brought to North America from European nations – utilized to manufacture the settler state and 'eliminate/assimilate Indigenous peoples into the national body' (TallBear 2018: 147). As I understand it now, settler sexuality encompasses the intersecting systems of patriarchal, heteronormative (as well as homonormative), gender binary, monogamous and biologically privileged relating, which are systemically enforced by state, religion and scientific action. Although not explicitly termed settler sexuality, other theorists have also pointed to colonial sexual scripts, and particularly heterosexual monogamous marriage, as a method of racialized nation building. For example, Martha Ertman discusses the racist language in the landmark 1878 *Reynolds vs. United States* anti-polygyny ruling, detailing polygamy as 'natural for Asiatic and African people' while at the same time 'barbaric' (Ertman 2008: 287). This is not a unique or antiquated example of the ways in which settler sexuality has been employed as a racialized legal tool. Today, there are approximately 1,049 privileges and protections for monogamous marriage in the United States, which operate to control citizenship, property ownership and monetary capitol – thereby maintaining the white, settler hegemony through biological family heritage rights (Duggan 2004). Viewed alongside settler sexuality, the seemingly personal relationship practices from my childhood become repositioned into a broader system of violence and state control. From this broader lens, individual relational practices not only exist within systems, but also garner power as potential sites for everyday acts of resistance.

Karen, the WIT organizer and my second mom, shares a time she witnessed me – even as a young child – enacting such resistance to prescribed family norms. At the age of four or five, my closest friends were two other WIT children; the three of us would often run around making mud pies, waging crab apple wars and playing any sort of pretend together. As she likes to tell it, one particularly sunny day, smiling ear to ear, we decided to hold a terrace wedding. I would be the blushing bride, but who would be the groom? Both boys, of course, and without a blush in sight at this unconventional solution. By Karen's account, the entire play-event was a beautiful waltz, 'there was no doubt, no hesitation, just three friends laughing and embracing in the love of children'. Taking each boy by the hand, I married my two best friends that day – a curious premonition to my future relational ethic.

Unconscious relational ethic building

By the time I entered high school my very own relational code was already brewing. While most teens were steeped in the toils and tribulations of body insecurity and who-likes-who, I was so numb I could barely self-relate, let alone relate to others. In the previous year I had experienced my first serious flirtation with Logan, a clever, ambitious and talented boy who always kept me on my toes. We had a puppy play, not-quite-dating friendship which abruptly ended in a terrible car accident. Only our closest friends knew of the connection, and at the time I felt I lacked relational validity to claim any particular grieving needs. Instead of asking to participate in the mourning rituals of his passing, I suffered silently, holding tightly to the unfinishable business between us. Given time, I may have found a healthier grief process. However, not long after this, my mom's brother was diagnosed with terminal cancer. When my uncle joined our home, my family constellation became a revolving door of people always there to help, yet somehow never reachable across the desert of grief blistering within and between us. School relationships took on a similar distant characteristic, though I certainly had friends who cared; one in particular managed to reach across the abyss.

I met Jack in an after-school activity programme. He had a deep, throaty laugh that came as easily as his ability to charm a room. As a high school student, he possessed the unusual trait of accepting everyone exactly as they were – and so, naturally, half the school considered him a best friend. Somewhere between afternoon drives and warm hugs, Jack stoked a tiny fire of joy back into my world. Just as truly as I lacked the words to define and claim my almost-romance with Logan, I had no words to describe the complexity of feelings that accompanied Jack's influence. He became more than a friend, indeed, much more. Definitely not a lover, but there was romance, a kind of familial romance, which I struggled to reconcile into the 'family', 'friend', 'partner' boxes of my settler-colonial cultural context. Around the same time, I was navigating a starry-eyed appreciation for a senior student named Crystal. She was smart in every sense of the word; sharply intelligent, self-assured and seemingly effortlessly beautiful. She also happened to be dating Jack. In the beginning, my relationship with Crystal was a shadow-ship: she lived largely unaware of me, and I followed her every move, desperate to conform to her shape. In my mind, Crystal epitomized the monolith of 'womanhood' – and the more I tried to emulate her, the more dissonant I became with gender identity. As I recall, the tensions between us three grew into a silent hallway drama studied fiercely by other students. Jack's friends tolerated me like an untrained and overzealous puppy (because, at least cultural-relationally, I was not 'trained'). Students I barely knew started taking 'sides' by telling me how I should or shouldn't behave. And quickly, so quickly I hardly registered the transformation, I became a villain in Crystal's perfect (re: relationship escalator) love story.

Through the years, I have come to understand this as one of the most striking things about non-monogamies: they are rarely characterized by those we love, but rather those who also love our loves. And in this way, Crystal became my first metamour.[3] While I endlessly tried to imitate her femininity, she steamed at my perceived impropriety. She begrudged my indifference to the family/friend/partner behavioural expectations around Jack, and on several occasions reprimanded me

---

3. Metamour describe a partner's partner. Here, I take liberties, using it to describe the unique relationship between two people who share caring for someone else, regardless of negotiated relational status.

for transgressing beyond the strictly friend-zone (a relational boundary which eludes me even today). If I'm honest, a part of me enjoyed jesting as the 'other woman'. For one, it made me feel closer to that ever enigmatic 'womanhood' construct. But more significantly, I appreciated the safety of it. You see, if Jack had Crystal, then I could still have Logan, and my ocean of grief, and the lonely individualism that held me together. If Crystal performed the role of 'perfect girlfriend' by shouldering the impossible burden of heterosexual and gendered expectation, I was free to love as fully as I craved. Liberated by her success (in contrast to my own apparent gender and relational failure), the emotions stored behind my wall of mourning found new purpose in my friendship with Jack. Looking back, I terribly disregarded Crystal's feelings and bids for boundary setting – I was absolutely a toxic metamour. But at the time, I found comfort in the nearly-queer of our situation. Even as my nonconformity became a source of painful social animosity, I found peace in myself for perhaps the very first time.

As Katrin Tildenberg suggests, 'sexual scripts tell us what is sexy and sexual; how, when, why, with whom, and with what consequences we can have sex' (2014: 5). With Jack and Crystal, the theoretical notion of settler sexuality was far from my awareness, but the underlying sexual scripts were endlessly transgressed, negotiated and (re)enforced. Through this journey, I began to consider different ways of doing relationships, and soon found a growing desire to rewrite sexual and relational story arcs. While not exactly conscious of the thoughts, I felt increasingly uncomfortable with the scripts prescribed to me on the basis of sex and longed to disturb the limitations set forth by the gender binary. Additionally, although I could not yet conceptualize alternatives, I began to wonder how disrupting the expectations of monogamous relating might offer greater personal and relational potential.

Roleplay as healing

Arin remembers our first summer together as a crimson blur. It began the night of a high school graduation party. I spotted Arin in the corner and, emboldened by my impending move to Setauket, I darted across the room for a hug. Even back then, they wore masculinity more like a fine silk robe than a performative suit of armour. Their high school experience, much like mine, was marred by cruel social retaliation brought by an inability to conform to gender and sexuality expectation. During these years, the hallways were filled with heated debates on topics such as gay marriage rights – which would not be legalized until the year after we graduated – and the 'Don't Ask, Don't Tell' policy, which banned openly gay people in the US military. Every day we navigated casual slurs and conservative opinions repackaged from parents, pastors and the media. All the while, adulthood loomed for us in waves of precarious citizenship. Looking back, we were both full of the same trauma, a craving to finally fit the aspirational mould we had been measured against for so long. At the time, the LGBTQ+ rights movement represented liberation – I certainly could not yet see the ways in which an assimilation project fails to confront the settler-state for controlling its citizens (controlling queers like us) through normative sexuality.

Arin caught my hug and from there, as they describe it, my long red hair and bright red hoodie became a jetting comet they gripped all summer long. Through our shared trauma we embarked on a romantic comedy of a fling – three months of rose-tinted glory authored completely through the language of normative sexual scripts and gendered expectation. Each decision we made was a role-play, a farce to fill deep wounds in need of healing before we could face queer possibility. Between carefully planned dates turned awry and sunset make-out sessions gone wrong, we began to interrogate our mutual desire to feel worthy of settler-colonial love stories. From uncomfortable truck-bed star gazing to bug-bitten park picnics, we nourished each other in profound acceptance – indeed we learned we did not need the relational traditions of our upbringing. In my memories, the soundtrack of that summer was a stream of unabashed laughter, tender whispers and one deep sigh as we found empowerment in beginning to confront compulsory relationality – that is settler sexuality – together.

Conscious relational ethic building

It was the year of the cicadas in Setauket and the high-pitched whir of their collective being enveloped every evening of my first semester on campus. My assigned dormitory was a women's suite, shared with three other students, each uniquely talented and extraordinarily ambitious. Most nights were spent lounging in the warm breeze of an open balcony door, chatting about everything from petty campus dining complaints to our farthest imaginings of the future. During these times, we often found healing together, just as my mom enjoyed with her WIT group. Between us nothing was held back, especially not the passionate romance spilling over from my previous summer. On one such night, my suitemate, Beatrice (Bea for short), sat across from me – her curly hair heavy with the day's humidity. 'It doesn't sound over,' her eyes were wide as she debriefed another Arin update. I scoffed. As an eager feminist, my semester agenda included classes, clubs and student activism; it did not include being distracted by a high school romance, or anyone else who might limit my opportunities for exploration.

Despite these convictions, the fall air brought cicada lullabies, late-night calls and a clinging sensation that Arin had become something much more than a summer fling. One night, as I left my suitemates to another lively rendition of the day, Arin's voice came distorted through the phone. 'I just can't lose you,' their voice was full of tipsy conviction, 'I feel like I'm losing you and I just can't lose you.'

Even now, I find my response bewildering. Despite having never fully considered the idea, it came resolutely, 'Ok, I don't want to do monogamy, are you willing to work with that?' Looking back, this decision is an unsurprising evolution from the expansive kinship network of my childhood. Just as those relationships were established to meet my mother's feminist needs, and her mother before that, my determination in this moment was driven of feminist desire. Happily, Arin's own queer feminist journey met mine in non-monogamy.

Our first year after must have seen dozens of check-ins, negotiations and boundary discussions. We seemed in constant personal and relational reimagining, which showed up as ever-changing needs and desires. Having previously caricatured prescribed relationality, we had a good idea of what we *didn't* want. But finding what we *did* was often a trick of trial and error. From cover of college hook-up culture, were fortunate to avoid stigmatization, but we still had no blueprints for doing committed non-monogamy. These were such collaborative and personally constituting times that, in true non-monogamous fashion, we eventually came to mark two anniversaries. One recognizing the queer joy we found together, and another to honour our investment – against the odds of discrimination and minority stress – to cultivating strong polyqueer family building.

Relating as an abstract painting

Arin's queer journey began before we started dating, but for me, it would take nearly the entirety of our nine-year partnership to come into queerness. Therefore, when we stumbled on the term 'polyamory', I remember feeling great relief to have a label for the otherness I felt. The term not only validated my relating, but it became a route through which I could conceptualize my queerness, even as I was not fully prepared to deconstruct heterosexual and cisgender convention. In everyday practice, polyamory became a belief system through which I could unambiguously assert feminist and queer resistance.

At the time, this resistance was no better exemplified than relating with Bea. To honour the transformative potential between us, we tested many relational descriptors – best friends, siblings, platonic lovers, to name a few – though none adequately encompassed the richness of our bond. Visualized, our connection resembled a collection of abstract paintings, the colours of family, friend and partner strewn about strategically, though not particularly precisely. Each painting in the collection was liminal, filled with different expectations, needs and desires to fit the moment. As we developed our relational negotiation skills, we improved at expanding and combining various relationship patterns to make new colours and achieve different ways of being close. My interest in relationship anarchy influenced this intimacy tailoring, although Bea never subscribed to relationship anarchy herself. For me, as a genderqueer person socialized as a woman, experiencing this emotional intimacy with a bisexual woman became an important site for feminist realization and affirmation. Our connection provided an energy-replenishing kinship, which necessitated neither performance nor cognitive labour. Together, we could abandon the social isolation and behavioural self-monitoring often expected of feminized people within the monogamous heteropatriarchy, thereby galvanizing one another to engage more effectively in everyday power shifts (Emens 2004).

Of course, as I have often come to appreciate, polyqueer relationality is more about relationship networks than individual relationships. Therefore, the recursive potential between Bea and I cannot be understood without relational context. Bea's husband, Dave, is similar to me in many ways. He is strongly driven by a personal ethic, which is often informed by great compassion for others. He cares deeply for social issues and tries to be cognizant of his privileges. Unfortunately, even the most consistent commitment to deconstructing power dynamics cannot prevent power-laden interactions from arising. Not long after Bea and Dave began dating, one such situation occurred, the effects of which still weigh heavily between us. It happened during a chance meeting at the campus gym. The lead-up (which may offer important context) is lost to time, but in my recollections, Dave randomly insisted that I promise to never kiss Bea. At first, I was confused at Bea's apparent lack of autonomy in the matter. Then, frustrated at the presumption that we might *want* to kiss. And finally, overwhelmed with the underlying restrictions tied up in this seemingly small act of control: did *no kiss* actually mean *no kiss or any other action considered sexual by a settler-colonial prospective*? Or perhaps, *no kissing and no emotional intimacy on par with kissing under a hetero-monogamous mindset*? Or maybe even, *no kissing, but actually, nothing beyond the hegemonic friend-zone*?

I did not feel empowered to challenge him. Instead, I later implored Bea for an explanation, pointing to the interaction's biphobia (stereotyping that bisexual people can't be faithful) and polyphobia (stereotyping that polyamorous people will 'steal' your partner). In retrospect, he was speaking not merely from stereotypes, but discomfort informed by past trauma. Nevertheless, this situation followed a tired pattern: that a heterosexual man, when threatened by queer, feminized relating, may presume enough entitlement to insert himself in the relationship and dictate relational parameters. Still, when Dave spoke, he set a firm border. Here I evoke Jamie Heckert's conception of borders and boundaries:

> Whereas borders claim the hardness of walls, whether physically as in Berlin (1961–1989) or the West Bank, or psychically as in the carefully trained performance of the (mostly male) bodies that patrol and enforce them, boundaries suggest a softness, a gentleness that offers security without control. Whereas borders claim the unquestionable and rigid authority of law, boundaries have a fluidity, and openness to change; more a riverbank, less a stone canal. Borders demand respect, boundaries invite it. Borders divide desirables from undesirables, boundaries respect the diversity of desires.
>
> (2010: 7)

With this border, Dave evoked the shaming mechanisms of settler-sexuality to reify control over his relationship with Bea and, in doing so, exerted control over each individual relationship between the three of us. Despite my growing commitment to relationship anarchy, and Bea's commitment to our kinship, neither of us challenged Dave's interference. At least for me, Dave's border brought back the weight of my shortcomings as a metamour with Crystal, and a deep fear of losing Bea if I fought too hard against the systemic pulls of settler-sexuality.

Epistemologies in conflict

In an exploration of the open-relationships in China between gay husbands and heterosexual wives (tongqi), Jingshu Zhu (2018) argues that the polyamorous principles of authenticity and transparency are not universally applicable. She points to veiled communication in these marriages as an act of care, a mechanism to avoid the shame and public denunciation associated with deviating from expected relational scripts. While Jingshu's argument is set in a Chinese context, I too have experienced the limitations of honesty as a tool of care. Although I often think of the people in my life in terms of the abstract paintings of relationship anarchy, I rarely share these views because reciprocity often surfaces as an impassable monogamous value. When I do express myself, those I care for sometimes read my honesty as a burden – they feel a need to tidy my feelings and solidify our connection into a mutually and socially understood relationship box. Unable to cope with the tensions between differing relational dogmas, they often end the relationship altogether. In this way, declining to share my internal 'queer bonding' experience is as much of an act of self-preservation as an act of relational care (Klesse 2019). Even with Bea, these tensions eventually played themselves out. At first, rather than threaten the precarity of our relationship, we engaged in silence as an act of care. In fact, it was not until Bea and Dave opened their relationship that we addressed our closeness candidly. Still, identifying our desires for greater kinship came slowly – always cautious of Dave's border. For a long time, Bea was fiercely protective of my role in her life, holding space for me even as our relationship dogmas grew and changed. However, the more hetero-monogamous her relationship with Dave became – with desires to get married, have kids and 'settle down' – the more she struggled to make me coherent in her life.

Polyrelational futures

At some point, much like Bea, Arin's desire to buy a house and 'settle down' became an insurmountable gulf between us. While writing this chapter, such tugs of settler-sexuality were constantly being navigated, negotiated, resisted and mobilized by my relational network. Bea and Arin, for example, both endeavoured to reconcile non-monogamous desire within the imaginaries and confines of settler organization – an issue which all polyqueer notions must at some point contend. While navigating the structures and restrictions of settler-sexuality is arduous, in their most resistant forms, my polyqueer connections have been profoundly healing. They have uprooted toxic gender binary and heteronormative notions and have given me tools to invoke feminist care more generously – not only within human connection, but also towards my internal world and the physical world around me. By inhabiting genderqueer expression and polyqueer relating as the foundations of queer groundless belonging, I personally engage in explicit resistance to the settler-colonial project and challenge my own desires for settler-colonial assimilation. In doing so, I hope to bring greater accountability to myself and queer networks for contending with nation-state complicity.

To conclude this polyqueer autoethnography, I would like to impart a cherished memory set in a Taiwanese classroom full of students from around the world. I shared this particular moment with another non-monogamous and genderqueer student, who grew up in Côte d'Ivoire under French colonial influence. During a class discussion on retirement, we began to imagine what ideal aging might look like from the perspective of our desired queer and expansive family constellations. For me, this thought-exercise was both inspiring and excruciating; as we compared our options to those of our monogamous peers, I became wholly aware that my imagined futures were completely – legally, socially, infrastructurally – beyond reach due to the tenacity of settler-sexuality. I realized that even if non-monogamous marriage became recognized by the state, full access to family building would entail an overhaul of entire systems of dyadic organization, including financial institutions, housing infrastructure, immigration policy and beyond. Furthermore, I began to understand that (re)producing settler-colonial violence by assimilating non-monogamous relationships into the constructs of settler-citizenship (e.g. via plural marriage rights) would only result in the normalization of certain non-monogamies, therefore reinforcing hierarchical citizenship through nation-state dictation of acceptable family building. As expressed by the Christian Klesse, 'the recognition of non-monogamous and polyamorous relationships and families demands no less than the thorough reformulation of our understanding of citizenship' (2019: 638). Presently, when I consider my future, I visualize a great emptiness filled equally with potential and precarity. Crucially, within these tensions exists an opportunity to resist polyqueer alignment with gendered, racist, classist, ableist and nationalist privileges – to rather mobilize polyqueer relating in service of a decolonial project which confronts, contends with, (re)imagines and resists settler-colonial control over citizenship, the land and the lives of Indigenous and queer people.

References

Ahmed, S. (2006). *Queer Phenomenology: Orientations, Objects, Others*. Durham, NC: Duke University Press.

Barker, M. (2005). 'This Is My Partner, and This Is My … Partner's Partner: Constructing a Polyamorous Identity in a Monogamous World'. *Journal of Constructivist Psychology*, 18 (1): 75–88. doi:10.1080/10720530590523107.

Barker, M. & Langdridge, D. (2010). 'Whatever Happened to Non-monogamies? Critical Reflections on Recent Research and Theory'. *Sexualities*, 13 (6): 748–72. doi:10.1177/1363460710384645.

Brunning, L. (2018). 'The Distinctiveness of Polyamory'. *Journal of Applied Philosophy*, 35 (3): 513–31. doi:10.1111/japp.12240.

Carlström, C. & Andersson, C. (2019). 'Living Outside Protocol: Polyamorous Orientations, Bodies, and Queer Temporalities'. *Sexuality & Culture*, 23 (4): 1315–31. doi:10.1007/s12119-019-09621-7.

Duggan, L. (2004). 'Holy Matrimony! As Politicians Square Off on Gay Marriage, Progressives Must Enter the Debate'. *The Nation*. Retrieved from http://www.thenation.com/article/holy-matrimony/.

Emens, E. (2004). 'Monogamys Law: Compulsory Monogamy and Polyamorous Existence'. *University of Chicago Law School Chicago Unbound*.

Ertman, M. M. (2008). 'Race Treason: The Untold Story of America's Ban on Polygamy'. *Columbia Journal of Gender and Law*, 19 (2): 287–366. Retrieved from http://ssrn.com/abstract=1270023.

Finn, M. & Malson, H. (2008). 'Speaking of Home Truth: (re)productions of Dyadic-Containment in Non-monogamous Relationships'. *Br J Soc Psychol*, 47 (Pt 3): 519–33. doi:10.1348/014466607X248921.

Hammack, P. L., Frost, D. M., & Hughes, S. D. (2019). 'Queer Intimacies: A New Paradigm for the Study of Relationship Diversity'. *J Sex Res*, 56 (4–5): 556–92. doi:10.1080/00224 499.2018.1531281.

Heckert, J. (2010). Love Without Borders? Intimacy, Identity and the State of Compulsory Monogamy.

Hostetler, A. J. & Herdt, G. H. (1998). 'Culture, Sexual Lifeways, and Developmental Subjectivities: Rethinking Sexual Taxonomies'. *Social Research*, 65 (2): 249–90. Retrieved from https://www.jstor.org/stable/40971272.

Klesse, C. (2019). 'Polyamorous Parenting: Stigma, Social Regulation, and Queer Bonds of Resistance'. *Sociological Research Online*, 24 (4): 625–43. doi:1.o0r.g1/107.171/1773/610 3670870840148188006902.

Lipsitz, G. (2007). 'The Racialization of Space and the Spatialization of Race'. *Landscape Journal*, 26 (1): 10–23. doi:10.3368/lj.26.1.10.

Littletree, S. & Belarde-Lewis, M. D., Marisa. (2020). 'Centering Relationality: A Conceptual Model to Advance Indigenous Knowledge Organization Practices'. *Knowl. Org.*, 47 (5): 410–26. doi:10.5771/0943-7444-2020-5-410.

Morgensen, S. L. (2011). *Spaces between Us: Queer Settler Colonialism and Indigenous Decolonization*. Minneapolis: University Of Minnesota Press.

Schippers, M. (2016). *Beyond Monogamy: Polyamory and the Future of Polyqueer Sexualities*. New York: NYU Press.

TallBear, K. (2018). 'Making Love and Relations Beyond Settler Sex and Family'. In A. E. Clarke & D. Haraway (Eds.), *Making Kin Not Population*. Chicago: Prickly Paradigm Press, pp. 144–64.

TallBear, K. (2021). 'Identity Is a Poor Substitute for Relating: Genetic Ancestry, Critical Polyamory, Property, and Relations'. In B. Hokowhitu, L. Tuhiwai-Smith, C. Andersen, & S. Larkin (Eds.), *Critical Indigenous Studies Handbook*. New York: Routledge, pp. 467–78.

TallBear, K. (2022). *Transcript: Dr. KIM TALLBEAR on Reviving Kinship and Sexual Abundance/Interviewer: A. Young*. Cascadia: For The Wild, https://forthewild.world/podcast-transcripts/dr-kim-tallbear-on-reviving-kinship-and-sexual-abundance-encore-284.

Tildenberg, K. (2014). 'There's No Limit to Your Love – Scripting the Polyamorous Self'. *Journal für Psychologie*, 22: 1–27.

Tuck, E. & McKenzie, M. (2015). *Place in Research: Theory, Methodology, and Methods*. New York: Routledge.

Tynan, L. (2021). 'What Is Relationality? Indigenous Knowledges, Practices and Responsibilities with Kin'. *Cultural Geographies*, 28 (4): 597–610. doi:10.1177/14744740211029287.

Vasiliev, R. (2004). *From Abbotts to Zurich: NewYork State Placenames*. Syracuse: Syracuse University Press.

Zhu, J. (2018). '"We're Not Cheaters": Polyamory, Mixed-Orientation Marriage and the Construction of Radical Honesty'. *Graduate Journal of Social Sciences*, 14 (1): 57–78.

Chapter 10

A REFLEXIVE CONSIDERATION OF THE APOCALYPTIC CHILD

E. Scherzinger

I

I was a teenager when Arcade Fire came out with their third studio album, *The Suburbs*, and it was my soundtrack as I rode my bike around the suburban Toronto neighbourhood where I grew up. Popping my headphones out of my ears, I would stop at my friends' houses as the sun was setting only to be rejected at the door by their parents, stating that they could not ride around with me. 'She hasn't finished her homework yet,' a frustrating, yet comforting, denial. The summers would bring popsicles, cicadas and all-day adventures: my first love and I would sit at the pond in the orchard near my parents' house, wholeheartedly believing that we were feeling truths and emotions that were entirely unique to human existence. Another sentimental suburban scene: sitting on the curb outside of my parents' house, waiting to see my best friend turn the corner and ride down the street. I once again listened to Win Butler crooning in the second chorus of the album's titular song: 'So can you understand / that I want a daughter while I'm still young? / I want to hold her hand / and show her some beauty before all this damage is done.' I took it at face value then, but now I know first-hand what the 'damage' was to be 'done'. Disillusionment weaves in and out of the album's songs, and, as I've aged, I consider the 'damage' the jaded cynicism that prevents adults from seeing beauty in the little things, which is why Butler wants to parent at a young age, a clear equation of youth with innocence. *The Suburbs* also consistently refers to some sort of war throughout many song lyrics and titles, like 'Culture War', utilizing a distinct Cold War aesthetic that features an overwhelming undercurrent of social anxiety, nuclear families and apocalyptic destruction. Across both readings, the 'damage' to occur seems to be the stripping of innocence from his unborn daughter, who stands as a beacon of ambivalence, both anxiety and desire.

As an adult, I understand the affective tenor behind these lyrics a bit more, as my everyday emotional state exists somewhere between anxiety and desire within what many would describe as a post-apocalyptic world. As such, I turn to autotheory to explore these affects about natality and innocence. Autotheory is a praxis of production that insists on subjectivity as representative, and also holds a rich and storied history in post-1960s contemporary intersectional feminist and disability studies. Standing as a methodological approach at the junction of autobiography, theory and autoethnography, autotheory 'takes the actually lived life as important critically, and as worthy of reflection and nuanced consideration in relation to critical and creative practices (which include fictionalization), without turning to fiction as a stylistic-legalistic crutch' (Fournier: 257). So, rather than focusing on the authoritative intention behind a text, an auto-theoretical hermeneutic practice attempts to co-produce a text's meaning in order to privilege the reader's lived experience within 'the ongoing, multidirectional process of citational practices that come to constitute meaning in culture' (Fournier: 199). I include feminist conceptualizations of autotheory as an artistic and critical practice of production in order to explore alternative hermeneutic practices for interpreting and reading the world: rather than simply engaging with what I assume Arcade Fire wants me to take away from their lyrics, I situate my own experiences of 'growing up girl' in order to probe at and question the natalism in their lyrics about suburban apocalypse that I find so fascinating. Indeed, rather than uncritically engaging with the reproductive futurity that has been imposed upon my white, feminine body my whole life, I intend to use autotheory to piece apart my concerns about having children in a world forever altered by climate change, disease and damage.

Grounded in affect, autotheory enmeshes cultural theory and philosophy with the writer's situated experiences. Maggie Nelson's *The Argonauts* is an excellent example of auto-theoretical non-fiction, mixing her existence as a queer woman with quotes and citational references in the margins of her text.

Arcade Fire's lyrics insist that a daughter is the one who will induce the 'beauty' before damage, clearly demonstrating a concern about the loss of girlhood innocence. As a child born in the throes of the 'stranger danger' era, my mother would not let me out of the house after it was dark, for worry of a stranger leaping from the bushes to kidnap and/or sexually assault me. In other words, even though I was raised in a suburban neighbourhood, typically framed as an idyllic location primarily centred on raising children, and thus structured around the maintenance of childhood innocence, my parents feared mythic evil-doers would strip that purity away from me. Little did they know that it would be, as is more often the case, someone that we knew: the boy down the street, a symptom of the patriarchal world at large imposing itself on me in a way that complicated my innocence entirely.

The anxiety over a child's – and particularly a girl-child's – loss of innocence is predicated upon the fact that white girls are uniquely configured as virginal and pure. Indeed, white girls' bodies are socially invested with not only weakness, but also hopes for nation-building via my reproductive capabilities. As such, white suburban girlhood is a contested site of reproductive futurity, growth and innocence. As Kathryn Bond Stockton (2016, p. 506) writes in her addition to her revolutionary text *The Queer Child*, 'Anglo-America, caught in a dream from which it won't awake, is steeped in fantasies of vaporous innocence. These are largely suburban-driven fantasies' that influence how adults treat and conceive of children. Stockton (2016: 514) continues, 'It is a privilege to need to be protected,' and it is this privilege that allows 'the all-important feature of weakness [to] stic[k] to these signs (white and middle class) and helps signal innocence'. As such, I was 'protected from what [I] *approach[ed]*: the adulthood against which [I was] defined' (Stockton 2016: 514) – an adulthood in which corruption would occur, according to Arcade Fire.

I could feel myself strain against this reading of my body, though, one that I ultimately resisted as a queer person. Looking back, I see that my desire (almost a compulsion) to sneak out after my parents had gone to sleep, to smoke weed and drink with my friends, to skip class and bike around the city were all attempts at understanding the tension between the innocence imposed upon my body and its sexualization by society macrocosmically, as well as older men leering at me, on a microcosmic level. Although I was relatively unaware of some of this objectification, thanks to a growing feeling of gender dysmorphia that would centre thoughts about my body in confusion, my body was still swelling under the weight of reproductive futurity. To escape into spaces and places that I was not supposed to occupy in the wee hours of the morning, then, was to queer the spaces of my upbringing. This term, coined by Lee Edelman, takes issue with the 'Child remain[ing] [as] the perpetual horizon of every acknowledged politics, the fantasmatic beneficiary of every political intervention' (Edelman 2004: 3). As such, Edelman introduces queerness into reproductive futurist discourses and renderings of the future to offer a counternarrative to the Child as 'the emblem of futurity's unquestioned value', effectively 'expos[ing] the obliquity of our relation to what we experience in and as social reality, alerting us to the fantasies structurally necessary in order to sustain it' (Edelman 2004: 4, 6). For example, politics requires a 'fantasy of the future' that includes the figurative Child to 'embod[y] the citizen as an ideal, entitled to claim full rights to its future share in the nation's good' (Edelman 2004: 11). I see now that, as a child, I was a pawn of reproductive futurism, a latent embodiment of the ideal female citizen, a child assumed to eventually become ripe for male consumption and heteronormative reproduction; however, this configuring of my youth and preteen body came 'at the cost of limiting the rights "real" citizens are allowed' (Edelman 2004: 11). These limitations, while put in place to prevent 'damage' to Arcade Fire's figurative daughter, bring about a unique kind of ruination to existing populations working outside of Western conservative renderings of the ideal Child.

The very real forms of ruination taking place and acting as, in Joseph Masco's terms (2008: 361), 'a form of nation-building' are centred on restorative nostalgia, a desiring impetus to 'transhistorical[ly] reconstruc[t] [...] the lost home', the locus of a nation's 'truth and tradition' (Boym 2001: xviii). In this context, I cannot help but think of the aestheticized politics of Arcade Fire's lyrics that I find myself returning to throughout my life. A decade ago, I was in the throes of that gloriously childish feeling of invincibility, feeling like I could take on the world, of being half-alive. Of course, I am aware that I often 'fall ill with nostalgia for a future, a time in which you clearly saw a future before you, before you felt the "tick tock" of a viral clock' (Stockton 2016: 512, emphasis removed). Stockton was referring to the movie *Precious*, and the child queered by HIV, but I think that this statement applies well to the way I look back on my childhood: nostalgic for a version of me before I was sexually assaulted, before I became impure, back when I embodied perfect girlhood. Now, I understood myself as queer, as mentally ill, as a chronically ill human being with a body that does not often work, as a piece of a world that I did not always want to exist in.

Perfect girlhood is typified by traditional femininity, what Samantha Holland (2002: 105) terms "'fluffy" femininity', and is weighted down by a lot of anxiety about the futurity of the nation and reproductive labour. In her interviews on alternative femininities and girlhood fashion, Holland's study participants defined 'fluffy' femininity as 'traditional' femininity, that which is 'malleable and not independent' (Holland 2002: 110). The paradox hidden within this indictment of traditional femininity is described as 'a problem that women encounter in childhood and must confront for the rest of their lives. This problem … raises the question of whether women can truly define who they are and how they present themselves to the world given the expectation that they meet definitions established by others' (Furman, quoted in Holland 2002: 110). Clearly, the anxiety of girls – and especially white girls – not meeting the patriarchal expectations of purity, innocence and heteronormative reproduction imposed upon them produces queer girls performing femininity outside of these restrictions. '[R] esponses' that are 'received when they do not adhere to the definitions of others' (Holland 2002: 110) range from affective to physical violence, attempting to restore '[t]radition' in femininity 'with a nearly apocalyptic vengeance' (Boym 2001: 43).

As a result, Stockton notes that 'the child from the standpoint of "normal" adults is always queer' (Stockton 2009: 7). Indeed, the Child is queered by innocence; as Stockton writes, 'One does not "grow up" from innocence to the adult position of protecting it' (Stockton 2009: 12). Instead, innocence renders the child 'fla[t]', 'vacan[t]' and signifying 'nothing' (Kincaid, quoted in Stockton 2009: 12). Thus, innocent children are 'foreign' and 'obscure to us' (Stockton 2016: 514), inhabiting a kind of paradoxical 'normative strangeness' (Stockton 2009: 30): the Child requires protection, but society demands the potential for abuse to hang over the Child in order to repeatedly confirm their innocence, their need to be protected. Stockton (2009: 33) writes, '[T]he child's need for protection and her weakness in these [abusive] moments, confirms the child's innocence.' However, in order to even go about the process of protecting the child, we must first position the child as a recognizable 'life that matters' (Butler: 14). Western sociopolitical frames are discursively circulated to produce 'norms that qualify […] a life' as recognizable and grievable (Butler, p. 3). These qualities are granted to children who conform to Western norms of innocence, and, more implicitly, whiteness and heteronormativity. In other words, the prospect of a white, heteronormative and middle-class child's death – a child whose 'future anterior' was once 'installed as the condition of [their] life' – reveals how some children are considered more grievable than others (Butler: 15). Braiding Stockton and Butler together, it is clear how the grievability of a child is premised upon their recognizability as a life that matters, a label determined by certain frameworks of normativity that deem certain children valuable, yet also queer.

I've come to notice this dynamic showing up more in apocalypse movies, one of my favourite subgenres of horror. From *A Quiet Place* (2018) to *Birdbox* (2018), children remain firmly at the side of an adult attempting to lead them to safety and survival. Often, the children of these films are framed as the most grievable of all the characters: in *A Quiet Place*, we are introduced to the Abbott family after one of their children, Beau, has been killed by the monsters while playing with a loud toy truck. Hearing Beau's toy, the blind monsters attracted to sound quickly grab him, leaving the viewer with a lasting image of John Krasinski, the boy's father, jumping and reaching towards the camera, attempting to save his son. The child, innocently attempting to play with his favourite toy and failing to grasp the gravity of the apocalyptic situation, leaves behind his parents and siblings, who grieve his absence for the rest of the movie.

I continually find myself frustrated with the way the apocalyptic child is represented. Of course, all children make mistakes, but this blatant image of innocence – a boy simply playing with his toy – swiped away by a corrupting monster in the midst of an apocalypse seemed incredibly forced. I cannot deny its effectiveness, though: it makes clear to the viewer that this apocalypse is a source of 'damage' to the white Child. Using the 'cinematic apparatus', movies that feature this genre of children navigating the aftermath of an apocalypse offer an 'ideal subject position' for societal ideologies on children to take up. The power of these post-apocalyptic films works to produce an idealized image of the apocalyptic Child: innocent, grievable and ripe for adult intervention and education on the 'appropriate' way to rebuild, often one that aligns with white neoliberal capitalism. This rendering of the Child, though, flattens the queerness inherent in this pseudo-innocent creature; there is no space for the apocalyptic Child to be anything other than a martyr of whiteness and capitalism. Indeed, to erase the strangeness of the Child is to excise 'anxieties about the future of gender, race, and sexuality from the narrative' (Dyer 2020: 5).

II

Now more than ever before, the apocalypse feels inevitable. Toronto is noticeably hotter than ever, and I find myself packing my parka away earlier each year. The United Nations has formally issued a red alert, cautioning whoever their warning is for that time is running out. Newspapers print images of people going to work on the American West Coast underneath a blood red sky, due to the smoke from climate change-induced wildfires. At the time in which I am writing this chapter, I am reaching the end of graduate school, and the unlikely tenure-track position, as well as the almost certainty of financial strain under capitalism, shift more into focus. The Covid-19 pandemic has scraped my mentally ill brain dry to the point that I feel incapable of any promised return to 'normal'. It takes multiple moments to remind myself that nothing will ever return to normal. Using Jacques Derrida, S. Trimble (2019: 81) notes that the concept of the 'return' is highly fraught; 'return' implies the reappearance of a repressed entity, often of a 'monstrous form'. To return to 'normal' would 'depen[d], of course, on the vanquishing of the monster' (Trimble 2019: 81). But who – or *what* – is the 'monster' in this real, impending apocalypse?

To answer this question would require a moralistic narrativization of Covid-19 and global warming that equates these entities with monstrosity, therefore telling a story in which Man vanquishes, or at least delays, these threats with his advanced technology, an adventurous feat made possible by limitless capitalist accumulation and at the cost of eventual planetary collapse. This figuration of Man, as Sylvia Wynter has theorized, is 'a "biocentric" vision of the human as a living organism imperiled by natural scarcity (Man2)', and this 'figure of Man took shape in relation to Others imagined as exploitable and/or killable' (Trimble 2019: 3). Man 2 is *homo oeconomicus*, according to Wynter, a figure that 'exposes the long colonial roots of a worldview premised on relentless accumulation' (Trimble 2019: 3). Importantly, Trimble notes a parallel between the apocalyptic Last Man and Wynter's *homo oeconmicus*. They write, '[T]he Last Man tends to hew close to the figure of economic Man, often deriving his authority from patriarchal white masculinity and its colonial coding as benevolent, capable, father-knows-best' (Trimble 2019: 4). Thus, there is a tension between monster and *homo oeconomicus*, in which the monster is the ultimate threat that brings about apocalyptic change, and yet the Last Man (Man2) needs the monster 'to begin the world again' (Trimble 2019: 4). As an example, Trimble notes how Major Henry West in *28 Days Later* seeks out the two main female characters, a white woman and a Black woman, to reproduce with his army and secure the next generation of humans within his zombie-proofed compound. This threat of sexual violence at the hands of white soldiers complicates the concept of the 'return to normal'. To begin again, to build a world in the image of pre-apocalyptic Western society, requires reproductive labour, and therefore feminine child-bearing potential; however, to do so through the means of sexual violence suggests that Major Henry West is the true monster, standing in as the repressed quality of white capitalist exploitation of femininity for nation-building gains. To vanquish the Major, then, is to eradicate the possibility of the return to Western neoliberal capitalism, and thus the return to exploitative labour, sexual violence and neocolonial institutions.

Indeed, reproduction is a required labour within an apocalypse, one that brings 'sedimented "histories of arrival"', in which 'reproductive and maternal labor unspools into the long and often difficult histories that inform where, when, and under what conditions women give birth to new humans' (Trimble 2019: 11). Rather than arriving to the world as a blank slate, 'young people in [apocalyptic] films are strange arrivals trailing long, deep, and often unresolved histories' (Trimble 2019: 11); however, societal assumptions of childhood dictate that innocence prevents these children from properly navigating an apocalypse without an adult already steeped in the sociopolitical ideologies of Western society. The apocalyptic Child requires, as is the case in the film version of Cormac

McCarthy's novel *The Road*, Man2 to carry 'good humanness in terms of economic productivity and security' into the post-apocalyptic world, capitalist neoliberal values that will then be reproduced in the new world via colonial grammars (Trimble 2019: 3). This hope for a new world that looks alarmingly similar to the contemporary one, fraught with all of its inequities and histories, is located in 'the figure of the child' (Trimble 2019: 11). Edelman's reproductive futurism speaks to this desire, in which the figural Child is made 'for the satisfaction of adults, an Imaginary fullness that's considered to want, and therefore to want for, nothing' (Edelman 2004: 21). In other words, we produce the image of a vulnerable, innocent Child, and then expect it to not have any of its own desires, which reach towards its own unique future. As such, any 'imagined desire' from the Child is felt as a threat, and so we feel 'justified running from it' (Stockton 2016: 506). This imagined Child 'enshrines [...] an insistence on sameness that intends to restore an Imaginary past', a pre-apocalyptic Western society founded upon problematic articulations of power. Deviation from this conformity to the new world renders the Child unvaluable, unimportant and ungrievable (Edelman 2004: 21).

As such, the reproductive futurism that lies at the heart of many post-apocalyptic texts sanctions various forms of violence against marginalized groups to secure the continuance of neoliberal capitalism. As I mentioned before, the apocalyptic film *The Road* treads in this white reproductive futurity, in which the main character justifies resource extraction and manipulation of people of colour for the survival of his son, who 'carries the fire'. I see the 'fire' in this instance as the responsibility that the Man tasks his son with: securing the futurity of whiteness. In one particularly telling scene, Viggo Mortensen's main character threatens a thief with his gun to give back what he has stolen, and then, conversely, steals the thief's clothes. The Man's son pleads with his father to not kill the thief. The two eventually walk away, but not before a stark image: 'Between the naked, shivering black man and the paranoid white man holding a gun, a smudge of gray on the filmic horizon stands in for the edge of what was once the New World' (Trimble 2019: 41). It is impossible to deny the racial and colonial dimensions of this scene, in which a white man violently extracts resources from a Black man in a bid to ensure the survival of his child, who is imbued with hope and desire for a better future by his father, 'a transference of depravity to young people [that] swell[s] adults' surety that they know best' (Dyer 2020: 131).

As I watch the slow onset of what feels like another global apocalypse, I find myself returning to these filmic representations of the aftermath and the characters that traverse them, and struggling with the heteronormativity and reproductive futurity in these narratives as both a queer person and, one day, a parent. There is a certain 'relation of cruel optimism [that] exists' between the heteronormativity of reproduction, my gender and my politics, which centre on anti-capitalist, anti-racist educational activism and disability justice (Berlant 2011: 1). In other words, the whiteness and heteronormativity inherent in reproductive futurism acts as a potential 'obstacle to [the] flourishing' of my politics and activism (Berlant 2011: 1). As much as I want to have a child and fulfil my lifelong dream of becoming a parent, I know that, despite my best efforts, my reproduction will be read to reach certain conservative conclusions by those around me. For example, my whiteness will produce whiteness, effectively reifying the grievability of some children and not others; my child will be considered 'grievable' in white supremacist capitalism. Further, if I have a child that can be read as a girl, I worry about their interpellation into nation-building narratives that situate their body as not only virginal and pure, but also a consumable, renewable resource that patriarchal sociopolitical institutions can exploit. I am concerned that the heteronormativity that dominates discourses on pregnancy and families will flatten my queerness while also attempting to restrict my child to an uncritical societal reading as an innocent, empty vessel. Akin to my experience of societal readings of my body in childhood, I am concerned that my pregnant body, and my child's existence, will be read as a reaffirmation of heteronormative capitalism and gender binaries, just as post-apocalyptic films reaffirm reproductive futurity and white childhood innocence. Indeed, these movies strive to begin again in a way that re-prioritizes whiteness, masculinity and the nuclear family. Assumed to be the cornerstones of Western society, these qualities in a post-apocalyptic context are saturated with restorative nostalgia, a type of nostalgia that attempts to 'retur[n] and rebuil[d] one's homeland with paranoic determination' and, if not reflected upon, 'breeds monsters' (Boym 2007: 15; Boym 2001: xvi). We can see how this desire for the return to pre-apocalyptic conditions spurs Major Henry West into sanctioning sexual violence, a political shift in nostalgia that connects exploitation 'to nation-building' (Boym 2001: 14). Indeed, the impetus to harness feminine reproductive capabilities in the name of Western futurity 'engage[s] in the antimodern myth-making of history by means of a return to national symbols and myths', one of which is the nuclear family, simultaneously a symbol and myth tied to ruination (Boym 2001: 41). As Masco notes, the media strategy of ensuring American preparedness for nuclear attack during the Cold War 'involved recalibrating domestic life by turning the nuclear family into a nuclearized family, preprogrammed for life before, during, and after a nuclear war' (Masco 2008: 374). The wreckage left in the wake of nuclear war was reimagined from an ashen, inhabitable landscape to 'a vehicle for individuals to demonstrate their moral character and for the nation to be regenerated through apocalyptic threat' (Masco 2008: 386). Thus, the apocalyptic Child, weighed down by their responsibility for the nation's futurity, must remain vulnerable yet capable of surviving mass destruction, innocent yet skilled enough to extract resources and exploit marginalized populations for the sake of restoring the nation.

In the current environment, no body wins: even thinking about birthing a child into the contemporary moment induces a terrifying feeling of precarity for not only myself, but my child, who has to be non-disabled enough to remain alive. I do not want my child to simply survive – I want my child to thrive in their radical subjectivity, to be as queer as they like, to not feel the unbearable weight of reproductive futurism, to live with the environment and the land around them and experience their sustaining and life-giving forces. Despite darkly joking with my friends that 'we only have 30 years left on this planet anyway', I feel this precarity quite deeply considering the state of the world; I feel 'a gut-level suspicion that hard work, thrift, and following the rules won't give [me] control over [my] story, much less guarantee a happy ending' (Hsu 2019: n.p.). So, I find myself faced with the question that spurred me into writing this essay in the first place: Is it irresponsible to bring a child into this world, when I am lucky enough to have the option to make the decision for myself? Is it even worth having a child if I will have to watch all of us become subsumed by an apocalyptic fireball?

III

Today is a better day. I might even call it a good day.

I have remembered all of my medications this week, spent time outside and slept well. My limbs have remained in their sockets, and my arthritis is not stretching the limits of my pain tolerance. As I write this, my partner is lying in the bed beside my desk, cuddling with my dog and keeping me company because I mentioned that I was feeling lonely. Today is a better day than most because I am cared for and loved.

Anxiety still follows me, and I constantly relive the realization that our partnership is one for life. I think back to my childhood outside of the sunbeams and sandboxes: me at ten years old, holding a knife to my wrist as raging tears fell on my skin, kicking myself for not being able to finally end it. I was a child when my mental illness made its grand entrance, as well as an untreated chronic illness that is still, at the moment of writing, a 'wastebasket diagnosis'. And yet, through the broken bones, hospital stays, medication, pain and wellness plans, I survived. I felt mostly alone, but I survived.

Quite often, I find myself returning to the concept of survival, and one could argue that this essay is an autotheoretical meditation on survival from someone who 'is told that, to this society, her care, even her survival, does not matter' (Hedva: 10). In this way, I use autotheory and writing as a mode of resistance. For me, writing has always been an attempt to translate my thoughts, to perform my meaning. This, Nelson suggests in *The Argonauts*, is a central tenet of autotheory. Nelson includes Judith Butler's critique of readings of *Gender Trouble*, indicating an attention to the multiplicity of, and potential meanings behind, her use of the term 'husband'. Butler writes, 'Performativity has to do with repetition, very often with the repetition of oppressive and painful gender norms to force them to resignify. This is not freedom, but a question of how to work the trap that one is inevitably in' (Butler, quoted in Nelson: 15). This conceptualization of performativity recognizes the dynamics of power that Western metaphysical and epistemological structures of interpretation enact. Crucially, though, the reflection 'from within' (Bal: 52) that is articulated yet always deferred is a characteristic of autotheory that recognizes the possibility of resistance against the hegemonic meanings imposed upon my words, my body. Thus, I see writing autotheoretically as sometimes my only form of resistance and survival.

Not only do sociopolitical and biomedical discourses shove my vulnerability and fragility in my face on a daily basis, but capitalism also appropriates my disabilities in order to 'perpetuate itself' (Hedva: 12), effectively situating my subjectivity as not quite worthy to continuously sustain via care and comfort, but not quite worthless to completely abandon. Of course, my status as a white person with feminine child-bearing potential affords me a lot of privilege within the biopolitical Western landscape; although I am already positioned as 'an abhorrence to the norm' (Hedva: 12) due to my status as a disabled person, my whiteness situates me within medical institutions as worthy of recuperation and rehabilitation. I am grievable because I am white, and am therefore meant to survive. This is a fact, and it stands in direct opposition to the experiences that Audre Lorde speaks to in her poem, 'A Litany to Survival', which Johanna Hedva, a disabled woman of colour, gestures to in her pontification on Sick Woman Theory. She (p. 8) writes, 'Sick Woman Theory is for […] those who, in Audre Lorde's words, were never meant to survive: because this world was built against their survival.'

Hedva offers hope for the survival of disabled and oppressed populations in the form of radical care work, and, because today is a better day, I feel that hope is more tangible than usual. I can recognize that care work is what is needed for survival to be a potentiality, even in the midst of an apocalypse that renders some populations disproportionately vulnerable and precarious than others. As Leah Lakshmi Piepzna-Samarasinha (2018: 87) writes, 'I want us to dream mutual aid in our post-apocalyptic revolutionary societies where everyone gets to access many kinds of care.' If I want my child to survive – and, beyond survival, feel *liberated* – then I need to return to my own practice and politics of care. Hedva (p. 13) expertly writes,

> The most anti-capitalist protest is to care for another and to care for yourself. To take on the historically feminized and therefore invisible practice of nursing, nurturing, caring. To take seriously each other's vulnerability and fragility and precarity, and to support it, honor it, empower it. To protect each other, to enact and practice community. A radical kinship, an interdependent sociality, a politics of care.

Piepzna-Samarasinha elaborates on this in their essay 'Cripping the Apocalypse: Some of My Wild Disability Justice Dreams'. Using dreaming as a methodology through which to enact change, they suggest that '[w]e could create visions of revolutionary futures that don't replicate eugenics – where disabled people exist and are thriving', rather than futures where disability is eradicated thanks to neoliberal capitalist notions of advanced health care (Piepzna-Samarasinha 2018: 128).

Clearly, I am extremely affected by the narratives that disabled people are told since childhood: 'we will die young, that our lives aren't worth living, and that we're up against everything' (Piepzna-Samarasinha 2018: 131). I hope that it breaks your heart as much as mine to read my reckoning with the lack of mainstream representations of disabled people in the apocalypse beyond burdening the 'ableds' who expertly traverse the wasteland; and the embargo on dreaming a post-apocalyptic future that includes disabled people as necessary. There is a lot of shame circulating in me that prevents seedlings of hope from growing, as well as 'grief mixed in with the rage, and survival, and a belief that you must be spoiled or entitled to ask for what you need' (Piepzna-Samarasinha 2018: 130). To be perfectly frank, I have never imagined my arthritic, hard of hearing, mad and chronically ill body surviving an apocalypse – never mind my own child, who may inherit some of the hereditary disabilities that I know so intimately; however, I am learning to recognize my disabilities as 'a set of innovative, virtuosic skills' (Piepzna-Samarasinha 2018: 126). As Piepzna-Samarasinha (2018: 134) notes in relation to the West Coast wildfires, it was disabled populations that 'shar[ed] the knowledge that being sick and disabled had already taught us', providing masks, air purifiers, detoxification herbs and anti-anxiety somatics.

I have spent my whole life assuming my status as burden, assuming that I will be one of the people 'abandoned when our cities flood' (Piepzna-Samarasinha 2018: 135), as I watched on the news when Hurricane Katrina made landfall. Even more recently, my best friend of six years decided to break off our friendship because I did not attend a protest with them that was organized by Indigenous people for the, at the time, recently discovered gravesite of children at a residential school in Kamloops, BC. Under the guise of accountability, this friend told me to buy a wheelchair so 'there's really no excuse for you not showing up'. These harsh words, and the loss of a friend, affected me deeply. As a disabled and queer academic, I have wrestled with the fact that many spaces, such as protests, are not safe for me to attend, and that my presence can also make that space dangerous for others. What if police assume my cane is a weapon, rather than a support? What if I get mixed into a struggle, and I break multiple bones? As my bones and muscles viscerally degenerate, I have taken to engaging with activism in more quiet ways, such as letter-writing, crafting banners and models, and actively engaging in mentorships of young, marginalized scholars in the academy. Yet, I still hear the voice of that friend telling me that my disabled body is not good enough. I have been told this multiple times throughout my life, and what these sentiments relay, at their affective foundation, is that there is an absolute hatred of disabled people.

Paulo Freire argues that humanization is an 'inescapable concern' of humans, and that we can point to historical moments in which 'both humanization and dehumanization are possibilities for a person as an uncompleted being conscious of their incompletion' (Freire, 2005, 44). Humanization is a central preoccupation of humans, and thus dehumanization 'is a *distortion* of the vocation of becoming more fully human' (Freire 2005: 44), a distortion that occurs, but is not indicative of, our capacities for liberation. Assuming dehumanization is a 'historical vocation would lead either to cynicism or total despair' (Freire 2005: 44); the struggle for freedom would be, ultimately, 'meaningless' (Freire 2005: 44). This is exactly how I feel when I am told that my disabled body is not good enough to attend a protest, be a friend, care for a child, survive an apocalypse. It feels meaningless to pursue life when dehumanization is 'an historical vocation' (Freire 2005: 44).

As Anna Borges states in her piece for *The Outline*, 'I wish there was a nicer way to say this, but I don't always want to be alive' (2019, n.p.). While this may be a shocking statement for some, suicide is a constant part of my existence as a mentally ill and disabled person. In fact, I would go so far as to consider myself friendly with my suicidal ideations. Borges relates the visceral affective responses to suicide in the news, and points out that the shock, 'alarm and urgency in these sentiments gives the impression that suicidality is solely standing on the brink, inches from death, waiting desperately for someone to notice and intervene' (2019: n.p.). While this experience may be true for some people, it is also worth noting that the acute danger of active ideation overshadows discourses on suicide. Sometimes, suicidal ideation is simply 'like living in the ocean. Not as sea creatures do, native and equipped with feathery gills to dissolve oxygen [...], but alone, with an expanse of water at all sides' (Borges 2019: n.p.). She continues:

> When you live in the ocean, treading to stay afloat, you eventually get the feeling that one day, inevitably, there will be nowhere for you to go but down. [...] I know [...] that my legs will exhaust and I will slip beneath the surface, but I don't want it to be soon.
>
> (Borges 2019: n.p.)

How could I not feel this way, when I look around at the world? I am reminded of the scene in *The Road* when the Man's wife commits suicide. She does not want to live in a post-apocalyptic world. I turned to my father one night at dinner during a conversation about survival in a world like the one depicted in *The Walking Dead*. I told my father that I would, most likely, commit suicide if that were the case. 'I can barely live in this world now,' I stated. 'How could I survive in a world with zombies?'

What I often fail to recognize is that I and my disability community have already cultivated the skills for survival – and, beyond survival, *liberation* – because I have been tasked with survival by sociopolitical institutions and economic structures who do not care for me. The constant dehumanization of disabled populations at the hands of the dominant class does not account for when they need us. In reality, dehumanization eventually leads 'the oppressed to struggle against those who made them so' (Freire 2005: 44). The moment in which change is possible is liberation for both the oppressed *and* the oppressors, thus configuring the liberated oppressed as 'restorers of the humanity of both' (Freire 2005: 44).

I know these concepts theoretically, but not cognitively. Perhaps it is my anxiety that is preventing me from taking a leap of faith, from believing that there is a moment of change possible. Perhaps I do not believe that humanity can be restored; however, I do believe in taking leaps of faith over and over again. Maybe this is cruel optimism. Maybe this is the journey of humanity into the abyss of forever. I am struggling, but I am trying.

References

Bal, Mieke. (2013). 'Imaging Madness: Inter-ships'. *InPrint*, 2.1 (5): 1–15.
Berlant, Lauren. (2011). *Cruel Optimism*. Durham, NC: Duke University Press.
Borges, Anna. (2019). 'I am not always very attached to being alive'. The Outline. 2 April 2019. Available at: https://theoutline.com/post/7267/living-with-passive-suicidal-ideation.

Boym, Svetlana. (2001). *The Future of Nostalgia*. New York, NY: Basic Books.

Boym, Svetlana. (2007). 'Nostalgia and Its discontents'. *The Hedgehog Review*, 9 (2): 7–18.

Butler, Judith. (2010). 'Introduction: Precarious Life, Grievable Life'. *Frames of War: When Is Life Grievable?* London, UK: Verso.

Dyer, Hannah. (2020). 'Introduction: Childhood's Queer Intimacies and Affective Intensities'. In *The Queer Aesthetics of Childhood: Asymmetries of Innocence and the Cultural Politics of Child Development*. Camden: Rutgers University Press, pp. 1–33.

Edelman, Lee. (2004). *No Future: Queer Theory and the Death Drive*, (ed.), Michèle Aina Barale, Jonathan Goldberg, Michael Moon & Eve Kosofsky Sedgwick. Durham, NC: Duke University Press. Print.

Fournier, Lauren. (2021). *Autotheory as Feminist Practice in Art, Writing, and Criticism*. Cambridge, MA: MIT Press.

Freire, Paulo. (2000). *Pedagogy of the Oppressed*. Translated by Myra Bergman Ramos. New York, NY: Continuum.

Freire, Paulo. (2005). *The Pedagogy of the Oppressed*. Freiburg im Breisgau: Herder & Herder.

Holland, Samantha. (2002). Just not 'girly': Clothes, appearance and 'alternative' femininities. Doctoral, Sheffield Hallam University (United Kingdom). Available at: https://shura.shu.ac.uk/id/eprint/19812.

Hsu, Hua. 'Affect Theory and the New Age of Anxiety'. *The New Yorker* 25 March 2019. Web.

Mamo, Heran. 'Halsey Says Pregnancy Has "Leveled" Her Perception of Gender'. *Billboard* 19 Feb 2021. Web.

Masco, Joseph. (2008). '"Survival Is Your Business": Engineering Ruins and Affect in Nuclear America'. *Cultural Anthropology, 23* (2): 361–98.

Nelson, Maggie. (2015). *The Argonauts*. Minneapolis, MI: Greywolf Press.

Piepzna-Samarasinha, Leah Lakshmi. (2010). *Care Work: Dreaming Disability Justice*. Vancouver, BC: Arsenal Pulp Press.

Stockton, Kathryn Bond. (2009). *The Queer Child, or Growing Sideways in the Twentieth Century*. (Durham, NC: Duke University Press.

Stockton, Kathryn Bond. (2016). 'The Queer Child Now and Its Paradoxical Global Effects'. *GLQ*, 22 (4): 505–39. doi: https://doi.org/10.1215/10642684-3603186.

Trimble, S. (2019). *Undead Ends: Stories of Apocalypse*. New Brunswick, NJ: Rutgers University Press.

Chapter 11

EXPLORING EMOTIONAL VULNERABILITY IN AUTOETHNOGRAPHY: UNPACKING AND RETHINKING EVERYDAY TRAUMA

Yi-Hui Lin

Introduction

Feminist autoethnography is a vibrant intellectual practice that raises new questions, prompts novel ways of understanding social reality and offers a means to bring together various moments in daily life to develop a better understanding of gendered structural violence. Through autoethnography, I want to address a particular way of voicing vulnerability and get close to the everyday to consider not only the web of situated relations through which subjects are constituted but also the possible ways to rethink, unlearn and potentially rework them. This cannot be done with a single focus on gender. Instead, it requires attention to the multiple dimensions of identity, such as race, ethnicity, class, citizenship, immigration status and disability, which can explain the variability in people's experience, with some more likely to be at risk of marginalization at different moments in life. This presents a way to draw out the plural and temporal contexts of how structures of power are organized around intersecting categories to frame social positions of individuals and may be extended to indicate that such selves are not unchanging. In understanding intersectionality as a situated accomplishment, I further push for the idea that this way of contextualizing the complexity of everyday life, thus elucidating the background in which agency is made possible, helps to go beyond a binary thinking of domination and resistance.

My engagement with autoethnographic strategies in this chapter involved working with post-structural feminist approaches that call attention to the limitation of conceiving a stable subject as the basis for feminist politics and, by extension, perceiving vulnerability as exclusive to an identity. Instead, vulnerability should not be fixed to any one identity, but rather seen in the context in which it is being produced. In this chapter, I reflect on moments of vulnerability I experienced growing up as a first-generation Taiwanese immigrant in a working-class family in the United States in the early 2000s. To offer contextual background, I was born in Taiwan and immigrated to the United States at eight years old where I was adopted by family members living there. Much has changed since I had those experiences. I am now in my late twenties and financially independent. I also write from a position of privilege as a non-disabled, heterosexual, cisgender woman with citizenship rights in my country of residence. The reason for writing this chapter is not to highlight my own personal struggles during a vulnerable time in my life, but to make known the structural elements that allowed the situation to arise and endure.

The autoethnographic accounts presented in this chapter are grounded in memory work, which is a writing method that allows the sensory and the emotional to come to the fore, particularly when expressing views that are not easily voiced (Bryant and Bryant 2019). In writing this chapter, I engaged with memories that have troubled me for years, and in this space, I paid close attention to the emotional dimensions of trauma, its invisibility and its connection to gendered forms of power, while paying attention to the affective and corporeal dimensions of spatial and relational dynamics. Here, trauma is loosely defined as situated in the interstices of the systemic experience of everyday sexism and the effects of more discrete events, such as sexual abuse (Cvetkovich 2003), and crafting my autoethnographic stories promotes reflection on the contour of these events and their accumulated effects. Ultimately, the type of feminist intervention I hope to explore in this chapter is vital in a postfeminist era, where notions of female empowerment and autonomy sit uncomfortably alongside of the visibly growing misogyny with its assertion that any remaining inequalities are the result of 'natural differences and/or [of] women's own choices' (Gill 2017: 607). This emphasis on responsibility distracts from the power structures that enforce women's and gender minorities' position in society. In undertaking autoethnographic writing, I hope that attention to the emotional vulnerability from childhood trauma and its social specificity can (re)contextualize the violence that often goes unnoticed and challenge the assumptions and practices that enable these events to happen, while also becoming mindful of how to resist the structures at work (Ahmed 2017).

Autoethnography and its political potential for affective resistance

As a method, autoethnography seeks to describe and analyse stories of the self within larger cultural contexts, allowing for descriptions of 'concrete moments of lived experience' that generate a broader understanding of individuals' and groups' lives (Ellis 2004: 30) to emerge. An analysis starting with the quotidian provides the context for us to redefine what should be called into question, challenged and resisted. Ahmed contends that 'theory can do more the closer it gets to the skin' (Ahmed 2017: 10), thus reminding her readers that 'good' theory should be relevant to and generated from ordinary life. This is what I wish to address by writing autoethnographically through the lens of my personal experiences, locating the mundane and private matters (Enloe 2011) within broader structures of social power. Below, I have blurred the boundary between autoethnographic accounts and theory as a gesture towards achieving this (van Amsterdam 2014).

This chapter is based on my journal entries, which were written retrospectively. Journal writing was a daily morning exercise that I undertook for two months in my bedroom. The method that I turned to during the initial writing process was akin to what Ahmed (2017: 22) describes as 'memory work', which involves writing down memories of events related to experience of self-perceived violence and injustice. The freewriting routine encouraged me to follow any train of thought to see where it led. In the early stages of writing, I found myself involuntarily closing my eyes, which allowed any unconscious awareness, thoughts and feelings to come forward. At other times, I followed an iterative process of writing and revisiting, which allowed me to unearth memories that had been forgotten, while inviting new thoughts, perceptions and emotions to arise (see Elbow 1987). The 'raw data', so to speak, emerged during this stage of freewriting, and the writing-up stage consisting of going back and forth between remembering, analysing and reassembling, while also referring to feminist literature for further reflection on the issue of resistance.

Autoethnography as a writing process allows different layers of consciousness – the embodied, affective, emotional and rational – to unfold, disclosing a range of perspectives that wouldn't have otherwise been visible (Ettorre 2017). My experience with writing in first-person illustrates this point clearly. Putting words down on paper provided a level of detachment from well-worn thought patterns. However, writing in the first-person voice ensured this detachment never went too far due to its confrontational nature and direct link to the vulnerable self. It tapped into a reservoir of bodily sensations and emotions that can be best described as feelings that are closely attached to a specific moment in the past that can be re-lived when a ruminative episode is triggered. Many early writing sessions were tearful and made me feel bad for days, but a part of me stayed detached. I was curious enough to wonder what these uncontrollable tears would reveal. This level of engagement and attention to my inner thoughts were emotionally laborious but would have been challenging to connect to when writing in the third person. In crafting my own voice in the autoethnography, I did not pay equal attention to every memory that emerged when writing. Instead, I attended closely to those for which an emotion was strongly present, to make sense of the embedded tensions and contradictions that would otherwise have gone unnoticed. Drawing on Ahmed's (2014 [2004]) understanding of emotions as performative serves to broaden the analytical perspective, developing the idea of emotion and affective sensation beyond the scope of individual experiences to one that views them as an embodied experience shaped by larger structures of political, economic, social and gender relations. Thus, engagement with one's emotional reaction can offer an alternative way to engage in the complexity of power relations that structure one's lived reality. This unlocks the subversive potential present when attuning to one's feelings.

Before I delve into my narratives, it is important to consider how resistance is used here. As resistance is an effect of and a reaction to power (Brown 1995: 49), I draw on Judith Butler's notion of gender performativity to understand what resistance might mean. Butler's account of subject-formation, while not sufficiently explaining the emergence of resistance, presents a useful starting point to challenge gender as biologically given and traces possible pathways to alternatives. In her critique of gender as biologically given, she argues that there is no such thing as an authentic 'woman', which exists prior to the cultural expression of womanhood. As she observes, 'This production of sex as the pre-discursive ought to be understood as the effect of the apparatus of cultural construction designated by gender' (Butler 1990: 7). On this view, the repetition of fluid gender norms in everyday life not only acts to further root them in society but also ensures the possibility to resist normalization. Despite the subversion from within, Butler was clear that intention and will to change do not causally precede action. In other words, to expect resistance to take form as an outright refusal of norms and practices through which people come to understand themselves as distinct individuals is unrealistic. Due to the all-encompassing nature of power, Iñiguez de Heredia (2017: 17) contends that 'a trap is created' when resistance is assumed to have taken place once the 'logic of power has been subverted' and transformed. If we can move past thinking resistance as defined mainly as an intentional act against oppression or measured solely on its outcome, we will be able to trace a pattern of actions that could be directly linked to harnessing change. Consequently, I am interested in how various acts carried out by individuals in a position of symbolic subordination relate to each other and to a concept of processual resistance.

Becoming breasted

I was raised by a mother, who having experienced gender discrimination first-hand, was serious about providing both her children equal opportunity and was dedicated to raising me outside traditional gender norms in Taiwan. Throughout much of my childhood, I had short hair and wore large T-shirts. There were no pink dresses, dance classes or Barbie dolls. Even compliments on appearance, such as 'what a *pretty* little girl', were politely brushed off. Growing up, I attended the same bilingual kindergarten, private English tuition and talent classes as my brother did. My mom made it clear to everyone in the family that I was to be given exactly what he had. The result? To this day I have never thought I could not do something because of my gender. This doesn't mean, however, there aren't ways in which I am held back. This demonstrates the incoherence and fragmentation in parenting and schooling regarding gender equality. For instance, despite my mom's good intention, there were other obvious contradictions in how I was raised. One of my earliest memories that offer an account of such contradiction took place when I was five. In one warm summer evening after dinner, I sat with my family in the living room watching television. Beads of sweat lined up around my forehead, waiting to slide. I turned to my mom miserably and asked if I could take off my shirt as both my brother and dad had done. It was a simple 'No', though she said I could change into a clean shirt. Of course, I protested the unfairness of it, but she simply shrugged.

For young girls, nakedness is highly regulated in many cultures, where exposure of breasts is commonly perceived as erotic and inappropriate. The expectation to cover up is extended from women to girls and put into practice long before their bodies have fully developed. Through the habitual practice of covering up, a woman's chest is interwoven into her identity at an early age and serves as a main marker of her own bodily existence (Young 2005). Social norms concerning bodies and clothing shape gender identity and are always mediated through multifarious practices, with varying influence. Likewise in the United States, where I lived for some time, Raby (2005: 32) observed that dress codes at schools teach students that clothing indicative of 'female sexual expression is incompatible with self-respect'. The school environment and its enforcement of school rules have the tendency to make girls responsible for the sexualizing gaze of their peers and the resulting distraction caused (Neville-Shepard 2019). All of these have a lasting impact on young women's body confidence.

As soon as the weather turns warm in Taipei, my male flat mates go around the apartment half-naked. Going shirtless is how they cope with the heat. One day, I crept out of my room wearing a sports bra and gym shorts. I thought at the time that there was no one at home, but as I was making coffee, I heard a door open. I panicked. With very little time to think, I hurried out of the kitchen and escaped to the other room, where the fridge is located. I quickly flung open the fridge door, and there I hunched in the corner, rummaging for milk until the door closed again. Female bodies that do not 'correctly' inhabit a space are noticed as being out of place, which can be an uncomfortable experience. In recognizing this, women change their behaviour in anticipation of attracting unwanted attention or criticism. However, these actions ensure further entrenchment of a gendered space, where, for instance, it remains common to see male toplessness in Taiwan during the warmest season of the year. As Löw (2006: 129) observes: 'Space is effected through the organization of perceptions, in particular of glances and the body techniques corresponding to them.' This highlights the co-constructive nature of gender and space and draws attention to the spatial process through which women come to experience themselves as embodied beings in relation to gender norms.

The embarrassment and shame that women themselves feel over what they wear serve as a disciplining device and demonstrate how gendered power is spatially reproduced in everyday life, but these experiences also take shape under the influence of postfeminist ideals that depict women as free and autonomous agents. I was perplexed by this seeming contradiction. A month after the coffee break incident took place, I shared my thoughts with my flat mates, and one of them admitted that for him walking around the flat half-naked was something he had to get used to. After his reassurance, I began experimenting with how to dress to keep cool in summer. To become shamelessly comfortable in my own skin took practice as I unlearned years of conditioning through which I had become less confident. My refusal to conform to gendered ways of taking up space is a form of feminist resistance. Importantly, it needs to be recognized that this moment of exercising agency was made easier with the support I received from my flat mates, thus highlighting how we are dependent on those around us in reimagining dominant social practices.

Sensing wrongs despite a lack of words

The gender divides in political, professional and daily life compound and are compounded by forms of gender biases and structural disadvantages. To be a 'girl' is not just to be pre-defined by one's biological sex, but to be addressed in a particular way because you are recognized as one. As the previous section has identified, this can manifest in how one is approached and responded to, and it extends to issues including unequal division of household chores and caring responsibilities, and everyday sexual violence. Ahmed (2017) underlines violence as a mechanism through which young girls come to learn their place in the world. As Ahmed explains, 'Girling is enacted not only through being explicitly addressed as a girl, but in the style or mode of address. Violence too is a mode of address' (2017: 26). In the section that follows, I discuss my own experience of sexual abuse. Words like 'abuse' and 'molestation' trigger distress. My mind goes blank, but bodily responses, such as tears, quivering and the ensuing exhaustion that present, are real. Nearly fifteen years have passed, and time has turned the past trauma into a scab. It does not bleed, hurt or prickle, nor has it healed properly, and like any unhealed wound, it aches when touched. Trauma can manifest in different ways. Currently, it is less about reliving events in flashbacks, but instead experiencing a deep sense of unnamable grief.

When I was eight, I moved to Southern California in the hope of receiving a better education. I was to be looked after by distant relatives, Kim and Ian, who had moved there previously. They became my legal guardians. These kinds of arrangements are not unheard of in Taiwanese society. In this case my parents would be sending money to cover the expenses of taking care of me. Despite having family there to support me, it was not an easy move for an eight-year-old to make. Growing up as a child of adopted parents who immigrated to the United States in their early fifties was a difficult experience, fraught with economic insecurity. Some of the challenges that my adopted parents faced were precarious work employment and struggles with career adjustment and development. For example, an excessive level of state licensing requirements in hairdressing made it impossible for Kim, who had left school at thirteen, to apply for her licence, despite forty years of professional experience and licensing in another country. Running a home hairdressing business without a license left Kim's husband feeling stressed, as he feared that a neighbour would report them to law enforcement. Ian worked as a substitute school custodian on an on-call basis. Contrary to the promise of the American Dream, moving up the ladder was incredibly difficult, and he was left with no choice but to stay on a zero-hours contract until a work-related injury forced him into early retirement. Before his retirement he occasionally made a decent wage in some months, while in others his work hours entailed fewer than ten hours of employment per week. The vulnerability to unemployment due to age, race and language barriers demonstrates that social and economic mobility is not guaranteed as working hard alone does not propel a person forward. For families confronted with economic hardship, barriers to accessing aid and benefits from the government only add to their struggles. The welfare and the immigration reform acts passed in 1996 restricted non-citizens' access to welfare, such as Temporary Assistance for Needy Families (TANF), food stamps and Medicaid (Schram, 2005).

On days when Ian was not contacted for work, he would sit in his dimly lit bedroom with all the curtains drawn. These periods were accompanied by a gradual increase in volatile mood shifts, with him directing emotional and verbal abuse at the children in the family. It was terrible witnessing either my brother or one of my stepsisters becoming Ian's chosen target, receiving endless put-downs, being yelled at or belittled for the smallest mistakes. When Ian's working hours were further reduced, his behaviour eventually escalated into sexual abuse targeting only the girls in the family. The imbrication of child sexual abuse and immigrants' exposure to precarity reflects one way that the broader relations of power operate in the production of gender vulnerability. There is one event I can still vividly recall. One afternoon, I was in the front room alone with Ian. The blinds were down, and the room was dark, even though it was bright outside. I walked past him as he sat in the room watching television. The next thing I knew he put his arms around my waist and pulled me toward him. He tried to hold me close as I struggled. From the reflection in the mirror on the wall, it appeared as if he was enjoying the fight I put up – a challenge for him to crush. It was not the unwanted touch during the nightly visits – one hand running up my leg from knee to thigh and higher up – nor the violation of privacy (a man trying to look at a child's naked body as she undressed in the bathroom and showered) that stuck in my memory. It was the employment of sheer physical force, taking any control way from me, that broke me.

In response to the abusive situation, I avoided spending any time alone with Ian and minimized contact whenever possible. If I was not around, I could not be wronged. Some of the tactics that I resorted to were to stay in my bedroom, delay eating times and try my best to identify his mood to avoid outbursts. In the evenings, I would stick close to my siblings, jam the door handle with a plank of wood before going to bed and remain vigilant throughout the night. Both conscious and unconscious emotional practices, such as numbing, distancing and dissociating from the situation at home, were exercised as means of carrying on living a normal life, so much so that anger, fear and sadness were never experienced in the first place. Kim also watched out for me and would wait for Ian to fall asleep before going to sleep herself. On days when I was unable to get rides with my siblings, Kim made sure she picked me up from school. Occasionally, Ian made hair dressing appointments at the time that Kim would need to pick me up from school. To avoid this happening, she faked appointments in that time so she would always be free to get me instead of him. Due to the unpredictability of Ian's behaviour, coping strategies were engaged to smother potential tensions before they had a chance to escalate. By illustrating the mundane tactics that grow out of a toxic parent–child relationship, these accounts offer a more agentic view of children's coping behaviours, as they navigate difficult situations beyond their control.

For any young person, however, it is not easy to seek refuge elsewhere or openly acknowledge harm when the abuser is also a caregiver. This is further complicated by the intersecting forms of power relations in society. At the time, I was living in the United States as an undocumented immigrant, and I remember being told by both guardians to keep this a secret, otherwise 'I would be put into a foster home or worse, be sent back home'. Violence does not occur in isolation from other forms of vulnerability, such as age, language barriers, social isolation, fear of deportation and economic dependence on adults. The broader contexts in which violence occurs then change the experience of the abuse itself, as well as the recourse to change. For a more comprehensive understanding of oppression, Johansson and Vinthagen suggest broadening discussions of resistance to explore the 'ongoing processes of negotiation between different agents' (2016: 418). This is evident in my relationship with Kim, which was fraught with ambivalence and conflict as the years passed by. Although I was protected from Ian, when possible, Kim prioritized her marriage and reputation within the Asian community over the safety and well-being of the young girls entrusted to her. This example challenges any assumption that there is an unconditional solidarity between individuals based on their gender against an identified perpetrator and further questions the dichotomy of victim and perpetrator. It also questions the notion that there is 'an easily identifiable origin of trauma' (Cvetkovich 2003: 33). This is a point that will be addressed more in-depth in the next section.

In 2009, another family member, who moved to Belgium decades ago, reached out and invited me to stay with her family for the summer. From the very beginning of my holiday, she sat down with me and started asking questions, touching on a wide range of topics, and then digging a little deeper to those she found interesting. After weeks of talking that felt like therapy sessions, I sat in the living room deep in thought, mulling over a decision that was about to change my life. I glanced through a window to the yard under the gentle hold of the late-afternoon sun and realized that the caring family home I had come to in Belgium stood in stark contrast to my American home. Unfortunately, access to institutional assistance, such as professional counselling, was a class privilege that I could not afford, with performance of care work relegated to close friends and family. I decided I needed to uproot once again and move back to Taiwan.

Silence speaks volumes

Sexual abuse is not just a physical violation, but one that has emotional and psychological effects on a victim/survivor. Bufacchi and Gilson (2016) explain that it is beneficial to broaden the way in which we speak about sexual violence, not only as acts of physical violence but also the trauma victims suffer; for a victim does not experience violence in one defined moment, but in many and within an indeterminate timeframe in the aftermath of rape. This understanding of trauma is applicable to other forms of sexual violation, including harassment and abuse. Cvetkovich (2003: 94) identifies the sources of sexual trauma as residing beyond the narrow confines of physical violence, to including a social culture of silence and secrecy around it, which 'creates its own network of psychic wounds that far exceed' the abuse itself. Trauma is often un-representable, as the very possibility to voice is often constrained by the inability to process and project outward what is felt internally and bodily in words. There are also other reasons why the silence around abuse seems unbreakable. While feelings of shame can lead to a victim's non-disclosure, it is often the social encounters a victim/survivor experiences that play a greater role, leading to silence (Phipps 2014). In feminist scholarship, silence and invisibility have long been associated with powerlessness (Enloe 2004). By bringing silence into analytical focus, two key questions can be posed: (1) How is silence enacted; and (2) how is it productive?

To answer the first question, attention should be directed to the wider relations at the community level and family dynamics, as both can play a central role in silencing victims/survivors of abuse. Within my family, fear of shame and embarrassment over what Kim's husband had done led to her concealment. Likewise, silence is maintained by what family members choose to validate or discount, which is indicative of the unequal influence of various voices and the power differentials between family members. Within my family, Kim is highly praised for her selflessness and the sacrifices she has made for the family. At sixteen, Kim became the sole breadwinner to her four younger siblings, mother and grandmother when her father died unexpectedly. She even turned down a marriage proposal a few years later and did everything she could to provide a decent education for her brothers. Therefore, she is granted immunity from criticism. The abuse that her husband committed was largely brushed aside as bad behaviour, and the seriousness of the crime either downplayed or entirely overlooked.

When I summoned the courage to disclose the abuse, my father was almost unresponsive. He only said, 'When you discipline a dog, you look at who its owner is.' Referring to the fact that Ian's wife is too highly respected in the family to be criticized. This disregard for my experience demonstrates how silence is actively maintained and jointly sustained in different ways, which can take the form of concealment and avoidance (Scott 2019). Nevertheless, disclosure in this moment was a form of subversion, despite not leading to the change I wanted to see. In this situation, the possibility of change also began with the disruption of the status quo. Seeing my dad respond this way destroyed any notion I had of a protective father figure, which became my turning point. I realized that the source of the problem isn't only the perpetrator of violence but also the culture of silence within my family and how I had located myself within this dynamic.

In addition to understanding the enactment of silence, the second question considers how silence is productive. To quote Scott (2019: 48), silence 'has a presence, history, and form, which shapes personal and social lives'. Things that are not said, done, seen or heard can be just as hurtful, sometimes more so than present acts of verbal and physical mistreatment. This leads one to explore how the unspoken secret of abuse, though widely known, has an impact on individuals and communities. The culture of silence around sexual violence does nothing but empower perpetrators to continue abusing victims (Whittier 2016). My younger stepsister, who decided to stay in the United States, would not have had to experience what I went through, had someone done something. Child abuse is further perceived as a 'private' issue, and like many family problems, sexual abuse is often kept within the family, with the issue being quietly dealt with and very rarely involving the authorities. One possible implication of this is the failure to provide support to children in abusive situations. Even when family friends realize what has happened, it is deemed socially inappropriate for them to get involved. They may respond with silence out of a feeling of respect for boundaries, but their reactions are important to how the problem is perceived by those around them. The lack of support or insensitive reactions from close contacts outside of one's household and members within the community can lead the victim to feelings of self-doubt about the seriousness of the situation (see Ahrens 2006).

Furthermore, the social and relational processes through which silence is enacted lead to exacerbated vulnerability. Fricker (2007) uses 'hermeneutical injustice' to refer to the inability of someone to make sense of and find the words to describe an experience they have gone through. For instance, there was no one to talk to or turn to for comfort as I made sense of my experience. The lack of a safe environment to speak openly about the abuse within my family has left a serious dent that even when voicing it became possible as I got older, disclosure was unpalatable. I found it hard to talk about my experience for many reasons. Often, I did not know what to say, what appropriate words to use and how much to reveal. I was worried I would be met with negative reactions or more silence. These anxieties were reinforced by my own uncertainty about what qualifies as 'molestation', how my experience should be defined and even whether the events could be recalled with total accuracy. This trauma is thus sustained by its underlying invisibility.

It took a while until I began setting boundaries with family members who were complicit in sustaining the silence and gradually limited my contact with them. Limited contact had its benefits. I started to process past events on my own terms. Repeatedly discussing these events with those whom I had chosen to build trust with was extremely powerful. This repetition made me realize that any feelings I had were valid. These feelings are neither right nor wrong. They just are.

Conclusion: Some reflection on resistance

This chapter contributes to discussions of feminist pluralist politics and its commitment to expanding ways of defining oppression as well as presenting a fuller account of agential practices. With a focus on childhood trauma, I put forward an exploratory account on lived experiences of injustice related to class, immigration and gender, while attending to resistance as a response to it. Back argues that attention to hope and repair amid everyday experience of domination is often overshadowed by accounts of vulnerability and structural exclusion (2015: 832), but any discussion of social struggles is incomplete without considering practices of resistance. From within the context of my own story, there are, thus, several possible understandings of resistance according to its degree of engagement against everyday forms of oppressions. Resistance refers to various practices, from actively voicing a direct challenge, cultivating bodily confidence and engaging in a routine of self-help strategies to adopting non-doings and enactments of non-presence. Resistance may also involve questioning the limits of what appears to be natural and trying to go beyond them. Equally important is to recognize that the ways in which resistance is realized in daily life is neither straightforward nor coherent. For instance, not all actions have the potential to harness an immediate change nor are they a direct challenge to established cultural norms. Unfortunately, making life liveable is more than what some can afford to do at times. We should, thus, recognize the decision-making capability individuals exercise to get on with living their life. This unease with assessing what counts as 'resistance' speaks to the challenge I encountered in writing this chapter. Representing this reality of struggle without romanticizing resistance is critical; yet I became increasingly mindful that I also needed to steer clear from glamorizing strategies of self-improvement, as that comes at a cost of diverting attention away from underlying power structures.

In unpacking these experiences, autoethnography has proven to be a useful tool. To begin with, writing daily ensured that I did not leap to conclusions in the moment, but instead contemplated events in light of the 'idea, feeling, emotion or sensation that emerges' and had them develop over time (Allen and Piercy 2005: 162). Autoethnography is also an intimate practice that helps an author reconnect to their emotions. For me, this created a space for an ongoing introspection of the self. In my experience, it was easy to recognize forms of oppression but harder to identify the ways I remained complicit or was able or unable to resist. This was evident in my writing process, where early versions of this chapter focused exclusively on exploring the structural dimension of social injustice, crowding out consideration of resistance. At the same time, paying attention to injustices and refusing to let go of them is exhausting work. Taking some distance from writing allowed me to switch off and gave me the energy to take my reflection further after I was well rested. Reconnecting with my emotions, once I had the strength to, became my greatest asset in questioning unequal relations of power. I was also able to re-engage with past events through a lens that credited myself with more agency.

We live in a world where sexual trauma and ordinary violence seem to be in danger of invisibility due to the perceived divide between public and private issues, often with the latter considered inappropriate or just difficult to speak about openly. In the quest to rethink resistance within situated contexts, autoethnography as a writing method opens a collective space to reflect critically on structural violence that is embedded in the daily life of individuals from vastly different backgrounds. As a method, it also privileges and recognizes emotions and affectivity as having an important role in making sense of those lived experiences. The nuance of diverse life experiences uncovered by this method enables feminists to generate inclusive knowledge and redefine key issues in non-essentialist ways.

References

Ahmed, S. (2006). *Queer Phenomenology: Orientations, Objects, Others*. Durham, NC: Duke University Press.

Ahmed, S. (2014 [2004]). *The Cultural Politics of Emotion*. 2nd edn. Edinburgh: Edinburgh University Press.

Ahmed, S. (2017). *Living a Feminist Life*. Durham, NC: Duke University Press.

Ahrens, C. E. (2006). 'Being Silenced: The Impact of Negative Social Reactions on the Disclosure of Rape'. *American Journal of Community Psychology*, 38 (3–4): 263–74.

Allen, K. R. & Piercy, F. P. (2005). 'Feminist Autoethnography'. In Sprenkle, D. H. and Piercy, F. P. (eds.), *Research Methods in Family Therapy*. New York, NY: Guilford Press, pp. 155–69.

Ayalah, D. & Weinstock, I. J. (1980). *Breasts: Women Speak About Their Breasts and Their Lives*. London: Hutchinson.

Back, L. (2015). 'Why Everyday Life Matters: Class, Community and Making Life Livable'. *Sociology*, 49 (5): 820–36.

Brown, W. (1995). *States of Injury: Power and Freedom in Late Modernity*. Princeton, NJ: Princeton University Press.

Bryant, L. and Bryant, K. (2019). 'Memory Work'. In Liamputtong, P. (eds.) *Handbook of Research Methods in Health Social Sciences*. Singapore: Springer. https://doi.org/10.1007/978-981-10-5251-4_88. Accessed 18 May 2022.

Bufacchi, V. & Gilson, J. (2016). 'The Ripples of Violence'. *Feminist Review*, 112 (1): 27–44.

Burkett, M. & Hamilton, K. (2012). 'Postfeminist Sexual Agency: Young Women's Negotiations of Sexual Consent'. *Sexualities*, 15 (7): 815–33.

Butler, J. (1990). *Gender Trouble: Feminism and the Subversion of Identity*. New York, NY: Routledge.

Cvetkovich, A. (2003). *An Archive of Feelings: Trauma, Sexuality, and Lesbian Public Cultures*. Durham, NC: Duke University Press.

Elbow, P. (1987) 'Closing My Eyes as I Speak: An Argument for Ignoring Audience'. *National Council of Teachers of English*, 49 (1): 50–69.

Ellis, C. (2004). *The Ethnograpic I*. Walnut Creek, CA: AltaMira.

Ellis, C. and Bochner, A. (2000). 'Autoethnography, Personal Narrative, Reflexivity: Researcher as Subject'. In Denzin, N. K. and Lincoln, Y. S. (eds.), *Handbook of Qualitative Research*. Thousand Oaks, CA: Sage Publications, pp. 733–68.

Enloe, C. H. (2004). *The Curious Feminist: Searching for Women in a New Age of Empire*. Berkeley, CA: University of California Press.

Enloe, C. (2011). 'The Mundane Matters'. *International Political Sociology*, 5 (4): 447–50.

Ettorre, E. (2017). *Autoethnography as Feminist Method: Sensitising the Feminist 'I'*. London: Routledge.

Fraser, N. (1995). 'False Antitheses'. In Benhabib, S., Butler, J., Cornell, D., & Fraser, N. (eds.), *Feminist Contentions: A Philosophical Exchange*. London: Routledge, pp. 59–74.

Fricker, M. (2007). *Epistemic Injustice*. Oxford: Oxford University Press.

Gill, R. (2017). 'The Affective, Cultural, and Psychic Life of Postfeminism: A Postfeminist Sensibility 10 Years On'. *European Journal of Cultural Studies*, 20 (6): 606–26.

Hlavka, H. R. (2014). 'Normalizing Sexual Violence: Young Women Account for Harassment and Abuse'. *Gender & Society*, 28 (3): 1–22.

Iñiguez de Heredia, M. (2017). *Everyday Resistance, Peacebuilding and State-making: Insights from 'Africa's World War'*. Manchester: Manchester University Press.

Johansson, A. & Vinthagen, S. (2016) 'Dimensions of Everyday Resistance: An Analytical Framework'. *Critical Sociology*, 42 (3): 417–35.

Lloyd, M. (2005). *Beyond Identity Politics: Feminism, Power & Politics*. London: Sage Publications.

Löw, M. (2006). 'The Social Construction of Space and Gender'. *European Journal of Women's Studies*, 13 (2): 119–33.

Neville-Shepard, M. (2019). 'Disciplining the Female Student Body: Consequential Transference in Arguments for School Dress Codes'. *Women's Studies in Communication*, 42 (1): 1–20.

Phipps, A. (2014). *The Politics of the Body*. Cambridge: Polity Press.

Raby, R. (2005). 'Polite, Well-dressed, and on Time: Secondary School Conduct Codes and the Production of Docile Citizens'. *Canadian Review of Sociology and Anthropology*, 42 (1): 71–91.

Schram, S. F. (2005). 'Contextualizing Racial Disparities in American Welfare Reform: Toward a New Poverty Research'. *Perspectives on Politics*, 3 (2): 253–68. http://www.jstor.org/stable/3688029

Scott, S. (2019). *The Social Life of Nothing: Silence, Invisibility and Emptiness in Tales of Lost Experience*. New York, NY: Routledge.

Van Amsterdam, N. (2014). 'Othering the "Leaky Body". An Autoethnographic Story About Expressing Breast Milk in the Workplace'. *Culture and Organization*, 21 (3): 269–87.

Whittier, N. (2016). 'Where Are the Children? Theorizing the Missing Piece in Gendered Sexual Violence'. *Gender & Society*, 30 (1): 95–108.

Young, M. (2005). *On Female Body Experience: 'Throwing Like a Girl' and Other Essays*. Oxford: Oxford University Press.

PART III

CRITICAL PEDAGOGY AS FEMINIST INTERVENTION

.

Chapter 12

FEMINIST PRAXIS IN EXILE: A COLLABORATIVE AUTOETHNOGRAPHY

Gülden Özcan, Simten Coşar

Introduction

This work is a collaborative attempt to historicize our experience as feminist academics in neoliberal settings across three different countries (i.e. Turkey, Canada, the United States) in the last two decades. We narrate how we learned to act as women academics in certain male and nationalist and/or racialized settings in neoliberal moment(s). We refrain from victimhood accounts as well as the charm of heroic feminist stances. Our situated knowledge as feminists from different generations, with different class backgrounds and ethnic identities invite us to be alert to the assumed levelling along feminism – in singular. It also orients us to opt for a collective structural account of neoliberal academics through our experiences. We tell individual stories – not individualized, isolated ones as storytelling makes it impossible. We tell our stories in terms of our relations to the socio-economic contexts that host neoliberal universities, to our presence on neoliberal campuses, to the academic circles that we happen to join, and from which we are excluded.

Ethnographic writing and feminist autoethnography are significant sites of knowledge production that enable the subjects to share their realities as constitutive parts of broader sociopolitical structures. Behar notes that 'ethnographic work is inherently paradoxical, being "a process by which each of us confronts our respective inability to comprehend the experience of others as we recognize the absolute necessity of continuing the effort to do so"' (Brodkey in Behar 2003: 271).

Assist Prof Gülden Özcan, University of Lethbridge (Alberta, Canada); Prof Simten Coşar, Carleton University (Ontario, Canada). As this manuscript was under revision Dr Özcan passed away on 11 May 2022. She was under breast cancer treatment since April 2021. Dr Coşar returned to Turkey in July 2021. She is affiliated with Carleton University as an adjunct associate researcher until June 2023. Her MS progressed; she is starting a new medication programme. For Information about Dr Özcan: https://www.ulethbridge.ca/retired-faculty/obituaries/özcan-gülden; https://www.kudoboard.com/boards/XgYFjLCC?fbclid=IwAR1puS3LvK9oMlJAItDXquXCTKPyjm_s6GKKTzBApUs8X2DXJ9OhC7Ft54U.

We try to grapple with this paradox by telling our experiences together to make sense of our particular realities as well as the neoliberal world of truth claims. By locating ourselves through our experiences into a certain moment in the history of knowledge production we hope to bring in knowledge of immediacy to account for the meaning of neoliberal production systems in universities. Likewise, by bringing in our experiences in juxtaposition to each other we hope to bring in horizontal knowledge production as deviant form in neoliberal times (Coşar & Bektaş 2017). And finally, we refrain from two autobiographies told in dialogue, and try to keep in line with feminist collaborative autoethnography that offers the space for 'a keen understanding of what aspects of the self are the most important filters through which one perceives the world and, more particularly, the topic being studied' (Behar 1996: 13).

Engaging in autoethnography, we take risks – a popular term in neoliberal times. We risk limiting our accounts to partiality, subjectivity, cultural boundedness, which, in effect, define our narrative (Foley 2010: 474). We try to come to terms with this risk by situating our experiences into the neoliberal order of things as well as with our states of existence on the university campuses. Offering accounts of neoliberal academia that involve our experiences as constitutive elements brings in ordinary language 'to evoke the richness and complexity of everyday life' (Foley 2010: 475). Besides, ours is another example of autoethnography where 'the act of writing itself becomes a way of being and knowing' (ibid.).

In our collaborative account we try to interrogate, reflect on and theorize about the unfolding of neoliberal knowledge production patterns across twenty years. We frame the narration along (1) spaces of knowledge production; (2) means of knowledge production; (3) distribution/dissemination of knowledge and (4) contestations in everyday academic life. We believe that building our accounts and conversation on these themes helps us problematize the class-gender-race intersections in experiencing – both as teachers and as students – exploitative mechanisms in neoliberal higher education systems. We further try to observe how we have navigated the neoliberal academia without compromising collaboration, even in dire times of personal, institutional crises. Here we emphasize collaborative feminist production as interventions to male-oriented, profit-driven everyday practices in the neoliberal academia. The main argument of the paper is that feminism as praxis has always been in exile metaphorically and literally in academia, and collaborative feminist knowledge production reveals the promises of production in exile as a form of strategy for struggling against neoliberal exploitation across class-gender-race.

Spaces of production

As we are sitting across the screens at home, with voices coming from other rooms filled with family members … as we communicate via Zoom mostly in the past one and a half years, not only because we are in different countries and/or continents but because the Covid-19 pandemic never seems to give a break, we question whether we would have preferred this way of knowledge production and sharing even if it were not for the pandemic. For we have been trying to live not only through the pandemic but also with our 'disabilities' that turned out to be ever more challenging in risky times. For example, living in pandemic conditions helped Simten to come to terms with the reality of her limitations with multiple sclerosis (MS). It made it easier for her to refrain from detailing her underlying medical conditions to her colleagues at work – homework, rounds required two-hour-long bus ride in her latest visiting scholar position. It also affected her preferences when applying for jobs. In neoliberal settings this meant bending one's expectations, hopes for future work opportunities in a totally foreign country after her unintended retirement in Turkey. At one point, Simten found herself calculating the *pros and cons* in application forms, to mark the disability option. In the neoliberal ableist work settings you take one step backwards when you do that. Your academic record, accomplishments in teaching and publishing, the promises that you make are almost automatically levelled down since chronic MS pain and fatigue does not guarantee high energetic performance and consistent flexibility, leading to cost-benefit calculations in terms of workplace arrangements and time considerations. For Gülden her breast cancer diagnosis came in the midst of the pandemic, *relieving* her from the worrisome aspects of forced in-person teaching but at the same time introducing pay-cut, and probable negative effects for her future career prospects as an early career scholar. More importantly, her diagnosis coincided with an incoming burnout – incessant teaching load through summer, fall, and winter, multitasked writing processes, multitasked grant applications and intensive presentations at academic meetings and in social justice workspaces; excessive service work, ranging from graduate thesis supervision to jury membership and to union and professional organization work turning a workday into a never-ending time span. Neoliberal times ask for consumption, but first self-consumption. You happen to step in works, collaboration and cooperative projects that might suit your stance against neoliberal academic requisites. But the fine line between neoliberal elasticity and volunteer work melds in the neoliberal workspace.

There are two major spaces of academic knowledge production: institutional setting (i.e. the university) and personal setting (i.e. home and neighbourhoods). Since one can think, research, write and teach differently in a hut than in a palace, our class positions directly relate to the way we exist in the academic production processes. The institutional settings we came to occupy in the last two decades have been informed by neoliberal higher education policies in Turkey, Canada and the United States. And on another level, private institutions' and public institutions' adaptations to such policies were effective in the way we have positioned ourselves on the campuses, in administrative bodies, academic meetings, and the classrooms.

Our shifting class positions over the last two decades have also been effective in the way we bring knowledge production into our personal spaces and keep it at a distance. Over the last two decades, Simten moved from a fresh PhD to full professor and then to retired scholar, all lived in a middle class lifestyle. Gülden moved from an undergraduate to a fresh PhD from working-class background to tenure-track Assistant Professor – with emerging middle-class living standards. Our personal spaces shifted from shared study rooms, multipurpose bed-and-study rooms, shared houses, desk-searching to study rooms of our own, neighbourhood cafes so long as they were affordable in non-pandemic times, to office spaces and study-rooms of our own. Our personal spaces are also directly implicated by the institutional frameworks in which we have come to relate to knowledge production. Our experiences in private and public universities help us catch the significance of neoliberal elasticity in the differences and similarities among the private and public campuses and in classroom settings as spaces of knowledge production and sharing.

Classrooms can be considered as foreign landscapes for feminist racialized women academics from working class and marginalized ethnic backgrounds. University campuses are never meant to be spaces of existence for us; they are merely spaces of production. Briefly, starting from the moment we stepped into academic life in public and private universities we encountered maleness, Turkishness and whiteness, and (upper-)middle class credentials, required for relating to knowledge. This was so when we were questioned about the reasons behind our involvement in feminist theorizing. Likewise, we were called into *equal* working conditions with cis-male academics regardless of our share in domestic work, including care-work both at home and in some contexts in our relations with students as women academics. Neoliberal settings are seemingly welcoming to women academics – with their architectural claims where everyone can communicate with everyone, and with the claims to initiate innovative, flexible, student-centred knowledge relations one might get the illusion of inclusion. This is true also for the LGBTIQ+ academics in North America, and certainly not in Turkey. However, innovation, flexibility and communication are based on male norms, racial and class hierarchies. The inclusion works so long as non-male bodies are *oriented* (Ahmed 2007: 149–68) to male, ethnicized, racialized class standards – as well as the rhythms of working and walking through the campus, and budgets. This is clearly an almost impossible task if one does not have upper-middle-class background, hegemonic Turkishness as one's ethnic identity in Turkey and white upper-middle-class identities in North America. Thus, you fall short of communication with your peers if your budget does not let you eat regularly in the private universities' cafeterias. This most frequently relates to non-academic criteria to integrate into the academic world – eating, drinking, speaking codes that require the habitus of the upper-middle class (Bourdieu 2010 [1984]). You need to get the basic sense of drinking wine and eating ethnic dishes in North America, and mostly West European, aestheticized dishes in Turkey. Simten's ignorance of how to *aesthetically* eat a lobster – at an international meeting – and Gülden's ignorance of Asian food and inability to use chopsticks – at a Japanese restaurant as part of her job interview – are the simplest examples of the preset habitus baggage that silently separates the fit and the less fit ones in academic spaces.

The spatial constitution of naturalized inequalities in academic life is reproduced through generations. Neoliberal forms of this reproduction might be observed in the presumed scarcity of office spaces, in hierarchical placements among academics, and in the mainstreaming-as-malestreaming of gender sensitive ethics in work relations. The overlap between hierarchical placement and physical placement is evident in the unequal distribution of workspaces for graduate students and faculty. An additional inequality emerges when academics step onto campuses temporarily, as *visitors-at-risk*. Simten's visiting experiences in North American universities attest to the normalization of inegalitarian spatial distribution. One might endure almost forced sharing of space, despite safety concerns while the alternative would turn out to be a narrower, windowless, less functional office. Another example is about safety concerns of a woman graduate student who tries to avoid the traumatic implications of meeting her harasser frequently. She demands the move of his office to another floor. The administrative response turns out to reproduce the men-women, graduate student-senior faculty asymmetries: her office gets moved to another building, impairing all spatial ties with her peers.

Gülden's experience as a graduate student was about 'taking space' among white entitled graduate students who easily took or crowded the spaces physically and vocally. Racialized graduate students are so visible that they are pushed into invisibility by the forceful performance of entitled bodies and voices – they are forced into passive stance that makes it difficult to claim the space; and this is not because of personal attributes of kindness, shyness, but the reluctance of the privileged ones to hear them. Such asymmetries put the racialized academics out of space. Thus, we are more than frequently non-existent in the encounters with senior, white, male-female academics in the hallways. Racialized, gendered – *worse still* feminist – academics are not heard in the meeting rooms; their sentences are traded with the more important statements of white, male academics – so we are invited to live in a vanishing state of physical and verbal presence.

Although our voices are heard, and our bodies are well monitored in classrooms, the gendered and racialized politics of everyday academic life continues there, too. More than often, we are incited to continue with Western (Political) Theory as the Theory-as-such. Simten was questioned when she integrated feminist perspectives into her course contents in Turkey's universities. Feminist academics are constantly invited to compete with female and male peers – and in Turkey LGBTIQ+ competitors are pushed into absence – on supposedly *equal* grounds, and regardless of the inequalities they experience due to class and ethnic backgrounds – a clear difference from the liberal campuses in North America. The time spent travelling to the campus, the hurdles of poor public transportation, financial difficulties that make it impossible to own cars are treated as beside-the-point and purely personal problems. Women academics are mostly treated as (potential) mothers, with motherly tendencies. Keeping emotions at bay is a requisite as emotions are deemed contrary to the rational world of social science, but at the same time we are expected to act motherly, caring in our classrooms. Yet, we have to struggle to fulfil our actually existing mothering roles in the rather inconvenient campus settings for breast-feeding, diaper-changing, kindergarten, as well as compensations for childcare and elder-care expenses, let alone our special needs-based expenses. These aside, in North America with ESL and in Turkey in the top-ranking private universities we have to polish our accents in English in order to appeal to the urban, (upper-)middle-class student groups. In North America we are expected to tailor down our knowledge-based expectations from the students who are treated as customers and/or products-as-graduates in neoliberal higher education markets.

We work on campuses, wide or narrowed down; all in place or scattered throughout cities; old and new buildings mixed, or they are divided across neighbourhoods and/or districts. Increasingly in the past decade we come across campuses as construction sites as an attestation to neoliberal extractivist capitalism. The construction plans seem to be developed in building campuses anew rather than renovating them for accessibility. They seem to be designed for infinite construction, making the neoliberal space more debilitating for racialized feminist academics whose location is almost always insecure. In one of the campuses that we worked in Canada, the grand opening of a new fancy and costly science building was coincidentally followed by significant budgetary cuts. The new building's operating costs increased expenses only in utilities by approximately $1.5 million. In the same budget year many admin assistant positions – the majority are women – were cut and much-needed new academic hires were delayed particularly for social sciences departments. These were all translated into even more service and teaching load for racialized women faculty members and insecurity when they refused to comply with new measures.

Insecurity is amplified with disability. Disability in neoliberal times is an asset to justify the infrastructural needs of racial capitalism while the disabled are increasingly dispensed with in their *dysfunctions* for a market that calls for speed, flexibility and dissatisfaction with performance (Nguyen 2018: 1–25). Spaces of production, dominated by white male norms tend to have crippling effects for lower class, women and racialized/ethnicized academics. As academics working in North America, pandemic times brought in a seemingly autonomous existence for our racialized, gendered and disabled bodies. Autonomy here does not diverge from neoliberal prioritization of flexibility in work relations. Pandemic times offered tentative, limited opportunity spaces for coloured, disabled women academics to manipulate time – so long as they could hold their positions. Simten found it more manageable to teach, participate in meetings, attend conferences online at home. She could manage to a great extent her daily practices according to the circulation of neural pain and fatigue rather than according to the home-office time pendulum. Gülden found it unfortunate to work off-campus since she harmonized her home-office schedules by the time when the pandemic broke. She also found it fortunate to continue her academic work at home since it became easier to breastfeed her newborn.

We swing between the physical *pros* of staying and working at home and *cons* of neoliberal flexibility priorities, which risk our bodies. The pandemic state of affairs no longer asks for work–life balance aesthetics. Thus, we can navigate through our physical disabilities in the comfort of our home spaces. But we are constantly called into work overtime – reminiscent of *time-space compression*

(Harvey 1990). We recall participating in long academic discussions, critical feminist workshops, collaborative writing processes, rights-based advocacy meetings, let alone online classes. The spatial homogeneity creates the illusion that we could attend every meeting one after another. Here, feminist collegiality and friendship help us keep constant awareness of the neoliberal illusion of flexibility – of our bodies, the time and the space. One example is the biweekly meetings we had within the scope of Feminist and Queer Researchers Network, an online platform that connects feminist and queer researchers from Turkey in and outside the universities. The meetings were held to share and reflect together on our daily experiences during the pandemic. Another one is a feminist collective storytelling group that we had started before the pandemic, the Sewing Machine, which had already taken a regular course when the pandemic hit. It worked as a safe space where we turned our experiences into multidimensional narrations of imagination; we talked into the possible extensions of immediate life stories to mediated accounts of multiple characters who would meet in plots of different geographies. The way we wrote together has been a collective production process.

Means of knowledge production

Feminists step into academic workplaces as marginalized claimants to knowledge power. The marginalization of feminist knowledge takes a sharp turn when the academics are racialized and when they do not carry the established academic ethos on their (dis)abled bodies. Although class monopoly over knowledge production in the universities seems to be debilitated by the increasing peripherilization of campuses in Turkey, and by the increase in admissions of people with lower-class backgrounds to academic posts in Canada and the United States, white, male, middle- and/or upper-class assets of academic life persist. Gülden recalls the disadvantage that she was forced into by one of her professors – male, white, heterosexual – in her first year in Canada as an international ESL graduate student. Despite that she got As for written assignments, she was assessed with a B+ for the final grade since she rarely talked in the class, and since the participation portion of the final grade was only tied to participation in class discussions. This adversely affected her future academic prospects – both her PhD applications and her eligibility for grants and bursaries. She also felt it necessary to explain the B+ in one of her job applications, which required transcripts.

Peripherilization and lower-class admissions do not mean the recognition of racialized feminist voices in academic spaces. In Turkey peripherilization worked in two ways: First, more and more people from peripheral backgrounds gained access to academic professions, which had previously been populated by urban, bureaucratic, upper-middle-class people, mostly with family ties to the academic positions. Second, starting with the late 1990s an increasing number of universities were founded outside the urban centres. Racialized feminist women still must dare to speak up their claims to the male spaces in the universities.

Knowledge workers' access to the means of production is limited to the policy preferences of administrative bodies in the universities, and the broader neoliberal measures increasingly make it difficult to access required technology, library resources, accessible office and classroom spaces for academics. Feminist knowledge producers (even more so, racialized and those from the Global South) have been impacted more than others as the budget preferences challenged the need to subscribe to feminist journals, to make spaces accessible and inclusive for women, as well as to integrate feminist priorities into knowledge production processes. It is relatively recent that we could see gender studies – not feminist studies – listed among the key terms in application forms for promotion to Associate Professorship in Turkey. Likewise, working in male-dominant Political Science departments – not necessarily in terms of the number of heterosexual male staff – in most of her career, Simten had to justify the relevance of gender-related course proposals to the curriculum, as well as their particular social utility for students. She could bypass the interventions by administrators who indirectly questioned feminist interventions to History of Political Thought and Political Theory courses. She was not successful in convincing the university administrations to include subscriptions to feminist journals. Feminist knowledge remained in exile from library shelves and online databases.

Feminist knowledge is exiled to domestic spaces, spheres of non-public world in mainstream academic life. Its credits in neoliberal universities are mainly based on its capacity to attract funding – i.e. its capacity to speak to the project-based interests of the decision-makers on campuses. In a way, feminist academics are called to clean the academic houses in return of temporary budgets. They are left to arbitrary decisions of the householders on budgetary considerations. It is the Women's, Gender and Sexuality Studies (WGSS) programmes and departments that are among the first target groups to *amalgamate* in response to budget cuts, proposed by the provincial governments in Canada – certainly, overwhelming political tendencies matter in this respect: WGSS bodies are most at risk in provinces with conservative governments. Regardless of the benefits that these programmes offer to the broader society, to the campus and to other programmes they are dispensable in crisis times. Maura, one of Simten's interviewees from a public university in Ontario, Canada, notes shutdowns in women's studies programmes 'because there were not enough people' (2 November 2016). This lack of interest on the part of the students relates to the funding opportunities in the country. Another interviewee, Jay, underlines the lasting impact of 'defunding feminism' that had been started by the Harper government in 2016 (1 November 2016). There has been no major change during Trudeau's liberal government. Gülden, too, immediately experiences the sharp turn in the budget cuts during the Covid-19 pandemic under the conservative government of Alberta that target critical, interdisciplinary, feminist research and teaching programmes in the universities. Strong-Boag (2014: 207) adds to these first-hand account: '[T]he movements speaking for justice – whether feminist, Indigenous or labour – were all dismissed as "special interest" and unrepresentative of conservative "majority" supposedly represented by conservative loyalists'.

The dispensability of feminist knowledge is also related to mainstream academic language. Language as a means of knowledge production is a concern when we do not speak in the neoliberal, white, male vocabulary. The strict separation of the abstract talk from everyday language, the treatment of everyday experiences as mere data for *higher* conceptualizations and their exclusion from theoretical argumentation lock feminists into ghettos. We are called to behave ourselves when we raise the significance of racialized and gendered bodies for theorization. Gülden's experiences in critical security studies circles are telling of the racial neglect in critical research on the rise and development of national security and securitization of human existence. Insistence on the necessity to read security with an anti-racist lens is subject to silence and/or dismissal by the gate-keepers on the grounds that it cannot be abstracted (Howell & Richter-Montpetit 2020: 3–22; Lentin 2020). Likewise, our co-authored feminist intervention in reading the connection between national and social security policies in Turkey met a reviewer's masculinist denial of the relation between state violence against Kurds and the deepening economic crisis – despite the data we used to substantiate the links.

Hierarchies of knowledge speak in the vocabulary of white supremacy, colonizing the concepts that are developed from within immediate and indirect experiences, and struggles by the suppressed peoples and groups. Academic language also signifies the colonial division of intellectual labour across nation-states. The English language persists as the hegemonic scholarly language of knowledge production across the Global South. In many post-colonial settings and in countries with supposedly no colonial pasts instruction in English has been considered to mark privileged standards that bring in opportunities for upward mobility for the lower classes and international reputation for the upper classes. Academics are usually required to fulfil criteria that are associated with the high-ranking academic institutions in the Global North. Academic promotion is mostly based on publications in journals with high-impact factors in the Global North. This requires excellent command of English as one's academic writing language, and the capacity to teach in English in a country with a different official language.

Another challenge comes with grant applications. Always a matter of condensing academic research interests into marketable tasks, grant application processes exemplify the relation between free market mentality and modern universities. Neoliberal universities promoted this relation as a sine qua non for ideal academic profiles. Regardless of the sociopolitical contexts, adjusting academic language to project mentality has proved to be a constant. It takes a different effort to write down projects, emphasizing the *productivity, efficiency and manageability* of the research at hand. The language itself invites feminist academics to competition. As we *dared* to apply for a grant in Canada as a visiting professor from the Global South, and an immigrant postdoctoral researcher, we were advised to include an established, tenured, white, male academic as principal applicant. On another occasion in Turkey, Simten has participated in selection committees in the country's principal scientific research institution, TUBİTAK. The trend there is similar to other neoliberal settings: those who are well versed in free market terminology, with previous and similar research, funded by the same agencies, and with networking capacities tend to collect the fruits of the grant application processes. Inequity persists at the institutional level: the *prestigious* universities of the centre offer expert assistance to the academics in due processes. Research officers themselves are part of the neoliberalization process. The research offices in small universities of the periphery have relatively insignificant effects in the grant mechanism. Apart from the problems with pushing academic research to market-based funding search, the assessment processes are clearly subjective: claiming the objectivity of what is already subjective is one of the main venues where racialized, unequal and gendered knowledge is reproduced.

Knowledge dissemination and exchange practices

In the concluding part of the *Equity Myth* where the writers reflect on challenging the myth they explain the state of neoliberal affairs in academic worlds: 'Neoliberalism's rise has brought precarious work and an academic culture of "survival of the fittest," where fitness is defined as the productivity of those who publish in top-ranked journals and win the largest grants' (Henry et al. 2017: 300). Journals are ranked in line with their conformity to the dynamics of academic free-markets. They are ranked according to impact factors, which are determined according to the *number* of references that the articles they publish receive. We all know that referencing is more a networking asset than a thorough literature review.

Citation numbers and frequencies are correlated with the research agendas and research topics. Chosen research agendas are criticized when encountered with white academics in the Global North. Until she got her full professorship with a seemingly lifetime position at a public university in Turkey, Simten played in the rules of the game by seeking to publish in high-impact journals indexed in SSCI, and mostly, in English language. She tried to balance her academic research and writing interests with the requisites for promotion – this meant overworking, no proper vacation for years. As an early-career academic Gülden has similar overworking experiences. Only after she went on medical leave did she realize the dire conditions of overworking with almost no vacation for sixteen years. We have long explained this self-exploitative working rhythm by putting knowledge production and dissemination through academic writing into the centre of our commitment to writing in general – that it was not merely work, at all. The dynamics in the publishing sector almost turn geography into the destiny for the academics from the Global South. Unless one has access to solid networks it is hard for the academics to get their feminist theoretical works published in indexed journals of the Global North. Simten recalls reviewer notes inviting her to write less on theory more on the country she is associated with, or requesting brief historical background when discussing feminist knowledge production in Turkey *for those readers who are not knowledged about the country*. Gülden recalls resisting the expectations to do Turkey-specific research in her MA and PhD theses as she insisted on pursuing critical reading of European theory and history. These expectations echoed even right after her PhD defence. Then she was advised to develop a new research agenda involving 'Kurdish question' by a committee member after she revealed her Kurdish identity. In parallel, she receives invitations to contribute to edited volumes or journals on topics that do not directly speak to her theoretical works but which relate to Turkey. She has persisted in theoretical work, which she considered to be a means for recognition in white male-dominant academic life.

Universities as workplaces also take their share from neoliberal performance credentials. We are invited to perform ourselves as efficient producers, as abled and elastic bodies, as calculative and pragmatic minds. Feminist knowledges counter this performative frame since they rely on the immediate relation between feminist practice and theory. If understood in terms of Butler's conceptualization of performativity that resonates with Arendt's emphasis on acting together, performance is familiar for feminist vocabulary: human knowledge grows in our everyday experiences; it is not acted upon, it unfolds in acting together and it is theorized as a part of acting together (Butler 2009). But feminist academic knowledge is not immune to neoliberal infusion. This is observable when, for example, Simten refrained from sharing her ongoing research with her colleagues until it was out. Likewise, publishing in *credible* journals and in works by *credited editors* and publishing houses never seemed enough. Although she was involved in critical reading of neoliberal order of things, she could not refrain from the temptation to be present and visible, almost taking no break from work. For a long time she internalized the contention that writing offers a relaxing space in managing everyday difficulties – personal and professional. It was not too difficult to integrate academic writing into this relaxing space. It is no coincidence that she could distance to neoliberal performativity after her somewhat forced retirement from the university, and when she has performed as a visiting academic for five years in North.

Bringing feminist knowledge into the classroom always meets male challenges in different cultural contexts. In Turkey this might mean speaking ideology and depriving students of *true* knowledge. In the United States, except for women's/gender/sexuality studies programmes and depending on the state and the university it might mean men-hating discourse, potential discrimination against anti- and/or non-feminists and/or as Simten was told in response to a mid-term course evaluation that she voluntarily handed to a multidisciplinary classroom in a Feminist Political Thought course, it might mean 'preaching', not 'teaching'. In Canada it might mean repetitive talk on men's aggressiveness, women's victimhood and/or a set of memorizable inequality patterns that gives students free hand to bypass free-thinking. This is one of the main reasons why Simten for a long time evaded claiming feminist identity in the classroom in Turkey, while teaching feminist knowledge without naming it. Doing so might help one to go around possible patriarchal intrusions into the classroom dynamics for some time. This preference ties to hooks's distinction between teaching feminist theory in the abstract and sharing feminist theory in everyday conversation. As hooks underlines, 'theoretical talk emerges from the concrete, from my efforts to make sense of everyday life experiences, from my efforts to intervene critically in my life and the lives of others' (hooks 1994: 70). Gülden depicts her most problematic experiences in teaching in Canada in relation to Middle Eastern men. She connects this to their stance vis-a-vis white women academics whom they stand at a distance in terms of identity, and whose superiority in knowledge they find easier to accept. We are called into negotiations between presumed identities, derived from our skin colours, ethnic backgrounds, accents and geographical pasts on the one hand, and our knowledge and the way we produce and share it on the other hand. We do not dismiss our pasts; we wear them as sites of our experiences against racial assumptions. Feminist knowledge helps here.

In conclusion: Contestations in everyday academic life

Neoliberal knowledge production processes are not identical across countries, states and provinces. The discourses might be similar, the academic criteria might be the same and the spatial constructions of neoliberal knowledge regimes might overlap. However, the ways they are experienced differ. In all cases, the exploitative mechanism persists along class, gender and racial dimensions. Thus, our accounts are not exceptional; they represent systematic unfolding of neoliberal management on university sites. They represent the ideal-typical academic identities, and their possible implications in everyday academic lives. In this respect, they affect our academic prospects, our career plans and the way we write and speak.

The way we write and speak as well as the way we relate to each other on academic planes also give hints for developing alternatives and counter-dispositions. Alternatives emerge as we navigate neoliberal academia. This means more manipulating the neoliberal order of things than challenging it all at once. We tend to walk on a tightrope between individual performances through our works and our feminist considerations for collaborative work. This comes in with serial publications on the one hand and compromises from our times and spaces outside the work life, and mostly staking our health. Manipulation works relatively easily when it comes to benefiting marginalized students and early-career academics.

Feminist conversations help us explore ways and means to challenge the patriarchal intrusions into our syllabi, teaching styles and contents of lectures. We share observations of each other's works, and daily encounters on campuses and especially in and with administrative bodies are functional in getting to know the multiplicity of patriarchal hurdles, which await feminist knowledge production and the risks of integration into neoliberal discursive practices. Non-white, critical feminist knowledge production offers the grounds for countering extensions of colonial knowledge in post-colonial times: it enables feminist writing that reveals the hidden inequalities in the supposedly balanced meritocracy of the academic world. It turns upside down the separation between theory and practice by substantiating the inseparability of the two. It presents multiple examples of the exploitative unfolding of white, male, colonial knowledge through centuries.

As feminist academics we experience the radical implications of feminist solidarity that works against racist, class-based, patriarchal knowledge patterns. This, we could do to a certain degree, frequently having to adjust to neoliberal academic life through marketing our products, our knowledge, language and teaching skills. In classes, we search for ways to bypass male means of assessment by bringing in alternative forms of participation that consider the possibility of silence as comfort zones for vulnerable students and, thus, that do not necessarily ask for leading roles, or aggressive in-class performance.

Writing does not have to be a solitary activity; it does not have to be practised in 'a room of one's own'. Our writing processes are always a matter of fine-tuning. Co-writing and writing in any place offer spaces for contestation (Anzaldua 2015[1980]). We tend to produce collaborative texts that merge different planes of everyday life in feminist knowledge: collective story writing (Sewing Machine collective), feminist journal publishing (*Feminist Asylum: A Journal of Critical Interventions*). In all the examples, we learn and create together. These acts are not limited to the texts that come out of the writing process, but they speak into our academic engagements at every level.

Feminist knowledge is knowledge in exile. If exile means one's forced distancing from the lands that she was born into and grown, if it means forced dissociation from the lands where she accidentally comes to exist and grows into being, then it would be apt to locate feminist knowledge in exile in the broader modern knowledge systems. If exile connotes new territorial boundaries, new identity claims and new contradictions in one's claims to rights – void and potential – then feminist knowledge can aptly be situated as knowledge in exile: pushing the borders, staking them and established identities, but at the same time searching for established identities, a place secured in existing borders.

References

Ahmed, S. (2007). 'A Phenomenology of Whiteness'. *Feminist Theory*, 8 (2): 149–68.

Anzaldúa, G. (2015[1980]). 'Speaking In Tongues: A Letter To 3rd World Women Writers', In C. Moraga & G. Anzaldúa (eds.), *This Bridge Called My Back: Writings by Radical Women of Color*. New York: State University of New York Press, pp. 163–72.

Behar, R. (1996). *The Vulnerable Observer: Anthropology that Breaks your Heart*. Boston, MA: Beacon Press.

Behar, R. (2003). *Translated Woman: Crossing the Border with Esperanza's Story*. Boston, MA: Beacon Press.

Bourdieu, Pierre. (2010 [1984]). *Distinction: A Social Critique of the Judgement of Taste*. Translated by Richard Nice. London and New York: Routledge.

Butler, J. (2009). 'Performativity, Precarity, Sexual Politics'. *AIBR*, 4 (3): i–xiii.

Coşar, S. & Bektaş-Ata, L. (2017). 'Modernin Distopyası: Neoliberal Akademiyi Birlikte Oto-Etnografiyle Anlamak' (The Dystopia of the Modern: Understanding the Neoliberal Academia Through Collaborative Autoethnography), *Doğu Batı*, (80): 73–94.

Foley, D. E. (2010). 'Critical Ethnography: The Reflexive Turn'. *International Journal of Qualitative Studies in Education*, 15 (4): 469–90.

Harvey, D. (1990). *The Condition of Postmodernity: An Inquiry Into the Origins of Cultural Change*. Cambridge and Oxford: Blackwell Publishing.

Henry, F., Dua, E., James, C. E., Kobayashi, A., Li, P., Ramos, H., Smith, M. S. (2017). *The Equity Myth: Racialization and Indigeneity at Canadian Universities*. Vancouver: UBC Press.

hooks, b. (1994). *Teaching to Transgress: Education as the Practice of Freedom*. New York and London: Routledge.

Howell, A. & Melanie Richter-Montpetit, M. (2020) 'Is Securitization Theory Racist? Civilizationism, Methodological Whiteness, and Antiblack Thought in the Copenhagen School'. *Security Dialogue*, 51 (1): 3–22.

Lentin, A. (2020). *Why Race Still Matters?* Cambridge, UK: Polity Press.

Nguyen, X. T. (2018). 'Critical Disability Studies at the Edge of Global Development: Why Do We Need to Engage with Southern Theory?'. *Canadian Journal of Disability Studies*, 7 (1): 1–25.

Strong-Boag, V. (2014). 'Limiting Identities: The Conservative Attack on History and Feminist Claims to Equality'. Forum: History Under Harper, *Labour*, 73: 206–9.

Chapter 13

CONFRONTING CONTRADICTIONS, CHASING
A FEELING: 'WITCHY', FEMINIST PANDEMIC
TEACHING AS A SPIRITUAL ACTIVISM

Kascindra Shewan

Introduction

In the spring of 2020, during the first of many public health mandated quarantines, I submitted a proposal to teach an undergraduate Gender Studies course at a Southwestern Ontario university titled 'Witchin': Intersectional Investigations into Witchcraft and Occult Practices'. Delivered virtually during the winter term of 2021, I discovered with students how understandings of 'the witch' – a complex and shifting figure, archetype and/or identity – could be enriched through the employment of intersectionality as a theory and practice. When conceiving the course, I had hopes that an exploration of a magical and multifaceted topic would facilitate opportunities for play, enthusiastic and energetic enquiry, and development of a feminist communal learning experience amid the solemnness of/produced by the pandemic. While post-delivery conversations with students, course evaluations and personal reflection revealed that the course met at least some of those early aspirational aims, this chapter is more interested in what I did not anticipate when preparing for this course. Namely, the important role that the class content and discussions would play in helping me to address my burgeoning 'crisis of faith' regarding the possibilities of 'feminist academic activism' to enact meaningful change within and outside of the neoliberal university (Deschner, Dorion & Salvatori 2020).

In this piece, I employ feminist autoethnography as a method to explore my professional and personal feminist identities are evolving through the relational praxis of spiritual activism as envisioned by Chicana/Latina, and Black feminist scholars (Anzaldua 1999; 2002a; 2002b; brown 2017; Keating 2005; 2008; Peréz & Saavedra 2020), social work research (Sheridan 2012) and academic feminist theory (Shotwell 2016). More specifically, I trace how my initiation and practice of spiritual activism during 'Witchin' helped me make sense of the seemingly senseless thoughts, feelings, experiences and actions characterizing my experience of the Covid-19 pandemic as a precarious academic worker. I posit that spiritual activism accomplishes this via its promotion of a relational, non-binaristic model of thinking-feeling that encourages me/its practitioners to reimagine opposition and contradiction as something with which to engage instead of working against (Peréz and Saavedra 2020). Crucially, then, spiritual activism is figured as both a performative methodology and an object of analysis in this chapter; as I elaborate upon what spiritual activism is (its epistemological roots) and what it can do (its possibilities, its limitations) in relation to healing traumas related to crisis and uncertainty, I also explore its more general invitation 'to shift perspectives and adopt a much broader – though inevitably partial – point of view' (Keating 2005: 249). With respect to the latter point, I posit that spiritual activism is useful in mediating dominant understandings of, or approaches to, feminism(s) 'as critique/fighting against' with understandings of or approaches to feminism(s) as 'appreciation' or 'a fight for' (brown 2017: 165; Peréz & Saavedra 2020: 133).

Spiritual activism: Seeking opposition with which to engage

'Spiritual activism' is a popular term employed by a variety of knowledge producers (i.e. academics, activists, religio-spiritual workers/leaders) in as many contexts (Keating 2005: 253; Keating 2008: 67). However, the understanding of spiritual activism that inspires my praxis derives from Gloria Anzaldúa's work on geopolitical, metaphoric and identitarian borders (1999; 2002a), including how the term has been analysed and mobilized by Chicana and Black Feminist scholars (Keating 2005; 2008; Pérez & Saavedra 2020). Given that Anzaldúa's notion of spiritual activism developed over decades through various texts, I rely on Anzaldúa's friend and biographer AnaLouise Keating's succinct definition to inform my understandings and praxis. Keating (2005: 242) explains,

> spiritual activism is a visionary, experientially-based epistemology and ethics, a way of life and a call to action. At the epistemological level, spiritual activism posits a metaphysics of interconnectedness and employs nonbinary models of thinking. At the ethical level, spiritual activism includes specific actions designed to challenge individual and systemic racism, sexism, homophobia and other forms of social injustice. Spiritual activism is spirituality for social change, spirituality that recognizes the many differences among us yet insists on our commonalities and uses these commonalities as catalysts for transformation.

Spiritual activism, then, has two interrelated dimensions. On one hand, it values embodied ways of knowing that are rooted in recognition/honouring of connections/dependencies – 'spirit/energy/consciousness' – that unites all human and non-human beings and entities (Keating 2005: 242). This relational epistemology is linked to spiritual activism's second component: a commitment to attempting to understand the world in ways that avoid dualisms, most notably pre-existing identity categories such as (but not limited to) race, gender, sexuality, class and ability. Crucially, this is not a call to ignore difference or diversity, nor does spiritual activism attempt to deprioritize the need for identity categories and politics for specific kinds of political or material goals. Rather, spiritual activism puts forth an invitation to consider similarities across difference to make new alliances and/or coalitions (Keating 2005: 247). Spiritual activism also calls on its practitioners to apply these epistemologies in service of social justice work – in whatever form that may take. Put simply, and to quote Anzaldúa directly, spiritual activism calls for 'inner works [changes in the way the self comes to know], public acts [social activism]' (2002b: 572); it rests on the scientifically documented premise that thoughts impact matter (McTaggart 2007) and thus aims to bring attention to the inner/individual dimensions of social justice work.

I perceive clear connections between spiritual activism (the object of this chapter) and feminist autoethnography (the subject of this anthology and the methodology of this chapter). Indeed, that Anzaldúa herself, as well as other Chicana and Black feminist scholars writing on spiritual activism, uses feminist autoethnography to articulate their conceptualizations of the spiritual praxis suggests continuities (Lara 2005; Pérez & Saavedra 2020). Like spiritual activism, feminist autoethnography posits the value of a turn inwards – what Elizabeth Ettorre terms 'theorizing the self' – towards 'connecting personal (insider) experience, insights and knowledge to larger (relational, cultural, political), conversations, contexts and conventions' (2016: 14). Inner works, public acts. What is more, both spiritual activism and feminist autoethnography encourage the disruption of prearranged 'paths of knowing' (Ettorre 2016: 14), and posit the value of their aspirational, but uncertain, projects of employing these modalities towards producing more just, less violent worlds. For me, these connections make feminist autoethnography a particularly well-suited methodology for exploring my relationship with spiritual activism because feminist autoethnography as method allows me to perform spiritual activism.

This, however, is a project with many risks, and without guarantees. Like spiritual activism, feminist autoethnography garners criticisms for being a potentially self-glorifying, naval-gazing activity that risks promoting problematic ideologies like possessive individualism and/or essentialist thinking (Ettorre 2016: 8, 14; Keating 2008: 58). I also suspect that combining these two theories/practices compounds the potential for a narcissistic solipsism that ignores or is inattentive to broader structural phenomena. For example, I feel a tension between wanting to give credit to and share the important knowledge of women of colour scholars writing from a spiritual perspective that inspires me and helps me heal, but also have concerns about what it means to employ these theories/practices in service of narrativizing a white woman's experiences in an academic context that is often hostile to the experiences and perspectives of trans and cis women, racialized scholars (Johnson 2020). Spiritual activism itself, however, invites me to understand this tension as something to be worked with, rather than something that needs to be avoided, or argued away. It is still possible to talk about and bring attention to potential representational problematics of this work, while also acknowledging, as Leela Fernandes does, that identity-based deployments of Chicana, Latina and Black feminist works on spiritual activism limit the 'depth' of the theory/practice's 'vision'

(2003: 10). In doing so, with Anzaldúa, I choose to 'inhabit the contradiction' of 'personal agency and structural determinacy' that I believe is required to work on social justice issues in ways that work to reimagine 'walls as doorways' (Keating 2005: 59; 2008: 246). Both spiritual activism and feminist autoethnography ask me to enter the messy, complicated space of sitting in/with the idea of my own implicatedness in the very systems and structures I work against. I believe this risky project contributes to both the weakness, as critics have acknowledged, and the strengths of spiritual activism and feminist autoethnography.

A messed up situation: Personal reflections on living with/through Covid-19

The first confirmed case of Covid-19 in Canada – which also happens to be the first confirmed case in my home province of Ontario – was announced on 25 January 2020. At the time, I was a newly minted PhD graduate working as a sessional instructor in a Gender Studies Department and as an editor/researcher at a higher education research firm. Less than two months after the first confirmed case of Covid-19, the Government of Ontario issued a state of emergency as cases began to surge, overwhelming an understaffed and underfunded public health system. With this announcement came the closure of recreation programmes, libraries, public and private schools, day cares, churches and other faith settings, as well as bars and restaurants (limited to takeout or delivery options only). Provincial parks and municipal playgrounds followed, and long-term care residences went into lockdown (no visitors; residents cannot leave for outings). The news was flooded with daily announcements and recommendations from political leaders and public health officials. Stay home; limit contact to members of your immediate household was the message that was repeated to us. Follow these orders, officials told us, and we will be 'back to normal' in no time.

As I write this chapter nearly two years later, after traversing numerous lockdowns, re-openings and the development and rollout of the Covid-19 vaccine, Ontario is once more in another 'lockdown' due to the pressure the Omicron variant is putting on a public health care system that continues to deteriorate. This current reality makes it difficult – for a myriad of reasons – to write about what happened (the traumas) during the beginning of the pandemic (March–June 2020). So much has happened; it was and is overwhelming. There was/is loss (of lives, relationships, aspirations and experiences), economic instability (job loss, exploitation, housing crises) and disconnection (literal isolation but also the vast difference in pandemic experiences/traumas). However, there are some unique and important events that characterized my early experience of the pandemic.

The class I was teaching (the first one I had designed from scratch) shifted online, as well as my alternative-academic editor/researcher job. This ability to work from home is an immense privilege in many ways given that others deemed 'frontline workers' – such as my mother, a grocery store cashier/manager, and partner, then acting as an internet services technician – were required to labour with the general public despite the threat of the virus as they provided essential services. Working from home, however, posed other kinds of challenges. I learned to teach online for the first time with no experience or training. At my editor/researcher job, my wage was illegally decreased by $5/hour within three weeks of the lockdown notice, even as my responsibilities/duties and hours of work increased. There were also personal challenges during this time. For example, my family and I struggled to find my grandmother a spot in a government-funded long-term care facility as we could no longer afford her care at her private long-term care residence. Once accepted and moved into one such facility – a challenge in and of itself because of strict public health measures – she contracted Covid-19. It was incredibly difficult not being able to support her in person as she battled the virus in the pre-vaccine period. Perhaps obviously, my own pre-existing mental wellness challenges were also exacerbated at this time as I had suddenly regressed back to the lonely work-from-home environment that I had left only months earlier and was suddenly without a primary care physician following her announcement of retirement.

It was sometime amid these events during the first eight weeks of the pandemic that I began to acknowledge and speak what I was then terming 'a crisis of faith'. Although I was raised within a Christian household, around the age of eighteen feminisms became more than just political projects, but spiritual ones that helped me understand my 'purpose'. Feminisms helped me develop and articulate my raison d'être, my vocation in life as someone dedicated to building more equitable, just worlds for all by working with others to address experiences of marginalization and oppression. I manifested these beliefs in my professional life (my work on sexualized violence prevention) and everyday interactions. These working beliefs often took the form of attempting to suss out which kinds of privileges ought not to be privileges, but givens, and working towards ensuring that necessary conditions for thriving (and not *just* surviving) are extended to all. A hefty project even in the best of times, my overindulgence in news and social media that reported on or speculated about increases in gender-based violence, issues in food/job/housing security and all sorts of wellness challenges amid the pandemic began to wear down any optimism I had about building different, more equitable worlds. Populations that are made to be marginal (some that I was a part of and/or working with/for in the spirit of solidarity) were – unsurprisingly – being unduly impacted by the pandemic and resulting public health measures. I found myself increasingly buying into the idea that there was no hope for change: if we – feminists, persons invested in imagining and realizing more just worlds – could not figure out solutions to some of these problems before the virus, how were we going to do so during and after the pandemic which seemed – from preliminary scholarly and news media accounts – exacerbating these issues?

Interestingly, those despondent and anxious thoughts frequently turned inward. I worried that I was no better than people/communities/policies I was becoming so critical of, feeling-thinking so sorry for myself and my own situation when there were so many others living through more challenging circumstances. I became resistant to optimism, seemingly only able to perceive problems and challenges. I was, as Elena Trivelli so usefully puts it, 'feeling bad about feeling bad' (2014: 163). I was overwhelmed and underwhelmed. Wired and exhausted. Always on, 'plugged-in' into what was happening 'out there' with the virus, while never feeling so disconnected from my communities as I rarely left my home. Feminism(s) no longer felt like grounding belief systems, but more like a collection of naïve aspirational projects disconnected from the harsh realities and uncertainty of the crisis of the present.

The stories we tell ourselves: A crisis of faith or burnout?

In his work on spiritual activism, Michael J. Sheridan describes 'the twin perils' that social activists commonly experience: burnout and polarization. Burnout refers to individual experiences of 'physical, mental, emotional, and spiritual exhaustion' that can develop when efforts to address social justice issues are prioritized over 'important areas of self-care'. Sheridan notes that burnout can also be a result of internal conflicts or contradictions, as well as the secondary or vicarious trauma of witnessing social injustice (2012: 194). The second peril, polarization, occurs more so on the societal or interpersonal level, and refers to when a social issue becomes something akin to an 'us versus them' struggle that overshadows a capacity for 'mutual understanding' (Sheridan 2012: 194).

Sheridan's work provides a useful framework for making sense of my early pandemic experiences in a manner that challenges a neoliberal tendency towards individual over-responsibilization and leaves space for the possibility of personal agency amid systemic and/or structural factors. Indeed, even as I can perceive ways to enact individual resistance to feelings of despondency (i.e. therapy), Sheridan's work suggests that this is a project that is fundamentally in relation to broader sociocultural and political happenings. This latter point about the sociocultural factors that can contribute to burnout and polarization in social justice work is especially salient given the immediate activist context that preceded and continues to unfold during the pandemic (i.e. #MeToo, Black Lives Matter, Every Child Matters). Indeed, scholars are beginning to analyse and discuss how coverage of these activist movements and responses to Covid-19 in news and social media tended towards intense, passionate and often polarizing discourses that permeated everyday life for many in ways different from before these movements and the pandemic (Merkley et al. 2020). As Peter R. Grant and Heather J. Smith (2021: 297) further explain,

> the virus elicits widespread negative emotions which are spread contagiously through social media due to increased social isolation caused by shelter-in-place directives. When an incident occurs which highlights systemic injustices, the prevailing negative emotional climate intensifies anger at these injustices as well as other emotions.

Grant and Smith go on to argue that on top of the negative emotions that 'everyone experiences' during a pandemic, 'disadvantaged groups are likely' to experience negative emotions that are 'more frequent and severe' (2021: 300). Thus, they posit that 'the negativity created by the pandemic may amplify the anger and resentment of activists who claim that social disparities are disproportionately affecting the health and economic well-being of their disadvantaged group' (Grant and Smith 2021: 300).

This observation is especially important given that what Sheridan argues underpins the aforementioned 'twin perils' of social activist work (burnout and polarization) is righteous anger and moral outrage. For Sheridan, while both righteous anger and moral outrage can be useful in catalysing involvement in social activism, they 'do not often provide sufficient fuel for the long haul', and 'only lead to reactive anger, setting in place a cycle of hostilities that is sure to erupt at some point in the future' (Sheridan 2012: 194). Instead, Sheridan suggests a more sustainable to approach to social activism is one rooted in spirituality (Sheridan 2012: 195).

Based on these works, I suspect that at least part of my aforementioned 'crisis of faith' with feminisms that emerged during the early pandemic could be attributed to a form of burnout amplified by the unique challenges of the pandemic. Moreover, it is possible that my 'crisis of faith' with feminisms during this time was or is a shared experience – shared in the sense that other social activists have experienced what I felt, and shared in the sense I alone do not bear the responsibility for ugly thoughts/feelings (i.e. this is not simply an individual mental wellness challenge). My 'crisis of faith' might be thus attributable to something other than 'personal deficiencies' or an inevitable product of a world in crisis; while I might exist/think/feel/act in physical isolation from others, I am still existing/thinking/feeling/acting with others.

I'm not helpless: Teaching as spiritual activism

When my sessional teaching contract ended in late April 2020, I first experienced relief (I/we did it!), and then a keen feeling of loss. Without my daily interactions with students, I became (even more) lonely, hopeless and longed for feelings of community, support and solidarity that undergirded the small feminist learning community that developed in that recent course. I thus found myself craving some sort of guidance, and began engaging more intensively with my occult beliefs and practices (i.e. astrology, forms of divination, beliefs about 'spirit(s)') to help me become reoriented during this trying time. Most importantly, I was turning my passing interest in Tarot card reading into a daily practice to provide some sort of object of focus or clarity during a time when so many negative situations and happenings were competing for my attention.

During my daily Tarot reading sessions, I became increasingly fascinated with both the cards themselves and how the practice of 'reading' worked. For those unfamiliar, images on Tarot cards are rife with tensions and contradictions, something apparent even in generalized considerations of the cards themselves. They depict familiar situations and archetypal characters, but their meaning is ambiguous and contingent upon a variety of factors, including the mood/mentality of the reader, the knowledges and experiences they bring to a reading, and the position of the card (upright, reversed and/or within a spread). Interacting with the cards daily, a couple things occurred to me. For one, the cards reminded me of a lesson I learned from Feminist Standpoint Theory: the importance of perspective and position to knowledge production. When engaging with the cards, I was reminded that there were more interpretative possibilities than any one person can perceive on their own. What is more, because the cards are archetypal in nature, they reminded me of the participatory nature of knowledge production, that even though we can and often do talk about individual ideas and thoughts, these ideas and thoughts are contingent upon those that came before us.

From these daily interactions, I began to realize that Tarot – and many other 'witchy' practices – had obvious connections to feminisms as recognized by other scholars and activists had before me (Salomonsen 2002; Sollée 2017). I perceived these connections not only in terms of a relatively modern up taking of the figure/archetype/identity of the witch in feminist activism (i.e. the efforts of organizations like W.I.T.C.H. – Women's International Terrorist Conspiracy from Hell), but also in the ways such mobilizations of the figure/identity/archetype of the witch inhabitant a contradictory, liminal space that feminisms also seem to occupy. For example, the witch can be a colonizer, uncritically appropriating the beliefs and practices of marginalized communities which she does not belong; but she can also be a resistant figure, employing ancestral beliefs and practices to strengthen and support communities that continue to suffer due to colonial regimes and mentalities. Feminisms – academic or otherwise – can function in much the same ways: they can be sites of extraction and exploitation of knowledge from particular communities put in service for causes that do not feed back into such communities in meaningful ways; but they can also be a means to articulate, analyse, explore and validate marginalized experiences and positionalities. Out of these realizations regarding the interconnections between feminisms and 'the witch', the idea for 'Witchin' was born: a course that employed one of academic feminisms' most popular theories/practices, intersectionality, to study 'the witch'.

Persevering in the face of despair: Developing Witchin'

In her book of the same title, adrienne maree brown articulates her idea of 'emergent strategy', or how activists can best collaborate and shape change (2017: 1). According to brown (2017: 23), emergent strategies describe

> ways for humans to practice being in right relationship to our home and each other, to practice complexity, and grow a compelling future together through relatively simple interactions. Emergent strategy is how we intentionally change in ways that grow our capacity to embody the just and liberated worlds we long for.

Key to brown's concept of emergent strategy is an awareness of the fundamental interconnectedness of all beings: 'the health of the cell is the health of the species and the planet' (2017: 15). Thus, and not unlike spiritual activism, brown suggests we might think about how social justice issues can be addressed by paying attention to interconnectivity or relationality (brown 2017: 23). For example, she advocates for the usefulness of organizing social justice activism like fractals (complex patterns that are self-similar across different scales). In social activist work, emulating fractals would mean, 'practising at a small scale what we most want to see at the universal level' (brown 2017: 22).

When I designed and delivered 'Witchin", I now understand that I was enacting a form of emergent strategy. The course was the way I was able to begin to practice what I wanted to see happen at a larger level (aspirational feminist coalitional work) at a smaller scale (an online undergraduate classroom). Addressing one of my most troubling pandemic experiences – my struggle to accept the contradictions of feminisms during a time of great uncertainty – the course functioned as a means to transform these sticky crestfallen thoughts/feelings into objects of curiosity. Critically, the figure of the witch was essential to this transformation as they facilitated much needed distance from the immediate and personal contexts of how feminisms seemed to be failing me/us during the pandemic; the witch also connected these immediate challenges to those of feminists past and present who, as Valerie Renegar and Stacey Sowards explain, 'have often utilized contradictions as a way to navigate through a world that does not necessarily accommodate their values or rhetorical practices' (2009: 3).

While preparing for even delivering the course, however, I had a lot of concerns. I was no 'witch expert', at least not in the academic sense. For the last six years my research had most ardently been focusing on sexualized violence prevention. And even if I tried to quell and curb my feelings of ineptitude by foregrounding feminist, queer, socialist and anti-colonial theories in this course, I was concerned that out of ignorance I may produce some kind of unintentional harm: maybe an oversight on the syllabus, or maybe in a class discussion that veered outside of my sphere of knowledge. Additionally, I recognized that to propose to teach an online Gender Studies course during a global pandemic on a topic so as seemingly frivolous as witches was a risk. It was a risk because within the current neoliberal postsecondary education system learning is largely regarded as utilitarian (how will this help students [or myself] to get a job?) (Rustin 2016). And while I do not believe that all learning outcomes can be predetermined, as a working-class first-generation university student I understand first-hand the difficulties of translating less-specific educational training (i.e. non-professional degrees) into a means of sustenance (employment).

Despite these worries, I persisted with my idea for the course not because I suddenly felt secure in my knowledge and/or my ability to lead, and not because I had carefully crafted a term-long assignment (a critical digital class archive) that I hoped would address administrators' and students' potential uneasiness with enrolling in a course with no clear or easily discerned professional outcomes. Rather, I proceeded with the course because:

– I felt I had to: at this point I was preparing to quit my editor/research job because there was still no plan to reinstate my wages, and I was looking for a temporary employment until I could figure out my broader career plans.

- I thought it might help me (and potentially even some of the students in the
  course) find some footing – intellectual, emotional, or perhaps even spiritual –
  amid the challenges of the pandemic by focusing on a topic that brought
  together ideas of powerlessness and empowerment towards imagining
  different ways of navigating our world(s).
- I thought it would be fun during a time when it seemed like not much fun was
  being had.

I was, in so many ways, chasing a feeling, the feeling that there were indeed
other ways of living the pandemic, and if I wanted them to pursue them, it was
likely that I was going to have to try building them myself.

Against purity: Collective coalitional responses

Part of the challenge of a personal or spiritual feminism praxis for me is its
intersection with my professional life and means of material sustenance.
Specifically, I am thinking about how 'doing feminisms' in the context of the
neoliberal academy is difficult because feminisms call on us to make mistakes
and learn from them as we strive for new and better worlds (Halberstam 2011),
while the neoliberal academy is still quite invested in discourses of mastery and
the continual production of high-impact scholarship (Johnson 2020; Rustin 2016).
I believe it is this particular tension that causes me to frequently buy into the idea/
ideal of what Alexis Shotwell terms 'purity politics' (2017: n.p.). According to
Shotwell, purity politics is a term that refers to the belief that in maintaining one's
personal innocence or goodness in relation to any number of social justice issues
(i.e. climate change, systemic racism, fast fashion) is the best and most morally
correct political philosophy (2016: 5–6; 2017: n.p.). However, Shotwell argues that
personal purity is a 'simultaneously inadequate, impossible, and [thus] politically
dangerous for shared projects of living on earth' (2017: n.p.). Firstly, because we
are often, if not always, already implicated in unjust phenomena, aiming for the
impossible position of personal purity could discourage participation in social
justice or activist work before one even begins. Secondly, in focusing on one's
individual actions and implicatedness, one is less likely to aim to make larger,
systemic changes. Thus, she suggests that '*if* we want a world with less suffering
and more flourishing, it would be useful to perceive complexity and complicity
as the constitutive situation of our lives, rather than as things we should avoid'
(Shotwell 2016: 8 – emphasis original).

Shotwell's work encourages me to consider how a discourse of personal
purity has limited me in the kinds of feminist projects I undertake. For example,
I perceive this philosophy articulated even in my own understanding of enacting
feminisms as aiming 'to reduce harms more often than I (re)produced them'. Taking
Shotwell's incitement to ditch personal purity in favour of an activism orientation
that embraces complexity and recognizes complicity would mean recognizing that
I am likely already implicated in (re)producing more harms even as I strive to
reduce them. This is a difficult position, however, within the neoliberal academy

where increased competition for non-precarious, tenure-track jobs with health benefits is decreasing, and the pressure to produce research that is useful to the university (intrinsically or in terms of 'image/brand') mounts (Rustin 2016).

While I do not have an easy way to resolve or reframe this tension, looking back on my experiences through the lens of the works of the aforementioned scholars/activists/spiritualists has helped me better understand, and thus navigate, some of the challenges of being a junior, precariously employed academic during a global pandemic. On the one hand, my 'crisis of faith' in feminisms is likely at least in part due to experiences of burnout and polarization. Here, a too ardent focus on social justice work in a climate of increasingly polarizing perspectives on sociopolitical problems resulted in a lack of attention paid to caring for myself in ways that ensure that I can continue to do the work that is so important to me. On the other hand, my attempt to address this 'crisis of faith' (i.e. deliver 'Witchin') was hindered by intense worry about how my own individual actions (re)produce various kinds of injustices and harms. In this case, an overly inward orientation encouraged a lack of engagement with broader systemic issues in service of attempting to prevent myself (my ego, my academic feminist reputation) from criticism.

Spiritual activism, however, helped and is helping me find a kind of middle path between these two extreme positions. It does this by mobilizing the contradiction of inner work/outer change towards a recognition of the complex interaction between that which we are implicated within but is often out of the reach of our individual control (structural factors), and the small, often seemingly insignificant actions an individual can take towards addressing communal difficulties and challenges. In encouraging me to embrace contradiction as something to work with (rather than against), spiritual activism invites me to participate in the construction of new realities – such as the space of 'Witchin' – even as I traverse the challenges of existing ones. As Renegar and Sowards explain, 'the ability to engage in contradiction is a renunciation of conventional social norms, traditional argument structure, and consistency as desirable practices. This both requires and fosters agency through transcendence and counter-imaginations' (2009: 15). Spiritual activism thus encourages the development of a 'projective agency' that enables one to be hopeful about possibilities for the future even as one recognizes the challenges of the present. It provides me with a kind of mental and emotional 'flexibility that is necessary for facing new and complex social circumstances' (Renegar and Sowards 2009: 16).

Conclusion

> I do believe that what we pay attention to grows, so I wanted to stop growing the crises, the critique.
>
> (brown 2017: 41)

In conclusion, I want to take a moment to consider what the broader implications of this work might be. With scholars like Keating, a major purpose of this work has been to 'explore spiritual activism's pragmatic, social-justice dimensions'

(Keating 2005: 243). And, like Keating, I also feel the need to 'demonstrate that a politics of spirit [have a place in the academy and] can [be or] lead to [the creation of] new tools for social change' (Keating 2005: 243). Here, I am not so much calling on feminist academic scholars to adopt or even practice spiritual activism, but to remain open to the possibility that its theoretical postulations could have great implications for feminist academic projects. Specifically, and related to my aforementioned discussion of purity politics, I think an important function of spiritual activism can lie in the way it encourages us to reorient ourselves towards critique – a practice crucial to academic feminisms (Benhabib and Cornell 1991; Fraser 2013; Friedman 1997; Johnson 2018). To be clear, I am not calling for a kind of binary project (i.e. only certain kinds of feminist work welcome here). Nor do I wish to define critique as in opposition to projects that build rather than those that deconstruct. Rather, I am advocating for a deep consideration of what motivates our critiques of systems, structures, others, each other (as feminists) and even ourselves. I am suggesting that feminisms (academic or otherwise) require both deconstructive, critique-motivated work and appreciative, synthesis-motivated work in different measures and at different times. In fact, it may be that in order to sustain feminisms and their movements what is needed is a greater consideration of what motivates or underpins our critiques: not just what they do (or what we hope they will do), but how do they operate within the neoliberal academy?

Related to this point, I believe it will be increasingly important as communities continue to deal with and recover from the impacts of Covid-19 that we look for opportunities for coalition work and community-building. This work will likely require, in the words of brown, for us to not only consider what we are in a 'fight against' (i.e. espousing critique) but also what we are in a 'fight for' (2017: 165). Interestingly, Pérez and Saavedra make a similar observation when discussing the research methodologies of Norma Rudolph who speaks about the benefits of a methodological shift from problem solving to appreciation. They note that Rudolph discovered that when she shifted from asking communities what problems need to be solved – a question that can produce feelings of inadequacy or insurmountably – to what they thought they were doing well, her research partners began to dream rather than despair; they began focusing on their small successes, considering how to make these successes iterative, and began to tackle larger projects (Pérez & Saavedra 2020: 133). This kind of (re)centring of appreciation – of what we are doing well, what is going right in our feminist works – is a crucial part of social justice work. As brown argues, 'to really transform our society, we will need to make justice one of the most pleasurable experiences we can have' (2017: 30). Practically, in my research, re-centring appreciation has meant focusing less on what we are doing wrong in sexualized violence prevention work, to focusing on what is working well, and what it could be. In my teaching, this has meant continuing to develop and deliver courses that not only meet institutional learning mandates, but are emotionally and spiritually engaging as well. What I am positing, then, is that spiritual activism is a useful theory/praxis insofar that its postulations regarding interconnectivity, non-binaristic thinking, and embracing the contradictions of inner/outer change might open up new ways of thinking we will so desperately need as we confront a world forever new post-pandemic. Crucially, I understand feminist autoethnography as an especially important methodology that can facilitate spiritual activism. Indeed, feminist autoethnography has allowed me to resist the idea prominent in a critique-oriented neoliberal academy that we – researchers, academics, educators – ought to have it 'all figured out'. Instead, feminist autoethnography enables a reflexive mediation on the self as becoming – whether that becoming be personal, professional or spiritual; it brings our attention to ourselves as subjects constantly being (re)made, giving one space to resist a worldview that overemphasizes sociopolitical 'purity' in endpoints or outcomes. Instead, feminist autoethnography and spiritual activism encourage us to hold feminisms ideal futures without marginalization and oppression together with the imperfection of the sociocultural and individual/personal 'now'. Personally, these practices allowed me to become 'unstuck', to begin dreaming of different ways of being with others instead of mired in the impossibilities of the now; they have allowed me to persevere amid despondency.

References

Anzaldúa, Gloria. (1999). *Borderlands/La Frontera: The New Mestiza*. San Francisco: Aunt Lute.

Anzaldúa, Gloria. (2002a). 'El Mundo Zurdo/The Vision'. In Cherrie Moraga & Gloria Anzaldúa (eds.), *This Bridge Called My Back: Writings by Radical Women of Color*. 4th edn. Berkley: Third Woman Press, pp. 217–33.

Anzaldúa, Gloria. (2002b). 'Now Let Us Shift … the Path of Conocimiento … Inner Work, Public Acts'. In Gloria E. Anzaldúa & AnaLouise Keating, *This Bridge We Call Home: Radical Visions for Transformation*. New York: Routledge, pp. 540–78.

Benhabib, Seyla & Drucilla Cornell (eds.) (1991). *Feminism as Critique: Essays on the Politics of Gender in Late-Capitalist Society*. New York: Wiley.

brown, adrienne maree. (2017). *Emergent Strategy: Shaping Change, Changing Worlds*. Stirling: AK Press.

Castillo, Ana. (1994). *Massacre of the Dreamers: Essays on Xicanisma*. Albuquerque: UNM Press.

Deschner, Claire Jin, Léa Dorion, & Lidia Salvatori. (2020). 'Prefiguring a Feminist Academia: A Multi-vocal Autoethnography on the Creation of a Feminist Space in a Neoliberal University'. *Society and Business Review*, 15 (4): 325–47. https://doi.org/10.1108/SBR-06-2019-0084

Ettorre, Elizabeth. (2016). *Autoethnography as Feminist Method: Sensitising the Feminist 'I'*. New York: Taylor & Francis.

Fernandes, Leela. (2003). *Transforming Feminist Practice: Non-violence, Social Justice and the Possibilities of a Spiritualized Feminism*. San Francisco: Aunt Lute Books.

Fraser, Nancy. (2013). 'Prologue to a Drama in Three Acts'. In *Fortunes of Feminism: From State-Managed Capitalism to Neoliberal Crisis*. London: Verso, pp. 1–16.

Friedman, Marilyn. (1997). 'Autonomy and Social Relationships Rethinking the Feminist Critique'. In *Feminists Rethink the Self*. Ed. Diana Tietjens Meyers. 40–61. New York: Routledge.

Grant, Peter R. & Heather J. Smith. (2021). 'Activism in the Time of COVID-19'. *Group Processes & Intergroup Relations*, 24 (2): 297–305. https://doi. org/10.1177/1368430220985208

Halberstam, Jack. (2011). *The Queer Art of Failure*. Durham: Duke University Press.

Johnson, Azeezat. (2020). 'Throwing Our Bodies Against the White Background of Academia'. *Area*, 52 (1): 89–96. https://doi.org/10.1111/area.12568

Johnson, Pauline. (2018). 'Feminist as Critique in a Neoliberal Age: Debating Nancy Fraser'. *Critical Horizons*, 19 (1): 1–17. https://doi.org/10.1080/14409917.2017.1376937

Keating, AnaLouise. (2005). 'Shifting Perspectives: Spiritual Activism, Social Transformation, and the Politics of Spirit'. In AnaLouise Keating (ed.), *EntreMundos/ AmongWorlds,* New York: Palgrave Macmillan, pp. 241–54.

Keating, AnaLouise. (2008). '"I'm a Citizen of the Universe": Gloria Anzaldúa Spiritual Activism as Catalyst for Social Change'. *Feminist Studies*, 34 (½): 53–69. https://www. jstor.org/stable/20459180

Lara, Irene. (2005). 'Bruja Positionalities: Toward a Chicana/Latina Spiritual Activism'. *Chicana/Latina Studies*, 4 (2): 10–45. https://www.jstor.org/stable/23014464

McTaggart, Lynne. (2007). *The Intention Experiment: Using Your Thoughts to Change Your Life and World*. New York, NY: Free Press.

Merkley, Eric, Aengus Bridgman, Peter John Loewen, Taylor Owen, Derek Ruths, and Oleg Zhilin. (2020). 'A Rare moment of Cross-Partisan Consensus: Elite and Public Response to the COVID-19 Pandemic in Canada'. *Canadian Journal of Political Science*, 53 (2): 311–18. https://doi.org/10.1017/S0008423920000311

Pérez, Michelle Salazar, and Cinthya M. Saavedra. (2020). 'Womanist and Chicana/Latina Feminist Methodologies: Contemplations on the Spiritual Dimensions of Research'. In Carol A. Taylor, Christina Hughes, Jasmine B. Ulmer (eds.), *Transdisciplinary Feminist Research*. New York: Routledge, pp. 124–37.

Renegar, Valerie R. & Stacey K. Sowards. (2009). 'Contradiction as Agency: Self-Determination, Transcendence, and Counter-Imagination in Third Wave Feminism'. *Hypatia*, 24 (2): 1–20. https://doi.org/10.1111/j.1527-2001.2009.01029.x

Rustin, Michael. (2016). 'The Neoliberal University and Its Alternatives'. *Soundings*, 63 (63): 147–76. https://doi.org/10.3898/136266216819377057

Salomonsen, Jone. (2002). *Enchanted Feminism: The Reclaiming Witches of San Francisco*. New York: Routledge.

Sheridan, Michael. (2012). 'Spiritual Activism: Grounding Ourselves in the Spirit'. *Journal of Religion & Spirituality in Social Work*, 31 (1–2): 193–209. https://doi.org/10.1080/15 426432.2012.647967

Shotwell, Alexis. (2016). *Against Purity: Living Ethically in Compromised Times*. Minneapolis: University of Minnesota Press.

Shotwell, Alexis & Julie Beck. 2017. 'The Folly of "Purity Politics"'. *The Atlantic*. https:// www.theatlantic.com/health/archive/2017/01/purity-politics/513704/

Sollée, Kristen J. (2017). *Witches, Sluts, Feminists: Conjuring the Sex Positive*. Los Angeles: ThreeL Media.

Trivelli, Elena. (2014). 'Depression, Performativity and the Conflicted Body: An Auto-ethnography of Self-medication'. *Subjectivity* 7 (2): 151–70. https://doi.org/10.1057/ sub.2014.4

Chapter 14

TAKING UP SITES OF RESISTANCE IN THE
NEOLIBERAL UNIVERSITY: RE-IMAGINING WAYS
OF LEARNING AND BELONGING

Elizabeth Chelsea Mohler

Introduction

To begin, it is important to offer a brief discussion of the terms used in this research. I use the term 'disabled student' rather than 'student with a disability' as it is congruent with the theoretical framework of critical disability perspectives.

In this chapter, I unpack the inequities within neoliberal post-secondary institutions, using insights from disability studies. I present a critical analysis of what it means for disabled students to participate in post-secondary education, traditionally contested for its promotion of ableism and sanism, against the backdrop of neoliberal policy-orientations (Nishida 2016) and the decades-long move towards leadership by the 'business-oriented managerial elite' (Hill et al. 2022: 63). Within the setting of neoliberal universities, education has become corporatized, commodified and individualized and disabled academics are evaluated on the basis of the financial and market value of their work and their capacity to fulfil internalized expectations (Nishida 2016). As noted by Waterfield et al. (2017), 'disability is cast as individual responsibility, leaving disabled academics navigating accommodations without institutional support' (p. 2). This conforms to discourses concerning the normative academic, which is constructed through a prism and language concerning efficiency and productivity (Waterfield et al. 2017). Efficiency and productivity are the benchmarks against which disabled academics are assessed, requiring self-responsibility and self-governance in order to manifest as 'good enough' academics (Waterfield et al. 2017). Thus, while post-secondary environments have become increasingly diverse, disabled academics must still perform invisible forms of work (Katzman & Kinsella 2018) in order to prove that they have a right to participate and exist in academia. Invariably, this undermines their ability to fully participate and contributes to what can be considered the 'hidden injuries of neoliberal academia' (Dwyer & Black 2021: 1).

Thus, in this chapter, I untangle how the downloading of responsibility to disabled academics in the neoliberal university presents a unique set of learning challenges for them. To counter this, I present examples of disability-centred activism and self-advocacy against the backdrop of attempts to promote accessibility and inclusivity in the post-secondary setting. Drawing from my own experiences as a disabled academic, I emphasize the importance of collective action as a tool and mechanism for promoting and actualizing education justice and democratic ways of living (Nishida 2016). As a current PhD candidate who has navigated primary to post-secondary with a visual disability, the subject of accessible teaching and learning in the post-secondary setting is one that is highly pertinent and personal. My current focus is on health and rehabilitation sciences, particularly within the occupational science field. I navigate the multitude of responsibilities of being a teaching assistant, research assistant and full-time student and all the accompanying challenges in managing my own access needs. Invariably, drawing from my own experiences of disability, I am an advocate of social justice, and, in my role as a critical disability scholar, I am highly committed to leading conversations related to barriers to the full participation of disabled students in the post-secondary setting. Using a critical lens, I am especially concerned about unpacking the social and political structures that work to produce and reproduce inequalities and inequity.

This critical lens supports an understanding of the dimensions of power and how policies shape and reproduce sites of oppression. I have taken up critical perspectives, I embody critical perspectives, I am always disrupting and re-configuring, and I bring this into the different spaces I occupy. It is against this backdrop that in this chapter I unpack the challenges of accessible teaching and learning for disabled academics in the context of the neoliberal university. My narrative is rooted in the work of Dionne Brand and Reinaldo Walcott in the ways that I enact the struggle for equity, power and narratives of belonging with an ethic of care in the space of the neoliberal university.

Conceptualizing neoliberalism

Neoliberalism, 'a phenomenon of the capitalist world-system' (Deckard & Shapiro 2019: 11), is a theory of political economy that relates to discursive policies based on the idea that development and individual well-being can be advanced by 'liberating individual entrepreneurial freedoms and skills within an institutional framework characterized by strong private property rights, free markets, and free trade' (Harvey 2005: 2). Neoliberal propositions espouse the rolling back of the state in the affairs of the market and, consequently, promote free-market mechanisms (Kelly 2020). Individuals are believed to thrive within this framework when governments refrain from imposing regulation that interrupts the free operation of the market. Neoliberal ideology also prioritizes individualism and autonomy. It is accompanied by notions of 'responsibilisation', which requires that individuals 'accept responsibility for self but to shed and responsibility for others – except to participate in acts of surveillance control' (Davies 2006: 436). This aligns with neoliberalism's tendency to enhance competitiveness and individuality since individuals are conceptualized as economic units within a market economy (Davies 2006: 436). In a university context, this involves competing for resources and a reliance on metrics as a tool to quantify value (Feldman 2019: 214).

Implicitly, neoliberalism is purposed to promote economic growth and capital accumulation, which inherently collide with issues of civil rights, such as the free access to social resources (Romstein 2015). Giroux (2012) has provided an overview of how neoliberal ideology impinges on post-secondary education while concurrently pursuing corporate interests:

> privatization; downsizing; outsourcing; union busting; competition as the only mode of motivation; an obsession with measurement; a relentless attack on teacher autonomy; the weakening of tenure; educational goals stripped of public values; teacher quality defined in purely instrumental terms; an emphasis on authoritarian modes of management; and a mindless obsession with notions of pedagogy that celebrate memorization and teaching to the test.
>
> (p. 17)

In the context of education, neoliberalism constitutes a 'pillar of social practices based on one's own activity, i.e. participation' (Romstein 2015: 327). A corollary of this ideological framework is that individuals are responsible for their own well-being, regardless of their ability and condition, and difference is not embraced. Neoliberal principles of participation and the principle of taking over responsibility within post-secondary settings are questionable. We must question how such systems centre the calls from disabled students, Black students, Indigenous students, students of colour, students at all of the multiple intersections of oppression, who are marginalized within the university because of these orientation and competency requirements.

Invariably, drawing from Foucault (1995), disciplinary power permeates through the post-secondary setting to formulate a normative academic who is capable of being governed and regulated (Waterfield et al. 2017). As Morrissey (2013) notes, these institutions permit 'managerial practices of performance evaluation', which provide the impetus for administrators to categorize academics who do not fit within such normalized regimes, as unproductive and sometimes, deviant (p. 799). Neoliberal discourses of individualization, competitiveness and productivity engender regimes of performance, whereby the normative academic becomes the reference point for all academics to emulate (Waterfield et al. 2017). Academic contexts become places where particular standardized ways of working are normalized and homogenized (Brown & Leigh 2020: 50). Research by Waterfield et al. (2017) has documented how in Canadian universities, for example, a focus on strategic plans, branding exercises and marketing has placed pressure on academics to illustrate their value via 'indicators [such] as grant funding, patents, training of "highly qualified personnel", social media "likes", journal impact factors, and standardised indices for productivity, such as the h-index and the i10-index measuring citations' (p. 5). This is a global practice in post-secondary institutions all over the world and impacts university structures and processes (Feldman 2019: 230). This posturing concerning the normative academic is contingent upon objective measures of performance and requires a certain level of compliance within the university (Waterfield et al. 2017).

There are calls amongst some academics working within the neoliberal context to 'confront' and 'remedy' such working practices (Saunders 2007), with Giroux (2017) describing the tensions between neoliberalism and higher education as being a 'war'. However, with the rife casualization of staff and competition for jobs, this is challenging.

The neoliberal university: Accessible teaching and learning?

As I have argued, within the context of neoliberalism, universities have increasingly become platforms for individualism, whereby there has been a shift in discourse from one where universities are recognized as beneficial for all in society to one which emphasizes the individual gains received from attending university (Cameron & Billington 2017: 1358). As part of these discourses, individual responsibility for success is emphasized (Cameron & Billington 2017: 1358). On the other side of the spectrum, universities are under immense pressure to prioritize economic growth and employability as the key outcome of education in comparison to other outcomes that are not market-driven (Cameron & Billington 2017: 1358). These dynamics have been accompanied by a shift in the conception of what constitutes a valuable education, from a focus on learning and knowledge to what students can do to increase their marketability (Cameron & Billington 2017: 1358; Shanouda & Spagnuolo 2021: 530). For students with a disability, a primary outcome of learning is that getting on with life without any help is framed as an admirable achievement but this can be harmful. As aptly explained by Shanouda and Spagnuolo (2021), the neoliberal cultural project 'eschews transparency while increasing individualization and self-responsibilization – encouraging disabled students to embody market rationalities as a way of maintaining their presence in academia' (p. 1). In other words, neoliberal discourses espouse specific ideals of the individual who is able to succeed through their own effort and determination (Brand 2020, para. 2; Walcott 2020, para. 1).

The promotion of this ideal means that, in the post-secondary education context, asking for help becomes invariably problematized, which presents a challenge for disabled students. These ideas are exclusionary; they encourage disabled students to not ask for help when required since help is framed as a weakness within existing discourses (Shanouda & Spagnuolo 2021: 530). Within the neoliberal university, a survivor rhetoric that revolves around self-determination has become predominant and a consequence of this has been the oversimplification of life experiences (UCLA 2020, para. 1). This means that narratives of individuals that are able to overcome a particular set of odds have gained traction and that individuals that are unable to overcome the odds working against them are likely to engage in self-blame.

Within the context of disability, it is apparent that the neoliberal university nurtures individualism, ableism and sanism amongst students (Dolan 2021: 5) and a corollary of these trends has been the 'othering' of the learning experience for disabled students (Dolmage 2017). Ableism causes disability to be conceptualized as 'bad' while concurrently promoting able-bodiedness (Dolmage 2017). Indeed, research shows that 'ableism makes able-bodiedness and able-mindedness compulsory. [It] renders disability as abject, invisible, disposable, less than human, while able-bodiedness is represented as at once ideal, normal, and the mean or default' (Dolmage 2017: 17).

The downloading of responsibility to students in the neoliberal university presents a unique set of learning challenges for disabled students. For instance, one of the first representations of disability is typically seen in legal statements at the end of a syllabus that inform students of their responsibility for securing the required paperwork for their course, in their own time. A vignette of how this challenge may play out is as follows:

Student: I need the paperwork for my course.
Instructor: I just got hired! I'm precarious! I don't have it yet!
Student: Here is how that impacts me. I don't have access to the course outline, which makes it difficult to attain information about what modules are on offer in my course. I cannot make a choice if I do not have the information to do so.

In such a scenario, a collective approach to responsibility for the syllabus would offer more opportunities for students with disabilities to access learning. Aside from the fact that disabled students may be physically prevented from doing so, there is also the issue that even for disabled students who are able to self-manage, there is often a lack of information about the existing support in place to assist them in managing their access needs. Thus, it is apparent from the beginning that disability is constructed as a negative, legal and medical concept (Ramirez 2019, para. 7).

The downloading of responsibility to students with a disability also extends to expectations about managing their own accommodations and access needs. As a starting point, disabled students often meet peers who do not have insight into disabilities or who hold stigmas about disabled people. Some might even perceive academic accommodations for disabled students to be an unfair advantage (Dolmage 2017). Disabled students commonly find themselves in a position of having to explain their eligibility for accommodations and might not even know what the actual range of available accommodations might be (Dolmage 2017).

In a study by Price et al. (2017: 1), the scholars found that many students with mental disabilities in a college and university faculty are not aware of the protections that are available to them and, even when they are aware, they do not have an idea of the types of accommodations that they can request. The research also found that processes for requesting accommodations are often complex, uncertain, risky and/or confusing. Not all accommodation for disabled students has preferred requirements, such as flexible scheduling, access to quiet spaces and classrooms with natural light that would enhance the learning experience (Price et al. 2017: 1). Amidst these unique challenges experienced by disabled students, accessibility is widely conceptualized as being an individual responsibility as opposed to a collective one. Indeed, what might also occur for disabled students is that 'they have to go in to disability services, offer up their diagnosis, and have that diagnosis matched with a stock set of accommodations' (Dolmage 2017: 36). In other exchanges, students might be required to inform disability services and administrators what they need, compelling them to perform invisible forms of work in order to safeguard their place within the university setting.

Many universities legitimize the accommodation process through discourse that emphasizes the importance of self-advocacy amongst young adults, while providing few resources that students may access and learn from (Ramirez 2019, para. 7). As part of the accommodation process, students must engage with university administrators and college professors, many of whom are largely unfamiliar with disability. The hurdles experienced by disabled students also pertain to the extensive paperwork required for accommodation. While universities may offer disability services that assist with this, these services often use high standards that can be problematic for newly diagnosed students, who may be unfamiliar with the language used in describing these accommodations (Ramirez 2019, para. 7).

There is also the issue of the limited number of accommodations that often do not align with a student's individual programme of study (Ramirez 2019, para. 7). Some students may be able to access the resources and devices that they require to succeed in the post-secondary education environment. However, more often than not, the accommodations process serves as another bureaucratic barrier, accompanied by roadblocks that can be overcome, depending on the tenacity of the student (Ramirez 2019, para. 7). To overcome these obstacles, disabled students must have a strong support system, the backing of their professors and medical providers who are willing to provide support in the form of a legal note to support the accommodations process. These resources may not be available to all students.

Disabled students may also not seek accommodation at university due to the stressful nature of the process, or out of fear of being conceived of as incompetent (Waterfield et al. 2017). Some disabled students avoid disabled disclosure completely because navigating disclosure is an ongoing, energy-consuming process. Similar performance standards and disabling notions of lesser competence are also present within higher education environments (Waterfield et al. 2017: 6). Studies have shown how disabled students navigate disclosure through avoidance or selective avoidance, for example by only choosing to disclose when mandatory for securing accommodations (Stone et al. 2013).

Stone et al. (2013) also reveal that many disabled students espouse a flexible academic work life in order to avoid being physically present. This may include taking up teaching online or using distance technology for supervisor meetings. As has been argued by Waterfield et al. (2017), on one hand, this facilitates continued productivity; however concurrently, it is very isolating. The scholars document that

> Disabled academics implement personal strategies for energy conservation especially in teaching, and several acknowledged a long-term impact on career plans, especially regarding any ambitions for administrative positions. Others [experience] too much fatigue to pursue accommodations. Those who [seek] accommodations typically [do] so through informal channels. More than half of those who [seek] accommodations through formal channels face negative and often inconsistent responses.
>
> (Waterfield et al. 2017: 7)

Such findings have informed Stone et al.'s (2013) proposition that in universities disabled academics constitute 'unexpected workers'. They must perform emotional work by managing their identities as disabled people on behalf of others as they seek to help those others manage their discomfort (Nario-Redmond 2019). I propose that access to learning for students with disabilities at the post-secondary level can be improved if accessibility is perceived as a collective responsibility because such a framework would encourage inclusive practices. A collective approach would produce novel frameworks and practices that aim to ensure that all individuals, as opposed to the abled or certain categories of disabled students (e.g. those that are able to self-manage), have access to learning.

Resisting neoliberal inequities

Student activist efforts have been a traditional feature of higher education institutions (Hoffman & Mitchell 2016). University spaces invariably symbolize 'the beginning of the institutionalization of these movements within higher education and mark important spaces not only for the continued promotion of access and equity for minoritized students on college campuses, but also as spaces that have the potential to foster student activist movements aimed at changing the structures and systems of exclusion and injustice' (Hoffman & Mitchell, 2016: 277). According to Kimball et al. (2016), activism can be conceptualized as: (a) 'involvement in and commitment to social change'; (b) ideological motivation to resist 'aggression and suppression'; and (c) 'emotional engagement rooted in larger senses of identity, stigma, and purpose' (p. 247).

Activism is distinct from self-advocacy whereby self-advocacy 'includes the ability to communicate needs and wants, locate services, and obtain necessary supports' for oneself (Kimball et al. 2016: 248). The key distinction between activism and advocacy, as noted by Hoffman and Mitchell (2016), concerns the differing levels of change that they emphasize. Self-advocacy pertains to people advocating for change at the level of the individual self while, on the other hand, activism concerns seeking change at the wider community level. According to Hoffman and Mitchell (2016), 'activism can still involve the communication and obtainment of needs and wants, locating services, and obtaining necessary supports, but this is done beyond the level of doing so for oneself; instead, it includes a commitment to broader social change, aspects of ideological motivation, and emotional engagement at the level of group identity' (p. 247).

Disabled students are engaging in both activism and self-advocacy as a form of resistance against the workings of neoliberal post-secondary institutes. I have personal experiences as a disabled advocate who is working to change application and admissions policies. I have also worked to improve accommodations for graduate students and worked to create a culture of inclusion throughout the student experience. These are the forms of invisible work that disabled students are performing. I suggest that advocacy and activism can spark community and collaboration and that, through experiential knowledge of disability (both from students and faculty), change can be fostered. Indeed, Kimball et al. (2016) have shown how disabled college students have drawn upon foundational self-advocacy skills in order to pursue various forms of disability activism in the higher education setting, such as role modelling, doing and teaching self-advocacy (Kimball et al. 2016). Disabled students are also reducing stigma through collective action and storytelling (Kimball et al. 2016) and are engaged in a continued struggle to access accommodation (Dolmage 2017).

Cory et al. (2010) have noted that staff at post-secondary institutions typically focus on regulatory compliance issues, ignoring the importance of a philosophical stance on meaningful inclusion and disability. Such posturing can actively reform the distant and unconnected nature of disability services on many campuses. The scholars have documented a successful approach at Syracuse University:

> The work of addressing systemic change in ways of thinking about disability was accomplished through programs and outreach, as well as through conversations and protests over campus activities the BCCC [Beyond Compliance Coordinating Committee] felt were discriminatory or oppressive. The annual film series helped raise awareness of disability and were accompanied by discussions that framed the films in the context of the social construction of disability. Additionally, events such as the e-books protest and policy letter against the Tunnel of Oppression, and the meetings with administrators that followed these protests, allowed students to share their philosophy with a wider audience. Although disability service providers may not want to participate in protests on their campuses, they can provide outreach programs and engage in thoughtful conversations with faculty and staff about the representations of disability in campus programs. This case study also illustrates the power of having students who are served through offices of disability services involved in the process of creating the services. The Working Group that was formed in collaboration with University administration solicited direct input from the students on issues of accessibility on campus while allowing those students to be part of the solution process. It empowers the students and provides administration real expertise to solve problems. Disability service providers can also learn from this case study

how to work with and support student advocates. The Director of ODS [Office of Disability Services] maintained throughout all discussions that his office and the BCCC were working toward a common purpose. Although their strategies, mechanisms, and decisions may vary, the larger objective was the same. This strengthened the directors' relationship with the BCCC and kept it from getting adversarial, allowing him to maintain a positive working climate with the students. Disability service providers should identify as allies to students with disabilities, allowing them to support the goals of student advocacy groups. Additionally, through this case study, disability services staff can learn that student access to the staff and transparency of operations can support a positive advocacy spirit.

This case study reinforces my argument that advocacy and activism can spark community and collaboration. Through experiential knowledge of disability (both from students and faculty), change can be fostered. Invariably, as Braidotti (2020) notes, 'we are in this together but we are not one and the same' (p. 465), which indicates the need for collective action from within the disability community.

Conclusion

In this chapter, I have unpacked the challenges of accessible teaching and learning for disabled students in the context of the neoliberal university. Invariably, neoliberal universities are predicated on specific ideals of the individual who is able to succeed through their own effort and determination. The promotion of this idea means that, in the post-secondary education context, asking for help becomes invariably problematized, which presents a challenge for disabled students. The downloading of responsibility to students in the neoliberal university presents a unique set of learning challenges for disabled students in various aspects of the experience of education, including access to learning and education. The chapter has argued that access to learning for students with disabilities at the post-secondary level can be improved if accessibility is perceived as a collective responsibility as such a framework would encourage inclusive practices.

References

Black, A. & Dwyer, R. (2021). 'Reimagining the Academy: Conceptual, Theoretical, Philosophical, and Methodological Sparks'. In A. Black and Dwyer, R. (eds.) *Reimagining the Academy: Shifting Towards Kindness, Connection, and an Ethics of Care*. London: Palgrave Macmillan.
Braidotti, R. (2020). '"We" Are in This Together, but We Are Not One and the Same'. *Journal of Bioethical Inquiry*, 17 (4): 465–9.
Brand, D. (2020). 'On Narrative, Reckoning and the Calculus of Living and Dying'. *The Toronto Star*, 4 July. Available at: https://www.thestar.com/entertainment/

books/2020/07/04/dionne-brand-on-narrative-reckoning-and-the-calculus-of-living-and-dying.html?rf (Accessed: 18 July 2021).

Brown, N. & Leigh, J. (2020). *Ableism in Academia: Theorising Experiences of Disabilities and Chronic Illnesses in Higher Education*. London: UCL Press.

Cameron, H. and Billington, T. (2017). '"Just Deal with It": Neoliberalism in Dyslexic Students' Talk About Dyslexia and Learning at University'. *Studies in Higher Education*, 42 (8): 1358–72.

Cory, R., White, J. and Stuckey, Z. (2010). *Using Disability Theory to Change Disability Services: A Case Study in Student Activism*. Available at: https://files.eric.ed.gov/fulltext/EJ888642.pdf (Accessed: 18 July 2021).

Davies, B. (2006). 'Subjectification: The Relevance of Butler's Analysis for Education'. *British Journal of Sociology of Education*, 27 (4): 425–38.

Deckard, S. and Shapiro, S. (2019). *World Literature, Neoliberalism, and the Culture of Discontent*. London: Springer.

Dolan, V. L. (2021). '"… but if you tell anyone, I'll deny we ever met:" The experiences of academics with invisible disabilities in the neoliberal university'. *International Journal of Qualitative Studies in Education*: 1–18, DOI: 10.1080/09518398.2021.1885075.

Dolmage, Jay Timothy. (2017). *Academic Ableism: Disability and Higher Education*. Ann Arbor: University of Michigan Press.

Feldman, Z. (2019). 'Metric Power and the Academic Self: Neoliberalism, Knowledge and Resistance in the British University'. *TripleC: Communication, Capitalism & Critique*, 16 (1): 214–33.

Foucault, M. (1995). *Discipline & Punish: The Birth of the Prison*. New York: Vintage Books.

Gill, R. (2017). *Beyond Individualism: The Psychosocial Life of the Neoliberal University*. [Online] Available at: https://openaccess.city.ac.uk/id/eprint/15647/3/ (Downloaded: 18 July 2021).

Giroux, H. A. (2012). *Education and the Crisis of Public Values: Challenging the Assault on Teachers, Students, & Public Education*. New York: Oxford University Press.

Giroux, H. A. (2017). 'Neoliberalism's War Against Higher Education and the Role of Public Intellectuals'. In M. Izak, M. Kostera, & M. Zawadzki (ed). *The Future of University Education*. New York: Palgrave, pp. 185–206.

Harvey, D. (2005). *A Brief History of Neoliberalism*. New York: Oxford University Press.

Hill, R., Thompsett, F. and Lyons, K. (2022). 'Over the Horizon: Is there an Alternative to Neoliberal University Governance?' *Social Alternatives*, 41 (1): 63–9.

Hoffman, G. D. & Mitchell, T. D. (2016). 'Making Diversity "Everyone's Business": A Discourse Analysis of Institutional Responses to Student Activism for Equity and Inclusion'. *Journal of Diversity in Higher Education*, 9 (3): 277.

Katzman, E. R. and Kinsella, E. A. (2018). '"It's Like Having Another Job": The Invisible Work of Self-managing Attendant Services'. *Disability & Society*, 33 (9): 1436–59.

Kelly, A. (2020). 'Rethinking the Neoliberal University and Its Impact on Students'. *Journal of Academic Language & Learning*, 14 (2): 1–6.

Kimball, E. W., Moore, A., Vaccaro, A., Troiano, P. F., & Newman, B. M. (2016). 'College Students with Disabilities Redefine Activism: Self-advocacy, Storytelling, and Collective Action'. *Journal of Diversity in Higher Education*, 9 (3): 245.

Morrissey, J. (2013). 'Regimes of Performance: Practices of the Normalised Self in the Neoliberal University'. *British Journal of Sociology of Education*, 36 (4): 614–34.

Nario-Redmond, M. (2019). *Ableism: The Causes and Consequences of Disability Prejudice*. New York: John Wiley & Sons.

Nishida, A. (2016). 'Neoliberal Academia and a Critique from Disability Studies'. In Block, P., Kasnitz, D., Nishida, A. And Pollard, N. (eds.) *Occupying Disability: Critical Approaches to Community, Justice, and Decolonizing Disability*. Springer: Dordrecht, pp. 145–57.

Price, M., Salzer, M. S., O'Shea, A., & Kerschbaum, S. L. (2017). 'Disclosure of Mental Disability by College and University Faculty: The Negotiation of Accommodations, Supports, and Barriers'. *Disability Studies Quarterly*, 37 (2): 1–13.

Ramirez, K. M. (2019). *Academic Ableism: Fighting for Accommodations and Access in Higher Education*. Available at: https://disabilityvisibilityproject.com/2019/09/23/academic-ableism-fighting-for-accommodations-and-access-in-higher-education/ (Accessed: 18 July 2021).

Romstein, Ksenija. (2015). 'Neoliberal Values and Disability: Critical Approach to Inclusive Education'. Bulgarian Comparative Education Society, Paper presented at the Annual International Conference of the Bulgarian Comparative Education Society (13th, Sofia, Bulgaria, Jun 10–13, 2015). Available at: https://eric.ed.gov/?id=ED568664.

Saunders, D. (2007). 'The Impact of Neoliberalism on College Students'. *Journal of College and Character*, 8 (5): 13–19.

Shanouda, F. & Spagnuolo, N. (2021). 'Neoliberal Methods of Disqualification: A Critical Examination of Disability-Related Education Funding in Canada'. *Journal of Education Policy*, 36 (4): 530–56. doi: 10.1080/02680939.2020.1712741.

Stone, S. D., Crooks, V. A. and Owen, M. (2013). 'Going Through the Back Door: Chronically Ill Academics' Experiences as 'Unexpected Workers''. *Social Theory & Health*, 11 (2): 151–74.

UCLA Center for the Study of Women. (2020). *Open Letter on Research Productivity and Childcare*. Available at: https://csw.ucla.edu/2020/07/06/open-letter-on-research-productivity-and-childcare/ (Accessed: 18 July 2021).

Walcott, R. (2020). *Anti-Blackness: Institutional Constraints & Pedagogy*. Available at: https://www.ryerson.ca/fcs-news-events/events/2020/11/anti-blackness-institutional-constraints-pedagogy/ (Accessed: 18 July 2021).

Waterfield, B., Beagan, B. B., & Weinberg, M. (2017). 'Disabled Academics: A Case Study in Canadian Universities'. *Disability & Society*, 33 (3): 327–48.

Chapter 15

ANTI-CARCERAL FEMINISM: ABOLITIONIST CONVERSATIONS ON GENDER-BASED VIOLENCE

Maria Silvia D'Avolio, Roxana Pessoa Cavalcanti, Deanna Dadusc

Introduction: Conversation as a feminist practice

At the time we started writing this chapter we were working together as criminologists in the same institution in the southeast of England. We shared a position of 'other' to some extent, as migrant women whose first language is not English, at early stages of our career inspired by Black feminist abolitionist theory. This positionality provided a different lens through which we could make sense of our experience of British academic institutions. Together we sketch a challenge to carceral ways of knowing and being in our discipline and in diverse institutions. We began this writing project as a feminist praxis emerging out of regular conversations about feminism, coming from our shared concern about the exclusionary institutional violence and carceral feminist discourses we observed. These discourses consider increasing surveillance, control and law-and-order as solutions to address violence against women. We started writing this chapter one year into the global pandemic while we were reflecting on feminist alternatives beyond state-centric imaginaries (Michaeli 2020) to address and counter the multiple challenges we were facing. Those relate to the erosion of democracies, the social reproduction crisis, the growing inequalities, persecution that disproportionately affect women, racialized and feminized bodies.

We use *conversation* as a feminist method of relationality to reflect on these issues from a plurality of voices, a method that is increasingly used in feminist literature (e.g. see Ahmed 2016; Bhandar & Ziadah 2020; Davis 2016). *Conversation as praxis* puts emphasis on our shared lived experience and on the collective aspect of discourse building. In this chapter, we are in conversation with each other but also with the texts that we quote, acknowledging how feminist anti-racist authors, resistance movements and political discussions influence and shape our positionality. Through these reflections of our conversations, we intend to acknowledge how our 'feminist bricks' (Ahmed 2017: 16) inform our understanding of how important it is to think beyond the state and challenge carceral feminist approaches.

Our starting point questions mainstream and media discourses around violence against women and girls which frame violence as a social problem narrowly defined as attacks that happen on the streets and in the domestic sphere. Commonly proposed solutions revolve around 'educating our boys', criminalizing violence and harassment as well as policing and surveilling public spaces. We argue that this hegemonic view ignores other forms of structural and systemic violence that women face. These include invisible, everyday and institutional forms of violence against women, including the role of racism towards women of colour and migrant women, and how austerity and the institutionalized misogyny of the Criminal Justice System (CJS) affect women differently and disproportionately. Multidimensional forms of violence are often erased and ignored in mainstream discourses. Structural and systemic forms of violence suggest that individual-level solutions are not enough to address the root causes of violence towards women.

Feminist groups and movements shed light on the role of intersecting inequalities that challenge the homogeneous understanding of the category 'women'. Reflecting on our practice as feminist scholar-activists, in combination with examples emerging from the pandemic and recent forms of collective action, we argue that diverse feminisms provide fertile ideas to expose institutionalized racism and misogyny within the CJS, and help us understand complex forms of violence against women as systemic.

To address these critical issues, we structured our conversation around three key questions: (1) How do we define and challenge carceral feminism? (2) What are the effects of institutional violence on women? (3) How can we think and create beyond state-centric imaginaries?

How do we define and challenge carceral feminism?

Marias

After the murder of Sarah Everard by a Metropolitan Police Officer in the UK in 2021 (Cavalcanti et al. 2021), we had various conversations about the extent of violence against women. During that time, we attended an event organized by a group of our students. They were mostly women who felt the need to discuss what was happening. This was a good chance for us to observe how they were applying the theories we had been discussing in class to an episode that they were witnessing for the first time. This is when I realized that most of them were advocating for carceral feminist approaches and solutions to satisfy their need for safety.

Feminist geographer Leslie Kern (2020) offers a useful conceptualization of the use of *fear* as enabler of social reproduction and reinforcer of patriarchal institutions. This is a useful point for understanding fear as embedded in the outside world, a threatening place for women in contrast to the supposedly safe haven provided by home and the domestic space. Fear is displaced onto spaces that require surveillance to be deemed safe. This is when carceral feminism enters the picture: controlling and limiting women to protect them, all in the name of feminism. In this light, challenging carceral feminism means going beyond the rhetoric of 'women need to be protected from violence' by reflecting on the ways in which this approach enables social reproduction and social control of women and marginalized groups. When we think about the use of fear for social control it is clear how this relies on mechanisms of exclusion and segregation, in other words, social cleansing, by pushing minorities to the margins, both physically and metaphorically. This happens through criminalization of the 'unwanted' – who are considered dangerous and disorderly, pushed away, excluded from accessing services and punished by the CJS through incarceration. The conversation with our students highlighted how deeply rooted are carceral feminist approaches in offering seemingly quick solutions to ensure safety for women. These solutions, instead, are damaging for both women and minorities (Day and McBean 2022).

Deanna

The main problem with carceral feminism, which I encountered in my own experience, is on the one hand the full embracement of accountability practices that reproduce the criminal court logics; and on the other hand, the demonization of harassers, as well as of people who call out sex offenders. Some years ago, together with a group of women who experienced harassment for speaking up against sexual harassment within an academic context, we created a collective, named 'Witchy Solidarity'. Rather than calling out the individual who had harassed us, we decided to instigate a conversation on patriarchal power dynamics within the team, and to reflect on how and why certain abuses of power were enabled in the first place. Our attempt to engage in such reflection was rejected, as we refused to share evidence and details of the harassment. Instead, we were accused of being dangerous women, whose only intention was to ruin someone's reputation and academic career. Some of us were literally punished by withdrawal of their scholarships and denial of access to academic positions. Our refusal to share evidence was taken as evidence that we could not be believed. This demonization was used to silence us and not only was it harmful, but it also reproduced carceral dynamics, of investigation, trial and punishment. To paraphrase Julia Downes's words: it is not the abuse that kills you, it is the *silencing* (Downes 2017).

Months later, during a workshop we organized, someone complained about the fact that it took too long to call out one of the harassers, and said: 'I was sitting in a conference room next to this monster and I did not know he was dangerous.' This narrative reproduces the idea that the harasser is a monster, that sexual harassment is exceptional. It feeds into a reproduction of fear of an alleged 'evil monster', which often points to racialized strangers, and fails to recognize how this monstrosity is the norm, embedded in several aspects of our patriarchal society. Demonizing harassers also points to solutions such as locking them up and excluding them from society, but it does not acknowledge the need to change the patriarchal infrastructures that enable these behaviours, normalize them and even reward them. This makes it difficult for people to call out the 'white professor' as a potential harasser because everyone will be reacting by arguing that their stories are hard to believe, because 'he is such a nice guy, and he does not look like a monster'. The same goes for the 'white cop'. To most white people, white policemen do not look or feel like dangerous 'monsters', but that is exactly the problem with demonizing, and erasing the possibility of seeing how this violence is pervasive and institutionalized. This discourse insinuates fear of being assaulted on the streets by 'unknown' dangerous 'others', and erases the fact that workplaces, families and friendship groups are usually much more unsafe due to relations of power and subjection that normalize and enable harassment.

Roxy

Carceral feminism is problematic because no kind of criminal justice solution is a solution. Any kind of criminal justice approach only exacerbates existing inequalities. They are fallacious, because they assume that punishing individuals could be a solution to structural social problems. When I was doing my PhD research at a London university, I went back home to do fieldwork in the northeast of Brazil (2012–2016). At that time, local government officials, some upper- and middle-class people were celebrating a public security intervention that claimed to 'cut down crime' and they talked about it as a success. The UN gave international awards to this security intervention (Cavalcanti 2020). But this perspective of 'success' came from white middle-class Brazilians who felt safer. There are a number of issues with it. In the communities that are considered marginalized or peripheral, people's experience is different. More people were taken out of those communities and put in prison – not because of violent crimes but because of drug-related crimes – and more women struggled financially. There is an escalation of issues. Women are left behind having to deal with inequalities and incarcerated family members. Abolitionist feminists refute the use of these carceral tools – police, prison, detention, punishment – which simply exacerbate the struggles of poor and Black communities. But we are often asked, if you abolish prisons, what should be done about a rapist? When we are talking about abolition or defunding the police, we are not saying that we do not want any emergency services. We are saying that these institutions are putting police in schools, they are using police to deal with social problems and all this means that more people are being brought into the CJS. But the CJS is not suited to deal with these problems when they are the institutions that are part of a system reproducing inequities and creating violence.

Deanna

There is a great reading '*What about the Sex Offender*' by Adina Ilea (2018), which really shows how discussions around sex offenders are breaking down the abolitionist argument, because many feminists would say, 'yes we can have a world without prisons. But what about sex offenders? We do need prisons, we do need police to deal with the sex offenders.' This issue around sex offenders really creates the main fracture within feminist movements and abolitionist movements. Often it is this 'feminist' discussion that opposes abolitionist visions with the argument that women need to be protected.

Marias

That is the main issue with carceral feminism, that it exploits women to justify strong institutional intervention. It is paradoxical how this 'feminist' approach is actually exploiting women for other agendas. An abolitionist approach, instead, argues for a focus on social and economic justice through the investment in support and resources for survivors. Lola Olufemi summarizes brilliantly this alternative argument:

> The most pressing issue for survivors is not that their abusers go to prison, but that there is a safety net for them to fall back on that enables them to leave abusive situations. They need refuges, routes to economic stability and adequate welfare support.
>
> (Olufemi 2020: 24)

Roxy

We need to bust some myths. These are deeply rooted problems that come from a racial patriarchal capitalist order, so putting more people in prison is not sorting the situation out.

Deanna

Yes, and not only this is not solving problems, but as Marias was saying, feminism is used as a legitimation for putting more people in prison. So it is a double-edged sword thing.

Marias

It is true, with the discussion around sex offenders, even when people say they do not trust institutions, it is all going back to basic issues. All discourses made on prison abolition go back to a small, minor aspect of that. When we speak about violence and harassment, the focus tends to be on violence that occurs on the streets whereas violence perpetrated by people we know is much higher. The result is that when advocating for prison abolition we are always presented with singular examples of violence (the most common being 'would you like to see a convicted serial killer walking on the streets?') rather than addressing broader issues. This happens as much in the classroom, where it is expected because our students are still learning to develop their critical thinking, as in conversation with colleagues. Thus, we are continuously asking ourselves how to deal with criticism that only brings up these minor aspects of a broader problem. How can we shift the narrative to argue that this is more than an issue of individual physical violence but rather an issue of institutional violence and redistribution of resources?

Roxy

Carceral feminism legitimizes punitive approaches, as Michelle Alexander's (2010) book shows these 'security' and anti-crime approaches are applied selectively. The mainstream rhetoric of 'law and order' claims that there is a problem (e.g. drugs, welfare queens), and this is used to justify punitive approaches. What you get as a result is a mass incarceration system that is applied disproportionately to punish, exclude and segregate racialized communities. She also talks about the myth of the black male rapist being used to legitimize criminalizing perspectives. These myths, which we encounter in the classroom and in criminological debates, are used to question the possibility of anti-carceral feminist perspectives.

Deanna

Yes, and this clearly comes from a white/citizen perspective, a perspective where women feel safe and protected by the police. And, of course, when one does not inhabit this white/citizen bubble it is not possible to feel that the police are making their communities safer, but the opposite. It is this feeling, this affective relationship, which is not just about discourses but about affects, and how we feel in the presence of a cop, what a cop's presence does to us. Usually, when I see the police I move to the opposite side of the road. As my privilege grows in this society I feel it less, but most of my life I have been feeling the police presence as a threat due to gender, my mixed background, as well as due to my involvement in activist groups who are often criminalized. For me, this affective experience of the police is so important in developing contrasting approaches. The second issue, related to Michelle Alexander's discussion of myths around black male violence, is that when we speak about carceral feminism we also have to speak about migration and borders. Carceral feminist perspectives are also linked to anti-migrant sentiments fuelled by a demand for greater securitization of borders and the portrayal of migrants as a threat to women – where people on the move are figured as carrying values that supposedly threaten and take away women's rights. A good example is what happened in Germany on 2015–16 New Year's Eve 'assaults'. In these situations, several groups advocating for women's safety demand stronger borders and the exclusion or repression of migrants, arguing that migrants make 'our streets unsafe'. I think this all links together with the discourses of 'the stranger' and the 'other', which are used to dismiss and exclude our experience and the abolitionist anti-carceral perspectives we espouse at work.

Roxy

Verónica Gago (2020) talks about many forms of violence being tied together in sexist violence. There is economic violence, countless violence of unpaid and unrecognized domestic and reproductive work, a disciplining that comes from the lack of economic autonomy, the violence of these forms of exploitation, their materialization into the household, which implodes into domestic violence, the violence of defunding and looting public services, the burden of extra community work which we have seen during the pandemic. This shows how sexist violence is a much wider form of violence. Sexist violence takes place at our own institutions, for example when the work done by migrant women is dismissed, erased and appropriated by colleagues who take teaching material without permission, or who hinder the allocation of research time to some of us. The institution itself perpetuates these wider forms of violence, when it appropriates our work for the purpose of marketing an image of inclusivity, all the while maintaining cultural and structural conditions, including unequal pay for women, Black and ethnic minority colleagues (Cavalcanti 2019).

Marias

Absolutely! It is encouraging to see how these different feminist struggles are merging, creating bridges of solidarity across minorities, challenging capitalism, patriarchy and colonialism. A feminist movement that works is a movement that creates connections between these key axes of exploitation.

Deanna

To bring it back to bordering again, from a carceral perspective comes also the idea that we need war to liberate countries and import liberal values. Women's rights in the United States have been legitimizing wars and 'wars on terror', wars against certain cultures and societies, to liberate women. In all these discourses women are put at the centre as victims who need to be protected and liberated through military interventions. Their communities are destroyed and their children killed by these 'liberatory bombs'. This is a very colonial logic (Day and McBean 2022). A lot of bordering practices including the militarization of borders – not only in the form of war – use discourses around women's vulnerability as an excuse to demand more control and more security. Border controls are heightened to arrest and criminalize 'human traffickers' who are exploiting women. Once again, we see women centred as victims who need protection, but above all, it is the border regime that exploits, kills and harms them. We know that if these borders were not there and women had freedom of movement, they would not have to rely on traffickers. Freedom of movement, and the abolition, rather than the militarization, of borders would be the best way to protect women. Carceral feminism amplifies violence against women and legitimizes it.

Marias

This happens when the category 'woman' overlaps with other identities, because a wealthy white citizen woman will not face these challenges. The mechanisms you describe also relate to trans women and the discussion on toilets, shelters and women's spaces. We witness an exploitation of discourses of safety in this context. Discourses aimed at creating a univocal category of woman assert that women might feel unsafe in spaces that include trans women. Such rhetoric not only dehumanizes 'othered' women (e.g. migrant and trans women), but also reproduces the idea of the female innate vulnerability. This feminism presumptuously sets binary standards between who needs to be protected and who is inherently an offender.

Roxy

It legitimizes violence on 'othered' bodies. It is an intersectional issue.

Deanna

It is the protection of women that creates violence. This is violence in the name of protection. The discussion on trans women is central to carceral feminist discourses. Carceral feminism is not just about prisons but about a language of security and protection. These discourses are the main vectors of a patriarchal state. Carceral feminism reproduces this language. This is not just about the prison; it extends to many areas, including bathrooms.

Marias

Sex work is also under scrutiny. Black trans women become targets of carceral feminists who want to exclude and criminalize them through a social cleansing agenda, without acknowledging broader issues of capitalism, racism, institutional misogyny and so on. For example, the police stigmatize sex workers and discourage them from reporting violence and abuse, and xenophobic attacks and threats of deportation increased in the UK after the Brexit referendum (Oppenheim 2021). The control and policing of women's bodies, in this context sex workers and trans women, is aimed at obtaining social reproduction (Bhattacharya 2017) because it is about reproducing patriarchal values by creating this very strict, binary society based on the nuclear family, control and exclusion of diversity.

Deanna

When discussing the conflict around trans women, prisons were also central because, of course, we do not want prisons in the first place. A debate arose around whether trans women should be in women's prisons or not. Carceral feminists argued that by putting trans women in prison, women would be unsafe in prison. Besides the obvious transphobic issues of this discourse, this was also making claims that prisons are made unsafe by women. As if prisons can ever be safe. This transphobic feminism argues that we should protect women in prison from women in prison. Carceral feminism conceptualizes womanhood as monolithic, assigned at birth, white, citizenly. Any other form of womanhood is perceived as a threat to the white middle-class citizen.

Roxy

Ahmed (2017) reminds us that ultimately an anti-trans stance is an anti-feminist stance, it contradicts the feminist project against gender fatalism – the discourse that 'boys will be boys' and 'girls will be girls' that is fatal for many.

What are the effects of institutional violence on women?

Marias

Institutional violence is not just about the criminal justice system. Many institutions are violent, like the institution of the family, the workplace, education.

Deanna

If we are to speak about our experience we can start from here, from where we are now, what we have been doing today. We are sitting in this garden, during a pandemic. We just had a conversation about decolonizing the curriculum. We discussed how our emails and agenda points in meetings are silenced, shut down or openly challenged. We come from these conversations where we feel that when we try to do something, the only way is to create formal complaints. We constantly feel like Sara Ahmed's *feminist killjoys*. But this is disciplined all the time, with remarks of what is appropriate and what not. This goes back to the carceral logic, because you need to submit evidence for your complaint to have a chance, you need to identify a perpetrator, otherwise your complaint does not have an object. That is how complaint is prevented (Ahmed 2021): who wants to go through these formal processes of gathering evidence, pointing at a perpetrator, and eventually feeling disempowered by the process which will bring us into question? We know the perpetrators are our bosses who will never be questioned and there will be no change.

Marias

We are only allowed to work with the tools that are provided by the institution, and this implies a massive power imbalance.

Deanna

Yes, there is a parallelism here on the need to find alternatives to these punitive and carceral approaches, that want a formal complaint, evidence, a perpetrator. Court, appeal and so on.

Marias

And yet again, this is how carceral feminism focuses on individual experiences and solutions of punishment and accountability processes, rather than taking into consideration the support that is needed at a community level outside of institutional structures. It seems that each formal institutional solution is just grounded on individual responsibility to find the solutions, in a neoliberal style. That is why the only way for killjoys to survive within institutional settings is to create a community of solidarity. These can take many forms: they can be organized like the various autonomous research collectives we are part of, can be informal but continuous, or spontaneous and finite but structured. This very experience of conversing and writing this chapter together is a solidarity act. At this very moment, the three of us are a community unified by the need to share these experiences and thoughts amongst ourselves. We need this space of solidarity to elaborate on our positions and deal with the silencing that we experience in our institution and elsewhere.

Roxy

This fits with Ahmed's point (2017: 257) about how the institution is presented as a solution, when in fact it reproduces violence. Ahmed notes how institutions are 'built as promises of happiness', but when we expose this violence, 'the violence of organizations that identify speaking about violence as disloyalty' (2017: 257), we challenge the happiness myth of neoliberalism and global capitalism.

Deanna

What you say summarizes very well what carceral feminism does, it legitimizes institutional violence.

Marias

Actually, asking more from the institution, asking the institution to offer safe spaces for women is limited because of issues of power imbalance. To disclose violence, you need to expose people you work with, so this practice does not consider imbalances of power that are embedded in the institution.

Roxy

As killjoys, when we expose the problem then we become the problem (Ahmed 2017).

Deanna

When you show a problem, you are often told 'this is how the institution works'. When you address that the problem is exactly how the institution works, the answer is again 'this is how the institution works'.

Roxy

These logics are mechanisms to maintain the status quo. We have been told several times, in different ways, how the institution works, and how (apparently) nothing can be done when we point out the problems or alternative ways of seeing and doing our work. We are told 'wait for the curriculum review in two years', or 'we cannot talk about this now'.

Marias

It ends up being about discouragement. Discouragement as a means to avoid complaint and effort.

Roxy

It creates a hostile environment.

Deanna

What you said about the killjoy and the troublemaker becoming a problem, and as Sara Ahmed writes, every time you say something you can already see the eyes rolling and nobody listens to you. I feel that the reaction I get to all my emails at work is an eye rolling reaction. This is an epistemological practice. It is a method. It is by resisting power that we can unmask its dynamics. Of course, when white people walk on the street, many will mostly feel safe next to the police, they rarely experience or perceive police violence. But when a white woman attended the vigil for Sarah Everard and expressed a critique against the police who killed her, then it did not take long for them to experience police violence. It is in that moment, in the moment of complaint, that white feminists commemorating a white British victim realize that the police are violent. It is during this moment of complaint – and of reaction to the complaint – that things become visible. The complaint, the trouble-making, the killjoy, becomes a method. The resistance to power becomes a method to see power. This is also what activist research means for me: analysing relations of power from the positionality and the experience of challenging power, of analysing the reactions mobilized against any attempt of critiquing or subverting power relations, and from there creating points of visibility of this violence.

Roxy

When the killjoy talks then, it is important to support her:

> Don't let her speak on her own. Back her up; speak with her. Stand by her; stand with her. From these public moments of solidarity [...] we are creating a support system around the killjoy.
>
> (Ahmed 2017: 260)

This makes me realize that I am in a different position to other people who claim to be feminists. They would not support us because we do not fit their model of white feminism. If they respond it is always in a defensive way. We need sisterhood as a collective snap (Ahmed 2017).

Deanna

We are asked to take online training courses about employing correct behaviours in the workplace, but these are only aimed at disciplining people's reaction to abuse.

Roxy

Again, this brings us back to Ahmed's great questions, about why there is so much secrecy and silence about institutional violence, even among some feminists.

Deanna

Because people, even some feminists, benefit from institutional violence. When I called out someone for abusive behaviour in an academic setting, the most painful thing was that so many women were standing with him. Most of the abuse I got after calling him out was mostly from the women who were standing with him. Saying that 'he is such a nice guy' because they had an investment in his power. By being invested in his power, in a broad sense of power, disrupting his power would be disrupting theirs. This is the problem of being invested in white supremacy, being invested in capitalism, refusing to accept a critique that challenges power and privilege that are grounded in abuse.

Marias

We need to switch the whole paradigm of how we speak about institutions, and challenge all these bureaucratic processes of bringing evidence, of respecting hierarchies and seeking punishment.

Deanna

What we are doing in this conversation is situating our experiences within broader structures of domination. And what carceral and radical feminism is doing is speaking about individual experiences without looking at the role that structures of domination have in shaping these experiences. And that is where I feel we are speaking very different languages.

Roxy

We need alliances and solidarities, informal communities and support network groups to avoid isolation, to be connected in this constant struggle.

How can we think and create beyond state-centric imaginaries?

Deanna

For me it is important not so much to talk about crime, but to speak of criminalization, and how crime is used as a weapon to legitimize certain forms of state violence and to violate communities, to imprison them and to suppress resistance. It is crucial to study how the notion of crime is used and mobilized to bring forward certain agendas or to protect certain interests. Also, when thinking about feminism, discussions and conflicts around carceral/non carceral, safety/security/protection are central to discourses about sex work, body autonomy, the stigmatization of women and abolitionist approaches.

Roxy

Serious harms and forms of exploitation are not addressed because of the selective nature of criminalization, a system that is cut and shaped by many social markers – gender, sexuality, class, 'race'[1] and nationality.

Deanna

Well, you say the category of crime is applied selectively, but from an abolitionist perspective for me it is not about applying it in a non-selective way, it is about abolishing the category of crime and thinking about something else. Because the category of crime can only be used by the state against the people. It is a weapon of the state which cannot be used in a radical and transformative way. Accusing the state of state crime for me is an oxymoron. The state will never make itself accountable for crimes, and there are international criminal courts but again these mostly punish individuals and it is almost impossible to assess individual responsibilities in certain contexts. We really need to think about other ways to address social justice, and crime has nothing to do with it.

Roxy

I agree that individual 'solutions', like punishing individuals, cannot address deeply rooted massive social problems, such as police violence. We have to be careful because 'acts' such as torture, genocide, armed violence are often not legitimized as crimes if they are committed by state actors. Accountability is still important, we are not against that. When we critique the state or state approaches, we do

---

1. The single quotes are used to resist the essentializing categorization – the invented and imposed biological categorization – that comes with the word, because 'race' is a creation, a social construction, but yet with real material consequences. In doing so, I am adopting the style of Paul Gilroy (2002) in 'There ain't no black in the union Jack', for example, who also uses the quotation marks for 'race'.

not want to seem like the 'anti-state state' (Gilmore 2016), that formation where certain people gain political power by proposing rolling back or condemning the state when it comes to welfare provision, spending in education and health care, who are also simultaneously advocating for building and rolling forward the state when it comes to building prisons and spending on security and 'law and order'.

Deanna

When we think about abolitionism, carceral feminism or even prison reformers, we might say that we cannot really abolish these institutions because there is some 'good' in these institutions that should be preserved. And for me the 'good' of these institutions can only be perceived from, and argued from, a privileged positionality. When it is good for some people, it is always based on the exploitation and oppression of other people. The British state reducing inequality within Britain is often at the cost of increasing global inequality, bringing more wealth to Britain at the expense of other countries where wealth was historically stolen from. Solutions cannot come within the state or from the state because the state as an institution – as a colonial, patriarchal and racist institution – is built like that, and it is doing what was meant to do. It is not there to protect people, it is there to protect its citizens, some citizens, but at a high cost of exclusion and oppression of other people who are not citizens or who are not first-class citizens. This is what the state is, and what it has historically been – since its birth. And we have never seen a different way of working by the state. If we need to think about alternatives, then these must be outside and against the state as a violent institution. Violence is intrinsic to the state; it is not a failure of the state. It is impossible to say that there is a good state or a bad state. And that is why we have to think about autonomous forms of organizing and alternative spaces outside and against the state.

Roxy

In some way we are speaking about the same thing, but what we call it might not be the same. Whether we call it the State or an organization. Maybe that is where we diverge. Coming back to Gilmore, where she proposes and I agree, that we need an anti-capitalist world with water, health care, food, education for everyone and we do not want a carceral state. The question is, how can this be done in the cities and in the world as we have it today? There is some interesting feminist work on new forms of collective organizing, collective leadership, municipalism (Roth 2019; Roth and Shea Baird 2017) that speaks to these debates. We converge on the stance that is anti-capitalist, against exploitation, anti-racist. But do we risk throwing the 'baby' out with the bath water if we only propose alternatives beyond the state? In Brazil, in the 2000s, we had a government that was promoting policies and practices aimed at reducing inequality, expanding access to education, expanding welfare spending (e.g. through the *Bolsa Familia* programme) and so on, the programmes were not perfect but they led to the first ever drop in inequality in the country. It is not necessary to oppress others, or colonize and steal from other

States, to promote measures through the state that can reduce inequalities. An abolitionist stance can work to pressure the state or the government for better provision, while in the meantime developing alternatives, without imagining the state as a solution (especially not the only solution) to social problems.

Marias

Another element to consider is that the concept of state includes differences instead of solidarity. Because it is protecting the interests of someone over someone else. So even a 'good', a fair or a socialist state is still built on borders and is built on the protection of the interests of someone over someone else. We often recognize this distinction between 'us' and 'them' by inhabiting this latter in our experiences as migrant women in the UK. However, we need to acknowledge that migration affects people differently, as I became painfully aware when I experienced my European privilege compared to my international colleagues during my PhD. A privilege that let me travel without the need to obtain (and excessively pay for) a visa, access the health system and work temporary jobs without a working visa.

Roxy

Yes, states are founded on violence, from their very origins, as the work of Tilly (1992) has examined. There is also a difference between 'State' and 'government'. The State as a concept is imagined, complex, it is not one unified, uncontested idea.

Deanna

That is really important. The state as an institution is colonial and patriarchal. The government is about organizing. The government within the state will follow the patriarchal and colonial logic of the state. But there can be alternative ways of governing our lives, which are not necessarily following the logic of capitalism, the patriarchy or the colonial state. Autonomous organizing can be a form of counter-government, or better, of 'becoming ungovernable'.

Marias

It is important to think about a government outside the state rather than within the state.

Deanna

We had a lot of conversations on how the institution is presented as the solution, and how we reached a point of understanding that the institution is not the solution, and the institution of the university, of the prison, of the CJS, of the state – and that if we are asked about possible solutions, for me the solution is not to demand to fit within these institutions, or to demand for the institution to include us, because the institutions are built around our exclusion. What we need to do is to create spaces that are outside and against these institutions, rather than putting our efforts in trying to reform these institutions. Creating parallel, alternative, subversive and disobedient social relations, communities and practices that are outside the institutions, without demanding or without asking for permission but just doing it. These are the informal communities of solidarity without which we would not be able to survive the institution. Of course, we are condemned to be within these institutions, but we also need to create alternatives.

Marias

This goes back to what we were saying earlier, that we do not only need to create spaces of resistance and support networks outside/within the institution, but we also need to be in open contrast with the institution in order to expose its structural barriers. I guess Audre Lorde's 'the master's tools cannot dismantle the master's house' is the most used quote in feminism for a reason. This is not just about higher education but about many other institutions, for example the CJS or the family. Creating different patterns and interactions is a feminist struggle, especially if it intersects with other issues. It is a feminist struggle because it is relational. As a movement feminism is about solidarities and relations. It is by challenging relations within institutions that we can change institutions.

Deanna

It is a feminist issue also because it is about social reproduction and it is about refusing to reproduce those social arrangements. Angela Davis says:

> The problem was that many of us then thought that what we needed to do was to expand the category 'women' so that it could embrace Black women, Latina women, Native American women, and so forth. We thought that by doing that we would have effectively addressed the problem of the exclusivity of the category. What we didn't realize then was that we would have to rewrite the whole category, rather than simply assimilate more women in to an unchanged category of what counts as 'women'.
>
> (Davis 2016: 96)

This links to our previous discussion about the policing of bodies and womanhood. So, the question is do you re-write the whole category or get rid of the category and build something completely different? Rather than trying to shape the box around you, or taking the shape of the box, just exist outside the box. This helps us organize an epistemological and organizing strategy that takes us beyond the category of women and gender.

Roxy

This links well with the points Angela Davis raised in *Revolutionary Feminisms* (Davis 2020), especially when she reminds us that mainstream feminism, such as carceral white feminism, leans towards assimilation instead of radical transformation. She calls for international solidarity through understanding the intersectionality of justice struggles. These expressions of internationalism have been critical of nationalism and the nation state. The bottom line is that any approach based on exclusion is contributing to exclusionary practices. So, abolitionism can be seen as radical reconstruction (based on Du Bois's work 1935), a project aiming to rebuild new organizations for liberation.

Deanna

The carceral state is not just a state with prisons; it is a state built on exclusion and repression.

Roxy

In addition to that, we can say that resisting the carceral state is not just about abolishing buildings with bars such as prisons, it is about decolonizing our minds.

Deanna

Yes, it is about everyday social relations and how they are organized, and how they reproduce the structures of racism and the patriarchy.

Marias

In a simplistic way, an anti-carceral feminist stand that we can pursue in our discussions is to analyse criminalization as violence, by framing it in a system that overlaps patriarchy, capitalism and colonialism.

Deanna

Capitalism, colonialism and patriarchal forms of oppression are forms of violence that perpetuate harm against people who try to stand up against them. They are forms of violence that are seen as the norm and normalized and use the CJS, historically, as a technique to protect their power, as much as they use borders. These are all tools of colonial, capitalist and patriarchal arrangements to protect themselves and to attack any resistance.

Roxy

Women have a key role in leading this resistance. If we think about all the forms of violence discussed here and how they disproportionately affect Indigenous, Black women and feminized bodies, it makes sense that they are at the frontline of resistance against these forms of oppression and exploitation.

Deanna

In this context carceral feminism is reproducing all this violence using the same weapons. But then there are practices and movements of resistance against all of this, resistances that are criminalized, and that is where we find women being labelled, repressed, and discredited at work. The witch always comes back as a freedom fighter who is regularly criminalized, silenced and even murdered by the patriarchal, capitalist and colonial arrangements (Federici 2004).

Marias

It is quite telling that who is at the forefront of resistance is at the margins of society because they experience this violence, and they do not have a vested interest in these forms of power.

Conclusion

Our conversation reveals that concepts centred on the criminalization of violence and policing of spaces need to be challenged and rethought, since violence towards women is not abnormal but rather the norm. Violence is not produced by ignorance, but instead is the outcome of a racist-patriarchal-capitalist social order embedded in institutions and social arrangements. Our analysis suggests that the idea that the police 'protect' women needs to be challenged, since it is founded on delusory claims that Criminal Justice institutions address violence, when in fact they maintain and reproduce the status quo – a social order in which solutions to reduce violence against women often involve increased 'security'. More police power and more resources to the police and the CJS only serve to reinforce the mass incarceration system, and thereby reproduce inequities that disproportionately affect women, Black people and communities, Indigenous peoples, migrants and trans people. The complex struggles revealed throughout our conversation are a testament to the importance of continuing this dialogue as a form of feminist praxis. That is a praxis of resistance, in which the killjoy subverts social and cultural discourse, along with the witch who takes to the streets to fight her and her siblings' battles.

> Feminism as a movement to end sexism, sexist exploitation, and oppression is alive and well. […] To ensure the continued relevance of feminist movement in

our lives visionary feminist theory must be constantly made and re-made so that it addresses us where we live, in our present. […] We must courageously learn from the past and work for a future where feminist principles will undergird every aspect of our public and private lives. […] Feminism is for everybody.

(hooks 2000: 117–18)

References

Ahmed, S. (2016). 'Interview with Judith Butler'. *Sexualities*, 19 (4): 482–92.

Ahmed, S. (2017). *Living a Feminist Life*. Durham: Duke University Press.

Ahmed, S. (2021). *Complaint!* Durham: Duke University Press.

Alexander, M. (2010). *The New Jim Crow: Mass Incarceration in the Age of Colorblindness*. The New Press: New York.

Bhattacharya, T. (2017). *Social Reproduction Theory: Remapping Class, Recentering Oppression*. London: Pluto Press.

Bhandar, B. & Ziadah, R. (2020). *Revolutionary Feminisms: Conversations on Collective Action and Radical Thought*. London: Verso.

Cavalcanti, R. P. (2019). 'A Feminist Critique of the Neoliberal University'. Feminist Academic Collective (online). URL: https://feministacademiccollective.wordpress.com/2019/12/05/a-feminist-critique-of-the-neoliberal-university/ [Accessed 5th January 2023].

Cavalcanti, R. P. (2020). *A Southern Criminology of Violence, Youth and Policing: Governing Insecurity in Urban Brazil*. London: Routledge.

Cavalcanti, R. P., Dadusc, D., Schlembach, R., & Fatsis, L. (2021). 'Silencing the Streets: From COVID Exceptions to Police Crackdowns'. *The BSC Blog*, April 7. https://thebscblog.wordpress.com/2021/04/07/silencing-the-streets-from-COVID-exceptions-to-police-crackdowns/ [Accessed 22nd November 2021].

Davis, A.Y. (2016). *Freedom Is a Constant Struggle: Ferguson, Palestine, and the Foundations of a Movement*. Chicago: Haymarket Books.

Davis, A. Y. (2020). Abolition Feminism. In: Bhandar, Brenna and Ziadah, Rafeef (eds.) *Revolutionary Feminisms: Conversations on Collective Action and Radical Thought*. London: Verso, pp. 203–16.

Day, A. S. & McBean, S. O. (2022). *Abolition Revolution*. London: Pluto Press.

Downes, J. (2017). '"It's Not the Abuse That Kills You, It's the Silence": The Silencing of Sexual Violence Activism in Social Justice Movements in the UK Left'. Justice, Power and Resistance, 1 (2): 35–58.

Du Bois, W. E. B. (1935). *Black Reconstruction in America: An Essay Toward a History of the Part Which Black Folk Played in the Attempt to Reconstruct Democracy in America, 1860–1880*. New York: Harcourt, Brace and Company.

Federici, S. (2004). *Caliban and the Witch: Women, the Body and Primitive*. New York: Autonomedia.

Gago, V. (2020). *Feminist International: How to Change Everything*. London: Verso Books. Translated by Liz Mason-Deese.

Gilmore, R. W. (2016). 'Navigating Neoliberalism in the Academy, Nonprofits, and Beyond: In the Shadow of the Shadow State'. *The Scholar & Feminist Online*, Issue 13.2. Available from: http://sfonline.barnard.edu/navigating-neoliberalism-in-the-academy-nonprofits-and-beyond/ruth-wilson-gilmore-in-the-shadow-of-the-shadow-state/ [Accessed 17th May 2021].

Gilroy, P. (2002 [1987]) *There Ain't No Black in the Union Jack: The Cultural Politics of Race and Nation*. Routledge: Abingdon.

hooks, b. (2000). *Feminism Is for Everybody: Passionate Politics*. London: Pluto Press.

Ilea, A. (2018). 'What About "the Sex Offenders"? Addressing Sexual Harm from an Abolitionist Perspective'. *Critical Criminology*, 26, pp. 357–72.

Kern, L. (2020). *Feminist City. Claiming Space in a Man-made World*. London: Verso Books.

Michaeli, I. (2020). 'The Feminist and the Post-COVID-19 State'. *AWID*. Available from: https://www.awid.org/news-and-analysis/feminist-and-post-COVID-19-state?utm_source=social&utm_medium=twitter&utm_campaign=TNI-AURJ-webinar&utm_content=AURJ [Accessed 14th May 2021].

Olufemi, L. (2020). *Feminism, Interrupted: Disrupting Power*. London: Pluto Press.

Oppenheim, M. (2021). Violence and Threats Against Sex Workers from EU 'Surges since Brexit'. *Independent*. Available from: https://www.independent.co.uk/news/uk/home-news/sex-work-brexit-vote-violence-deportation-threats-b1850271.html [Accessed 14th May 2021].

Roth, L. (2019). *Feminisation of Politics and Activism* – RESHAPE Intensive Cluj. 14th November 2019. Available from: https://youtu.be/v4cFNDc8bNo [Accessed 17th May 2021].

Roth, L. & Shea Baird, K. (2017). 'Municipalism and the Feminization of Politics'. *Roar*, Issue 6, available from: https://roarmag.org/magazine/municipalism-feminization-urban-politics [Accessed 17th May 2021].

Tilly, C. (1992) *Coercion, Capital and European States, A.D. 990–1992*. Cambridge, MA: Basil Blackwell.

INDEX

www.ingramcontent.com/pod-product-compliance
Lightning Source LLC
Chambersburg PA
CBHW071850270326
41929CB00013B/2166

* 9 7 8 1 3 5 0 3 3 2 6 9 0 *